THE
FOOTBALL
ASSOCIATION
YEARBOOK
1992-93

THE
FOOTBALL
ASSOCIATION
YEARBOOK
1992-93

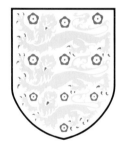

STANLEY PAUL
LONDON

Comprehensive details on the England team, including up-to-date appearance and goalscorer lists, are included in a new Football Association publication *The FA England Year 1992-93,* to be published by Stanley Paul in November 1992.

The publishers and the Football Association would like to thank the following for allowing use of copyright photographs: Action Images pages 10, 15, 22, 23, 54, 59, 66, 85, 88, 91, 95, 110, 112, 115, 122, 143, 163, 187, 202, 211, 251, 253; AllSport page 246; American Airlines page 7; Colorsport pages 18, 98; *Daily Mirror* pages 19, 47, 51, 113; the *People* page 101; *Reading Chronicle* page 191; Bob Thomas page 2.

Stanley Paul & Co. Ltd

An imprint of Random House UK Limited
20 Vauxhall Bridge Road, London SW1V 2SA

Random Century Australia Pty Limited
20 Alfred Street, Milsons Point, Sydney, NSW 2061

Random House New Zealand Limited
18 Poland Road, PO Box 40-086, Glenfield, Auckland 10

Random House South Africa Pty Limited
PO Box 337, Bergvlei 2012, South Africa

First published 1992

Set in Century Schoolbook by SX Composing Ltd

Printed and bound by Scotprint Ltd, Musselburgh, Scotland

A catalogue record for this book is available upon request from the British Library

ISBN 0 09 177292 3

Contents

American Airlines
– the official airline of the FA and the England team

In October 1991, it was announced that American Airlines was to be the Official Airline of The Football Association and the England team.

American Airlines, the Official Airline of World Cup '94, is the largest US carrier across the Atlantic with up to 115 non-stop flights per week from London (Heathrow, Gatwick and Stansted), Manchester and Glasgow to six US gateway cities and nearly 200 destinations beyond (including all nine World Cup venue cities).

The England players benefit from a special Most Valued Player Award, with American Airlines providing two return transatlantic Business Class tickets to the player making the greatest contribution to the England team at each home international. During the 1991/92 season, the presentation Crystal Eagle Trophy and air tickets were won by Stuart Pearce in the 1–0 victory over Turkey, Alan Shearer in the 2–0 victory over France (his international debut) and by Chris Woods in the 1–1 draw with Brazil.

When the appointment was made, the FA's Chief Executive Graham Kelly, said: 'We have been impressed by the commitment American Airlines has shown to the development of soccer in the United States and its desire to extend support to English football in particular. We are confident that the high level of service provided can only help the team in their preparations for the World Cup.'

Sir Bert Milichip, Chairman of The Football Association

THE FOOTBALL ASSOCIATION

Patron: Her Majesty The Queen

Elected Officers:

President:
H.R.H. The Duke of Kent, K.G.

Vice-Presidents:

W.T. Annable (1967), Nottinghamshire F.A.
E.G. Powell (1968), Herefordshire F.A.
J.C. Thomas (1973), Durham F.A.
P.J. Swales (1973), Manchester City F.C.
J.M. Ryder (1973), Cornwall F.A.
P. Rushton (1974), Worcestershire F.A.

Ex-Officio Officers:

Chairman:

Sir Bert Millichip (1970), West Bromwich Albion F.C.

Vice-Chairman:

C.H. Willcox, M.B.E., J.P. (1978), Gloucestershire F.A.

President, The Football League:

W.G. McKeag, B.A.(Cantab.) (1988), The Football League

Honorary Vice-Presidents:

His Grace The Duke of Marlborough, D.L.
The Rt. Hon. The Earl of Derby, M.C.
Air Marshal Sir Michael Simmons, K.C.B., A.F.C., R.A.F.
General Sir John Stibbon, K.C.B., O.B.E.
The Rt. Hon. The Earl of Harewood, K.B.E., LL.D.
Sir Walter Winterbottom, C.B.E.
E.A. Croker, C.B.E.

Honorary Members:

W.A. Wright, C.B.E.	D. Hawes
S. Cullis	R. Charlton, C.B.E.
T. Finney, O.B.E.	L.A.M. Mackay
Sir Matt Busby, C.B.E.	L. Underwood

Looking to Protect the Future

GRAHAM KELLY

Chief Executive of The Football Association

This has been a season when The Football Association has looked to the future not only with the creation of the Premier League but also with the attention that it has focused on the plight of young footballers.

Sir Bert Millichip, the FA's chairman, brought the handling of the country's best young footballers into the public debating chamber with his comments in late March.

The fact that so many of those – eight out of 34 – applying for a place in the final intake of the School of Excellence at Lilleshall were suffering from serious medical conditions, was a shock to everyone concerned with the game.

Football Association surveys conducted almost a decade ago revealed the size of the burden that was being placed on the youngsters in this country. Now the medical confirmation provided by the stringent examination of applicants for places at Lilleshall has demonstrated beyond any question the alarming effects of that burden.

The best players in this country are simply playing too much football too young. There is a responsibility on everyone connected with the national game to prevent that continuing in the future.

Young players are spending too much time at the mercy of well meaning but uninformed 'managers' and too little time with properly qualified coaches. More time must be spent developing skills on the ball rather than physical approaches to the game.

We find that the best players are playing for their schools, youth teams and district and county representative teams in the same week. If that is not enough, we tend to find that the best young footballers are outstanding at other sports as well putting added responsibility on them. They find themselves pressurised by their environment and their peers into physically overreaching themselves. It is at that time that the injuries and medical conditions that affect the rest of their lives are sustained.

So what can be done? The appointment of a youth coach by clubs throughout the country is of vital significance. All too often insufficient care is devoted to finding the right person for that crucial job.

In the *Blueprint for the Future of Football* published last summer, we

Graham Kelly watches Mark Wright of Liverpool hold the FA Cup aloft

contended that there had been no clear consensus on how the sport should have developed in the last 125 years. Indeed the various bodies within the umbrella of The Football Association have developed individual and sometimes conflicting views on the way forward during that time and especially recently.

The Football Association has always attempted to put forward the right principles, but not always has the governing body had the strength to overcome conflicting priorities.

The FA-licenced Centres of Excellence, mainly based at League football clubs, were a massive step in the right direction a few years ago but, for far too long, the players were restricted to just one hour a week. Practice makes perfect and that practice involves a constant repetition of patiently taught skills in a careful environment. Only gradually should the skills taught on the training field actually be transferred to the harsh realities of the competitive game.

In Europe, many of the bigger clubs have their nursery teams where the best young players can be taught the finer arts of the game. But in England they may be playing for three different teams at a weekend and their schools in the week. These are not controlled games but matches played in a competitive environment where the youngsters are searching for honours.

That pursuit of silverware is often to the detriment of the player and the game. There has to be a way to legislate, no matter how difficult that is, to curtail the number of matches played. Unfortunately managers or coaches often have no idea what other clubs a young player turns out for.

The FA is often criticised for not checking the growth of Sunday youth football, but it is difficult to prevent players from playing a game they love. More valid would be the criticism of the lack of sound guidance given to those who form teams at this level, coaches and players. It should be a priority to keep the country's best young players out of Sunday football, otherwise we will have more and more tragic cases of players being burnt out before their football career has even begun.

Amid all the furore about the Premier League last year, two lines in the 119-page Blueprint were overlooked, and these words mean so much to the future of the game:

'The Football Association should legislate for the age group, size of teams, pitch sizes and all other details concerning young players.'

I suggest that we work to that aim without delay. We should forbid the best players to play any football other than for their school and, under carefully controlled conditions, for their Centre of Excellence when they are older. One youngster with a serious medical condition is one too many and a blot on the image and intentions of the game.

Euro 1996

GLEN KIRTON
Head of External Affairs of The Football Association

At 2.30 on the afternoon of Tuesday, 5 May 1992, UEFA President Lennart Johansson emerged from a meeting of the UEFA Executive Committee in Lisbon to announce that the organisation of the 1996 European Championship had been entrusted to The Football Association.

A simple enough statement, but one that marked the emergence of English football from a long, dark tunnel. Two years previously, the fine impression made at the 1990 World Cup in Italy, with the England team winning the Fair Play Award and the fans behaving impeccably, led to the reinstatement of English clubs to the European competitions. The return was spectacular. Supporters were a credit to their teams; Manchester United won the Cup Winners' Cup, and England was rewarded with the opportunity to stage the European Cup Final, held in May 1992 when Barcelona and Sampdoria provided a Wembley feast to match any in the great stadium.

The success of the English clubs' return to European competition encouraged The Football Association to submit an application to FIFA to stage the 1998 World Cup Finals. The competition was fierce, with France and possibly Brazil in the running. The prospect of a split European vote, letting in the South Americans, persuaded us to negotiate with the French, which led to an agreement whereby we supported France for the World Cup and they, in return, backed England for the European Championship in 1996.

UEFA invited countries interested in staging the tournament to submit their applications by 30 November 1991. They called for answers on a number of important points, ranging from the grounds to be used, Government backing, assurances on the safety of grounds and a projection of the money that the tournament might generate.

From the moment that England's documents were submitted, it was suggested by many observers that this was the best bid and that the selection of England as host for 1996 was a formality. We did not take this for granted however and an advertising campaign was constructed by the agency Mitchell Paterson Aldred Mitchell under the slogan 'It can only happen in England'. The Football Association agreed to spend in excess of £500,000 on this and other means of reinforcing the message that England was the only logical choice for the 1996 Championship.

A formal presentation to the UEFA Championship Committee in Gothenburg on 16 January went well and indication was given that a decision would be made on 24 March. In the meantime, UEFA had decided that, in view of the growing number of countries affiliated throughout Europe, it might be necessary to extend the final tournament to sixteen teams. This strengthened England's hand as none of the other candidates – Holland, Austria, Greece and Portugal – looked capable of

staging a 31-match tournament on their own. A worrying development, however, was that talk began to circulate of a two-country Championship with the suggestion that Holland and Austria might put in a joint bid.

The 24 March meeting came, together with a discussion paper from Holland in which a twelve-country format was proposed. Nevertheless, the Committee decided that, for 1996 at least, it would stick to eight competing nations. Surprisingly, a decision on the host country was deferred to allow an inspection to be made of Portugal. Fortunately, this did not sway the thinking of the Committee and the Lisbon announcement, embarrassing as it must have been for UEFA President Lennart Johansson, was for England and not Portugal.

The Football Association's plans for the tournament envisage the use of four grounds: Wembley, Villa Park, Old Trafford and a fourth ground, preferably situated in the North East. This leaves a choice of Elland Road (Leeds), St James's Park (Newcastle) or the new ground being planned by Sunderland. If all three of these grounds fail to meet the necessary standards, The Football Association will opt for Goodison Park in Liverpool. The choice of the fourth ground will be made within the next twelve months.

UEFA insists that the grounds used are all seated. A minimum capacity of 30,000 is required, with a 50,000 minimum for the final. The Football Association has decided to opt for the maximum possible capacity and with the exception of Wembley, which accommodates 75-80,000, the grounds chosen have been selected on the basis that they will house at least 40,000 people.

The teams heading the two groups will play all three of their matches on one ground, Wembley and Old Trafford being the 'seeded' grounds. Wembley will be paired with Villa Park and Old Trafford with the North-East ground.

Wembley could also be used for both semi-finals and the final,

Glen Kirton

although there are some misgivings in UEFA circles about the prospect of using Wembley two days in succession for the semis.

All of these issues need to be addressed in the near future, but the most urgent priority for The Football Association is to establish an administration for the tournament and to hold talks with all of the agencies that will be as important in the staging of the competition as The Football Association itself. The list is a long one, but will certainly include the government, police, television companies, telecommunications agencies, commercial sponsors, official suppliers, the press, hotels and tourist organisations, British Rail, the airlines, the clubs, and, of course, the supporters.

In the meantime we have the chance of a dress rehearsal. In July next year The Football Association will be hosting the UEFA Under-18 Youth Tournament. Eight teams will be competing in two groups, based in the East and West Midlands. It would be a great advertisement for English football if we could get as much support for these games as we anticipate in 1996.

Watch this space for an up-date twelve months on!

Searching for a Modern Hero

**BBC Radio football correspondent Mike Ingham on a
season when the wind of change blew everywhere
except out of Africa.**

Blackadder's faithful punchbag Baldrick, alias Bristol City supporter
Tony Robinson, on his return from 'Comic Relief' tour of duty in Tan-
zania, told BBC Radio Sport in April that as far as the image of English
football is concerned in some African villages, Jim Finney is still
refereeing, Francis Lee still winning penalties, Jim Holton is getting
booked and John Mahoney is the 'Pin Up of the Month'.

The Randall and Hopkirk hairstyle, far from being deceased, is still
very much in vogue . . . Leeds United pose as League Champions and
Liverpool, having seen off a disappointing north-east challenge, parade
the FA Cup.

For many Third World countries faded *Goal* and *Charles Buchan
Football Monthly* inserts represent a link with the English game that
crackles through on short wave radio when the wind is in the right
direction. Locked in a photographic time capsule it doesn't matter that
Alec Lindsay's mutton chops are no longer part of Liverpool's Wembley
squad or that Bremner, Giles and Hunter now only talk a good tackle
from the press box. Leeds are still champions and Liverpool have the
Cup – so what's changed? Apart from domestic revolution that is . . .

What impact will The Football Association's new Premier League
have in the Masai Mara? Come to that what impact will it have in Mel-
ton Mowbray? England manager Graham Taylor will be one of the
principal beneficiaries . . . but the route to the new League has not been
without obstruction.

My first day as BBC Radio's football correspondent was spent in the
High Court. While my predecessor Bryon Butler was taking five for not
very many in a village green cricket match, I was waiting for his lord-
ship to get to the punchline and wondering what on earth I'd let myself
in for. I have a Law degree but was still in need of sub-titles during the
summing up – this was no place to be covering the national sport.

On the final whistle – deep into time added on – the result was victory
for the FA over the League by a couple of own goals, and the green light
to carry out the Blueprint proposals for a Premier League. As governing body of the English game, The Football Association was held to be
acting within its jurisdiction and all interested parties were free to re-
sign from the Football League.

The Lytham St Annes defenders in my view had, in true Sandy

Brown tradition, headed the ball past their own keeper. A Premier League could in theory have been administered in-house. A little foresight, vision and internal re-organisation might have pre-empted the breakaway, but the return to a 22-club First Division proved to be the final straw. It played into FA hands and made this renegade act inevitable.

We will now have a Premier League of 22, soon to be trimmed to 20 and perhaps reduced further when commercial considerations allow. The new League has become reality despite the fact that radical change in English football will always encounter a certain amount of opposition motivated by vested interest. But the only apparent difference the public will notice next season will be two more preparation weekends for the England squad before vital World Cup qualifying fixtures.

England's qualification for the European Championship in Sweden and selection as hosts for the next one were two of the highspots of a Gazza-less season that kept shooting itself in the foot and culminated with the lukewarm threat of a players' strike.

The championship itself was confirmed by an own goal and a place at Wembley decided by the lottery of a penalty shoot-out – fixture congestion one of the reasons for this final solution. If that's the case why persevere with the Zenith Data Systems Cup?

At the end of the Cup Final, the winners were inadvertently presented with losers' medals. It was that sort of season. Disrepute charges occurred as frequently as backpasses to the goalkeeper, and as for the bond scheme, with apologies to Ian Fleming, supporters suspected 'Goldfingers' at work.

Derby County and Blackburn Rovers went to extraordinary lengths to try to ensure their place in the Premier League. Kenny Dalglish, a born-again manager, took over at Blackburn after Don Mackay was sacked four games into the new season. Denis Smith bought most of the Sunderland players who went on to play in the FA Cup Final, and lost his job between Christmas and New Year's Day. The recently formed League Managers' Association must crusade harder for the security of its members and in this supposed time of change should take the opportunity to draw up its own Blueprint for better media relations. The paid-for exclusive story which very often leads to a disrepute charge should be condemned.

English football will be given a PR lesson at the USA World Cup in 1994. By then it will be sitting room only in the Stretford End, North Bank and Kop and we will have a better impression of football's evolution if not revolution.

Thirty years ago George Eastham's High Court victory changed the course of the English game – the twenty-first century will be the judge and jury of the Premier League. I wish it well.

CHAPTER ONE

The FA Cup

If the 1991 FA Cup Final will always be remembered as the final of 'Gascoigne's knee' then the 1992 version will go down as the final of 'Souness's heart'.

Graeme Souness, the Liverpool manager appointed in April 1991 to succeed Kenny Dalglish, announced on the morning after the FA Cup semi-final tie with Portsmouth that he had to undergo a triple heart by-pass operation. He was admitted to a private hospital outside Manchester for the surgery and less than a week after the operation, watched the semi-final replay from his hospital bed.

Souness was determined to make the final at Wembley when Liverpool faced Sunderland. He had announced at the start of the week that he would do everything possible to be with his team, even if there was some doubt on the doctors' part about the wisdom of his making the journey. Discharged from the Alexandra Hospital in Cheadle only 48

Left: Colin Clarke (Portsmouth) and Steve Nicol (Liverpool) challenge for the ball at Highbury

Graeme Souness at the first FA Cup semi-final

hours before-hand, speculation was rife about the prospects of him attending the match.

But Souness made it. Dressed in a black tracksuit he emerged from the Wembley tunnel moments before the playing of the national anthem. Ronnie Moran, a Liverpool servant for 43 years and the care-taker-manager while Souness had been in hospital, was given the honour of leading the team out onto the pitch. Throughout the game Souness was closely guarded by the medical men who were under strict instructions to prevent any shows of joy from their patient.

At half-time Souness was in the Liverpool dressing-room cajoling and motivating his players. 'It was,' said the Liverpool captain Mark Wright, 'a Churchillian performance. There was no ranting or raving, just firmly made points about our performance.'

Within minutes of the restart Liverpool had taken the lead through Michael Thomas. The doctor alongside Souness immediately enveloped the Liverpool manager in a careful bear hug.

'The doctor wanted to make sure that I did not jump up in celebra-tion,' admitted Souness afterwards. 'I felt fine though and if I can with-stand the pressure of that sort of occasion, I can withstand anything.'

'It took great strength of character for him to be here,' said Wright. 'I am pleased to see him and delighted for him. He brought me to Liver-pool and my loyalty lies with that man.'

Moran added: 'It was a great tonic for Graeme. He didn't get over-excited because he knew that if he had something might have hap-pened to him. He held himself well.'

But in the midst of the Liverpool celebrations there was disappoint-ment for Sunderland. Winners in 1973, they enjoyed some moments of encouragement in the first half in 1992 but faded away in the second period.

For their captain Paul Bracewell it was a fourth FA Cup final defeat. He managed briefly to hold a winners' medal after an organisational mix-up led to the losers receiving the wrong medals. But when reality had been restored, Bracewell reflected on this latest defeat. 'I don't think that I am jinxed,' said the former England midfield player. 'It is just a bit much having to play three of the four finals against Liverpool.'

There was only so long that Bracewell's bravery could last. When his defences dropped for a minute, he admitted that the defeat 'hurt like hell'.

Malcolm Crosby, the Sunderland manager, tried to be philosophical. 'It would have been nice for it to have ended in a Sunderland triumph but you can't be greedy. We did tremendously well to get there and I feel very fortunate to have led my side out at Wembley. A lot of managers never experience that pleasure in their careers.'

FA Cup Final 1992

Liverpool 2   Sunderland 0

For Steve McManaman the 1992 FA Cup Final will be a significant signpost in a career that came of age out on the hallowed turf as he became the precocious hero of an anticipated Liverpool victory. Six years earlier he had been there, too, but bedecked in a blue and white scarf as an Everton supporter watching his side succumb to two goals from Ian Rush.

Now here he was playing in the same side as the great Rush, sharing the glory of a final victory, and announcing to millions of television viewers right across the globe a talent that will surely serve his country in years to come.

Much of the pre-match debate had surrounded the fitness of John Barnes. Had he been able to play, then McManaman would probably have been watching the match from the substitute bench. As it was he came in despite not having played a full senior game since being injured in extra time against Portsmouth over a month earlier.

The focus on Sunderland was whether they might repeat their Wembley victory of 1973 when Leeds were hot favourites, a match fondly remembered for the final whistle embrace between goalkeeper Jim Montgomery and his manager Bob Stokoe. Both those famous characters were present 19 years on and in the first half they might well have been forgiven for believing that Sunderland might once again upset the odds.

There had been heavy rain in North London on the Friday and Saturday morning before the match and the pitch was heavy. Sunderland's young manager Malcolm Crosby had impressed on his players the need to control the contest in the middle of the field. And for some period of the first half they did just that. It was a time when young McManaman, shadowed on the right by Gary Owers and Kevin Ball, showed little of what was to come.

Though Michael Thomas might have given Liverpool the lead after only nine minutes, shooting too high as Tony Norman came out to close him down, it had been Sunderland who produced the better of the opportunities.

Bruce Grobbelaar had to save at his near post from Anton Rogan, John Byrne fluffed his shot from an excellent position and a goal-bound shot from Paul Bracewell was diverted involuntarily for a corner by Mark Wright.

Indeed, Sunderland believed they might have had a penalty when Rob Jones fell onto Peter Davenport in the 19th minute. But that was certainly cancelled out by Bracewell's challenge on McManaman a

Michael Thomas scores Liverpool's first goal in the 1992 FA Cup Final

The victorious Liverpool team with the Cup

Anton Rogan of Sunderland denies Ray Houghton the ball

minute before half-time. The young winger had switched from left to right and was cutting superbly inside the penalty area when his legs were whipped away. The Wearsiders were fortunate that a penalty was not given. What the incident did demonstrate was that a switch of wings might put the Reds on the path to victory. By keeping McManaman on his favourite flank in the second half, Liverpool almost certainly turned the game.

For within two minutes of the restart he was weaving inside and laying the ball in for Thomas, who let it bounce once and then, leaning to his left, struck it fiercely beyond Norman's fingers and into the net.

That goal from Thomas was repayment in full for the one he scored for Arsenal to deny Liverpool the League Championship three seasons earlier. It also unlocked the door for Liverpool and with Jan Molby controlling affairs like a conductor waving his baton, Sunderland were slowly submerged under an avalanche of superior football.

This was the Liverpool of old and Graeme Souness, only a month after undergoing heart by-pass surgery, must have found the experience therapeutic as he sat on the touchline flanked by his club medical staff.

Dean Saunders headed against the bar in the 69th minute and a minute later the second goal was delivered from the devastating boot of Ian Rush, his fifth Wembley goal in three cup finals.

It was a masterpiece of the finishing art. Saunders ran at the retreating Sunderland defence and when he laid the ball off Thomas pushed it into the path of the Welsh striker.

With a measured precision that has been his hallmark, Rush stroked the ball just inside the post and the Cup was on its way to Merseyside. It also broke the record of goals scored in Wembley FA Cup finals set by Stan Mortensen, who scored four.

For Barnes the disappointment of not being able to participate was offset by seeing young McManaman use the big Wembley pitch to offer his references for a bright future.

'I genuinely believe Steve will be an England player sooner rather than later,' he said. 'If he is playing this way at the age of 20 he is going to be some player even if he doesn't improve.

'But he will. He has always been a very good dribbler but now he is becoming conscious of the players around him and bringing them into the game.'

Generous praise from a man who is considered a master of the art of wing play.

It was not, perhaps, the most exciting or exhilarating of recent FA Cup finals, but it did ensure Liverpool a passage into next season's European Cup Winners' Cup and gave them a trophy in an otherwise barren season.

FA Cup Final Teams

LIVERPOOL

Grobbelaar

Jones Wright Burrows Nicol

McManaman Molby Houghton Thomas

Rush Saunders

Byrne Davenport

Atkinson Armstrong Bracewell Rush

Rogan Bennett Ball Owers

Norman

SUNDERLAND

Referee: Mr Phil Don (Middlesex County FA)
Attendance: 79,544

Penalty Shoot-outs

This will always be remembered as the season of the penalty shoot-out. For the first time in its history The Football Association was forced, by circumstances beyond its control, to introduce penalty shoot-outs after the replay of an FA Cup tie. The move was a result of requests by the Association of Chief Police Officers (ACPO) that police forces be given a minimum of nine days between a Cup tie and the replay.

It meant that in the majority of cases there could be no replay on the traditional Tuesday and Wednesday after an FA Cup tie – although the Merseyside and Teesside police forces both relented on at least one occasion.

Faced with the prospect of organisational chaos if an FA Cup tie went to more than one replay – as Arsenal's tie against Leeds had done the previous season – The Football Association reluctantly introduced the penalty shoot-out.

'You know that if you introduce this sort of method then one day you are going to have to use it,' said Graham Kelly, the FA's chief executive. 'And one day it is going to hurt as well.'

Although Manchester United, the 1990 FA Cup winners, had been knocked out in the fourth round by Southampton, the greatest controversy was caused when Portsmouth lost to the eventual winners Liverpool, on penalties, in the semi-final replay at Villa Park.

In the original game at Highbury Portsmouth had been three minutes from reaching Wembley when Ronnie Whelan snatched a dramatic equaliser to take the semi-final to a replay. In an enthralling game at Villa Park Portsmouth matched and came close to beating Liverpool – especially when McLoughlin hit the crossbar – before the tie went first into extra time and then to penalties.

Liverpool won 3–1 on the penalty kicks, but it was an unsatisfactory solution to a magnificent match and there was no hiding the disappointment of the Portsmouth players and manager, and of course the fans, who had helped create a splendid atmosphere at both games.

Their manager Jim Smith accused the penalties of 'trivialising' the competition and Ronnie Moran, the Liverpool caretaker manager, added: 'It is certainly a cruel way to go out of the competition. I know that if we had lost on penalties I would have been choked.'

But the FA point out that they had little option but to employ penalties even though they had wanted to avoid them at the semi-final stage of the tournament. Originally they had hoped that a second replay could be arranged but policing problems dictated that it was impossible. The replay of the Highbury semi-final had been scheduled for 8 April, the Wednesday after the first game. But the West Midlands

SMITHS
ACTION PACKED!
EST. 1920
SMITHS
SMITHS CRISPS CUP
Under 11 Six-a-Side
SMITHS CRISPS INDIVIDUAL SKILLS CHALLENGE
SMITHS CRISPS INTERNATIONAL SHIELD
Under 15 Schoolboys International – Wembley
SMITHS CRISPS CHALLENGE CUP
Under 15 Schoolboys International – Wembley
ENGLISH SCHOOLS F.A.
FESTIVALS OF FOOTBALL
North Tyneside, Jersey, Isle of Wight
INTERNATIONAL KIT SPONSORS
England and Wales Schoolboys

Police asked for the replay to be put back five days to Monday 13 April because they felt their resources were stretched by the need to man polling stations at the General Election which was to be held on 9 April.

With Easter approaching the following weekend and then England's commitments in Moscow, with a game against the Commonwealth of Independent States, the first free week for a replay was after the end of the League season and less than seven days before the final.

That would have created logistical problems with the distribution and split of tickets for the final as well as a host of other difficulties for Wembley Stadium and the Metropolitan Police in the Wembley area.

Graham Kelly certainly had sympathy for Portsmouth and especially their supporters. 'I felt so sorry for the Portsmouth fans. They had contributed so much to the atmosphere and no doubt they felt it was a cruel way to go out. They took the disappointment marvellously. They were a credit to their club.'

It was a scenario that had been predicted back in November when Scunthorpe became the first-ever team to lose in the FA Cup on penalties. Bill Green, the Scunthorpe manager, claimed that the competition had been devalued and added: 'It has been reduced to something along the lines of the Zenith Data Systems Cup or the Autoglass Trophy.

'The beauty of the FA Cup has always been the David and Goliath aspect of it - the minnows stretching the big boys over two or three matches. The Cup is in danger of losing that magic after 120 years.'

Green argued that there was no need for penalties at the early stages of the competition but the FA wanted a knock-out event that was governed by consistent rules throughout. The FA argued that it would be unfair if some clubs could, because of special arrangements or relationships with their local police have second replays while other sides had the option of only one extra game to solve the tie. The rules have to apply for everyone.

Scunthorpe, Colchester, Newcastle and Manchester United were all to lose on penalties, before the FA Cup semi-final once more focused attention on the issue.

At the same time it was revealed that FIFA's Football 2000 committee which was set up to investigate ways of improving the game, had suggested a rethink on the penalty shoot-out. The committee, on which Graham Kelly serves, had been recommending to FIFA an alternative to the penalty finish. 'The fact that FIFA have been looking at the matter so closely suggests that it may not be regarded as an ideal way of deciding a game,' he said.

Michel Platini, the former French international player and until recently coach of the national side which played England in the European Championship in Sweden, advocated a sudden death finale. Platini had been on the losing side in the 1982 World Cup in a penalty shoot-out and then was in the French side that beat Brazil by the same method four years later in Mexico.

Platini would no doubt have agreed with Ian Rush of Liverpool who said after the semi-final victory over Portsmouth: 'It is great when you win on penalties but it is a horrible way to lose.'

Penalties had become more common during the 1990 World Cup in Italy and it was then, after thousands of complaints about the standard of the competition, that FIFA formed their 'think tank' committee.

The pressing need for an alternative solution to drawn matches became even greater after the 1991 European Cup final when most observers believed that Red Star Belgrade deliberately played for the penalty shoot-out against Marseille in Bari.

Platini's suggestion, which received support from within the committee, was that the game should continue until a goal is scored. But that answer to this complex problem is not as simple as it seems. Because of policing and transportation problems Graham Kelly believes that there is a need for a time limit. 'Portsmouth and Liverpool looked as though they might never score. They could have missed the last bus home,' he said.

There were, in the wake of the Portsmouth exit, numerous other suggestions on the way to settle matches that finish in stalemate.

Corner counts is one suggestion, although it is not favoured within the game. Teams could deliberately play for corners in attacking situations in the case of a draw. Corners are not always a true reflection of the attacking intent of teams (Portsmouth and Liverpool had seven apiece).

Shots on target is another, although it is difficult to decide what does and what doesn't constitute a shot on goal. It opens up a great number of grey areas and also requires someone to be the arbiter. Like corners, it is regarded as a statistical rather than skilful way to decide a match.

In the Rugby World Cup it was suggested that, in the event of a drawn game, the team with the better disciplinary record should be adjudged the winner. That may be a welcome solution in some quarters but it again puts pressure on the match officials. As Graham Kelly says, until a better answer is devised, we appear to be stuck with the penalty shoot-out.

FA Cup 1991-92

PRELIMINARY ROUND

Haringey Borough 5   Watton United 0

When the deadline for entry to the 1991–92 FA Cup competition closed, no fewer than 558 clubs had been accepted.

It was perhaps ironic that one of those teams which started in the competition from day one should be situated just a mile from where the Cup was actually residing.

Tottenham Hotspur were still wallowing in their memorable victory over Nottingham Forest and the dust had hardly settled on the gleaming trophy when, in late August, little Haringey Borough played their first game in the competition.

The sense of occasion was not lost on Haringey, since they play their games *in* White Hart Lane!

Tottenham, whose ground is actually some yards *from* White Hart Lane, are given a constant reminder of the fact that their neighbours have the same address – a board by Haringey's Coles Park ground says 'Welcome to Haringey Borough – the only club to play in White Hart Lane'.

Haringey could have been forgiven for casting an eye down the road towards the Cup when, on a day when 154 ties took place, they beat their preliminary round opponents, Watton, 5–0.

Any dreams of a possible confrontation with Peter Shreeves, and his Cup holders, were ended when, in the first qualifying round, Haringey were drawn away to GM Vauxhall Conference team Redbridge Forest, where they lost 5–0.

PRELIMINARY ROUND   31 August 1991

(replays in italics)   *Result*

Brandon United	v	Shotton Comrades	7–1
Darwen	v	Hebburn	1–1
Hebburn	v	*Darwen*	*2–1*
Esh Winning	v	Netherfield	1–3
Alnwick Town	v	Chester-le-Street Town	4–3
Consett	v	Willington	5–0
Clitheroe	v	Langley Park	4–4
Clitheroe	v	*Langley Park*	*1–1*
Langley Park	v	*Clitheroe*	*1–0*
Bridlington Town	v	Evenwood Town	5–1
Ashington	v	Crook Town	3–1
Prudhoe East End	v	Bedlington Terriers	0–2
Garforth Town	v	Whickham	4–1
Darlington CB	v	Horden CW	3–2

30

Spennymoor United	v	Easington Colliery	1–0
Stockton	v	Billingham Town	2–4
Great Harwood Town	v	Eccleshill United	6–0
Durham City	v	South Bank	4–0
Penrith	v	Ferryhill Athletic	1–0
Shildon	v	Washington	3–1
Blackpool (wren) Rovers	v	Thackley	3–2
West Auckland Town	v	Denaby United	3–5*
Seaham Red Star	v	Peterlee Newtown	3–2
Sheffield	v	Congleton Town	2–0
Burscough	v	Leyland DAF	†
Irlam Town	v	Curzon Ashton	0–0
Curzon Ashton	v	*Irlam Town*	*4–1*
Knowsley United	v	Atherton LR	5–1
Prescot AFC	v	Chadderton	3–2
Newtown	v	Glossop	4–2
Liversedge	v	Maine Road	3–1
Salford City	v	Warrington Town	0–0
Warrington Town	v	*Salford City*	*1–0*
Ashton United	v	Rhyl	0–0
Rhyl	v	*Ashton United*	*1–0*
Radcliffe Borough	v	Nantwich Town	0–1
Newcastle Town	v	Ossett Albion	2–0
Harworth CI	v	Maltby MW	2–1
Lancaster City	v	Winsford United	1–5
Armthorpe Welfare	v	Vauxhall GM	1–1
Vauxhall GM	v	*Armthorpe Welfare*	*1–2*
Worksop Town	v	Brigg Town	3–1
Ossett Town	v	North Ferriby United	2–0
Rossendale United	v	Heanor Town	2–4
Belper Town	v	Arnold Town	2–0
Grantham Town	v	Ilkeston Town	1–5
Eastwood Town	v	Farsley Celtic	2–4
St Helens Town	v	Borrowash Victoria	1–3
Holbeach United	v	Hinckley Athletic	2–3
Rocester	v	Oakham United	1–3
Dudley Town	v	Lincoln United	1–4
Sandwell Borough	v	Alfreton Town	1–2
Boston	v	Harrogate Town	2–3
Irthlingborough Diamonds	v	Wednesfield	2–2
Wednesfield	v	*Irthlingborough Diamonds*	*3–3*
Irthlingborough Diamonds	v	*Wednesfield*	*1–2*
Tamworth	v	Lye Town	2–2
Lye Town	v	*Tamworth*	*1–3*
Oldbury United	v	Blakenall	1–2
Solihull Borough	v	Spalding United	1–0
Hinckley	v	Bridgnorth Town	2–4
Racing Club Warwick	v	Rushall Olympic	2–1
Stourbridge	v	Long Buckby	1–0
Hinckley Town	v	Boldmere St Michaels	3–1
Willenhall Town	v	Wellingborough Town	6–1
Hednesford Town	v	Northampton Spencer	1–1

Northampton Spencer	v	*Hednesford Town*	*1–1*
Hednesford Town	v	*Northampton Spencer*	*1–0*
Stamford Town	v	Paget Rangers	2–1
Walsall Wood	v	Raunds Town	1–1
Raunds Town	v	*Walsall Wood*	*3–1*
Banbury United	v	Stratford Town	4–1
Highgate United	v	Chasetown	0–3
Malvern Town	v	Halesowen Harriers	3–2
Tring Town	v	Hemel Hempstead	0–3
Chalfont St Peter	v	Flackwell Heath	2–0
Evesham United	v	Rothwell Town	3–1
Rushden Town	v	Friar Lane OB	3–2
Edgware Town	v	Southall	4–0
Waltham Abbey	v	Stevenage Borough	0–1
Desborough Town	v	Vauxhall Motors	††
Braintree Town	v	Bury Town	2–1
Mirrlees Blackstone	v	Great Yarmouth Town	2–1
Aveley	v	Felixstowe Town	2–0
Barton Rovers	v	Bourne Town	3–4
Wisbech Town	v	Burnham Ramblers	4–3
Collier Row	v	Saffron Walden Town	2–2
Saffron Walden Town	v	*Collier Row*	*2–3*
Leyton–Wingate	v	Eynesbury Rovers	6–0
Hitchin Town	v	Tiptree United	1–1
Tiptree United	v	*Hitchin Town*	*1–0*
Purfleet	v	Gorleston	3–1
Kings Lynn	v	Haverhill Rovers	5–2
March Town United	v	Histon	1–1
Histon	v	*March Town United*	*2–1*
Walthamstow Pennant	v	Langford	3–2
Arlesey Town	v	Clapton	0–1
Sudbury Town	v	Barking	2–2
Barking	v	*Sudbury Town*	*2–2*
Sudbury Town	v	*Barking*	*2–1*
Letchworth Garden City	v	Potton United	1–1
Potton United	v	*Letchworth Garden City*	*2–0*
Haringey Borough	v	Watton United	5–0
East Thurrock United	v	Royston Town	1–0
Canvey Island	v	Harwich & Parkeston	0–2
Lowestoft Town	v	Rainham Town	1–0
Barkingside	v	Baldock Town	1–1
Baldock Town	*v*	*Barkingside*	*5–0*
Ware	v	Milton Keynes Borough	5–1
Ford United	v	Hornchurch	2–1
Halstead Town	v	Hoddesdon Town	3–2
Basildon United	v	Brimsdown Rovers	0–1*
Wolverton	v	Uxbridge	1–0
Witham Town	v	Welwyn Garden City	3–1
Newmarket Town	v	Biggleswade Town	1–1
Biggleswade Town	v	*Newmarket Town*	*2–2*
Biggleswade Town	v	*Newmarket Town*	*1–0*
Leighton Town	v	Kingsbury Town	3–2

Darenth Heathside	v	Croydon	0–3
Yeading	v	Rayners Lane	8–0
Cheshunt	v	Tilbury	0–3
Burnham	v	Feltham & Hounslow Borough	1–1
Feltham & Hounslow Borough	v	*Burnham*	*0–4*
Beckenham Town	v	Wingate & Finchley	1–0
Egham Town	v	Wembley	0–1
Dulwich Hamlet	v	Harefield United	2–1
Hertford Town	v	Northwood	3–2
Horsham YMCA	v	Erith & Belvedere	1–2
Shoreham	v	Sheppey United	0–3
Molesey	v	Ringmer	4–0
Corinthian	v	Merstham	6–0
Chertsey Town	v	Worthing	2–2
Worthing	v	*Chertsey Town*	*4–1*
Chichester City	v	Chipstead	1–3
Faversham Town	v	Eastbourne Town	0–0
Eastbourne Town	v	*Faversham Town*	*0–4*
Whyteleafe	v	Ashford Town	2–0
Tunbridge Wells	v	Burgess Hill Town	0–2
Canterbury City	v	Arundel	1–0
Leatherhead	v	Corinthian Casuals	3–1
Cove	v	Slade Green	2–1
Chatham Town	v	Steyning Town	1–3
Lewes	v	Three Bridges	4–3
Metropolitan Police	v	Hastings Town	2–4
Tooting & Mitcham United	v	Redhill	2–0
Whitstable Town	v	Eastbourne United	0–1
Hampton	v	Haywards Heath Town	3–0
Hythe Town	v	Croydon Athletic	4–4
Croydon Athletic	v	*Hythe Town*	*2–1*
Langney Sports	v	Southwick	0–1
Lancing	v	Wick	4–1
Epsom & Ewell	v	Walton & Hersham	1–5
Oakwood	v	Havant Town	0–3
Newbury Town	v	Horndean	1–0
Selsey	v	Malden Vale	2–1
Bracknell Town	v	Portfield	2–2
Portfield	v	*Bracknell Town*	*2–1**
Buckingham Town	v	Abingdon United	1–0
Sholing Sports	v	Maidenhead United	0–6
Totton AFC	v	Lymington AFC	2–2
Lymington AFC	v	*Totton AFC*	*3–2*
Horsham	v	Hungerford Town	2–1
Bournemouth	v	Abingdon Town	1–0
Calne Town	v	Westbury United	1–2
Fareham Town	v	Thatcham Town	1–5
Thame United	v	Eastleigh	1–1
Eastleigh	v	*Thame United*	*0–2*
Chard Town	v	Witney Town	1–2
Cwmbran Town	v	Paulton Rovers	1–0

33

Glastonbury	v	Keynsham Town	1–0
Gosport Borough	v	Clevedon Town	1–3
Barry Town	v	Ton Pentre	3–1
Radstock Town	v	Devizes Town	0–2
Bridgend Town	v	Chippenham Town	2–0
Yate Town	v	Bristol Manor Farm	4–1
Frome Town	v	Exmouth Town	3–1
Shortwood United	v	Weston–super–Mare	3–0
Melksham Town	v	Welton Rovers	1–1
Welton Rovers	v	*Melksham Town*	*1–2*
Dawlish Town	v	Maesteg Park	1–2
St Blazey	v	Minehead	0–3
Clandown	v	Ilfracombe Town	1–3
Torrington	v	Barnstaple Town	3–1
Bideford	v	Falmouth Town	2–3

* *after extra time*

 † *walkover for Burscough, Leyland DAF removed from competition*

†† *walkover for Desborough Town, Vauxhall Motors withdrawn*

FIRST QUALIFYING ROUND

Harlow Town 4   Leyton-Wingate 1

Whenever Harlow Town take part in the FA Cup it is difficult to forget their famous victory over Leicester City, a team that included a young, fresh-faced Gary Lineker, back in 1980.

When they entered the 1991–92 Cup competition they were not as hopeful. Indeed, they had to search for a ground to play their first qualifying round tie, against Leyton-Wingate.

Problems over their own ground meant that Harlow travelled over the Essex border into neighbouring Hertfordshire to borrow the Buryfield ground of Ware FC.

The move did not prevent Harlow from securing a 4–1 win, even if the crowd was disappointing – just 61 hardy souls.

For Harlow sweeper Gary Armstrong the Cup run was a reminder of former glories. Armstrong had been a member of the Gillingham team that held Everton to two goalless draws in the fourth round in 1984 before losing in a second replay.

Armstrong, who ended his days as a professional in Finland, helped Harlow through to the first round after victories over Tiptree United, King's Lynn and Gravesend & Northfleet.

Their reward was a trip to face Third Division Peterborough United, but there the glory ended when Harlow, along with Armstrong, lost 7–0.

FIRST QUALIFYING ROUND   14 September 1991

(replays in italics)

Att				Result
193	Workington	v	Gateshead	0–1
135	Alnwick Town	v	Brandon United	1–1
182	*Brandon United*	v	*Alnwick Town*	*0–1*
130	Netherfield	v	Billingham Synthonia	3–2
169	Newcastle Blue Star	v	Hebburn	5–1
108	Annfield Plain	v	North Shields	0–4
106	Ashington	v	Consett	0–4
316	Bridlington Town	v	Blyth Spartans	3–2
71	Northallerton Town	v	Langley Park	1–0
142	Cleator Moor Celtic	v	Gretna	0–7
154	Spennymoor United	v	Bedlington Terriers	0–1
66	Darlington CB	v	Murton	1–3
244	Whitby Town	v	Garforth Town	0–1
140	Dunston FB	v	Guisborough Town	1–0
121	Penrith	v	Billingham Town	4–2
100	Durham City	v	Tow Law Town	1–0
402	Morecambe	v	Great Harwood Town	1–0
89	Norton & Stockton Ancients	v	Guiseley	0–4
70	Seaham Red Star	v	Shildon	3–0†
126	*Shildon*	v	*Seaham Red Star*	*2–1*
123	Denaby United	v	Harrogate RA	1–0
298	Fleetwood Town	v	Blackpool (Wren) Rovers	3–2
300	Prescot AFC	v	Accrington Stanley	0–5
106	Knowsley United	v	Sheffield	2–0
121	Curzon Ashton	v	Bangor City	1–1
305	*Bangor City*	v	*Curzon Ashton*	*1–2*
355	Buxton	v	Burscough	4–2
342	Caernarfon Town	v	Colwyn Bay	1–1
795	*Colwyn Bay*	v	*Caernarfon Town*	*2–1*
317	Rhyl	v	Newtown	1–0
290	Warrington Town	v	Hyde United	1–0
220	Marine	v	Liversedge	4–0
174	Flixton	v	Mossley	1–1
376	*Mossley*	v	*Flixton*	*2–1*
386	Winsford United	v	Nantwich Town	3–0
	Harworth CI	v	Droylsden	0–1
50	Bootle	v	Newcastle Town	2–1
321	Eastwood Hanley	v	Northwich Victoria	2–1
167	Heanor Town	v	Armthorpe Welfare	0–2
270	Ossett Town	v	Southport	0–1
403	Stalybridge Celtic	v	Worksop Town	4–0
417	Skelmersdale United	v	Macclesfield Town	0–4
173	Borrowash Victoria	v	Belper Town	2–0
425	Farsley Celtic	v	Emley	0–1
161	Horwich RMI	v	Ilkeston Town	1–0
358	Harrogate Town	v	Frickley Athletic	2–2
429	*Harrogate Town*	v	*Frickley Athletic*	*3–3*
382	*Frickley Athletic*	v	*Harrogate Town*	*3–2*
199	Alfreton Town	v	Hinckley Athletic	1–0

Att			Result
319	Lincoln United	v Gainsborough Trinity	3–1
231	Goole Town	v Oakham United	0–1
150	Bridgnorth Town	v Matlock Town	1–2
209	Solihull Borough	v Wednesfield	3–0
498	Blakenall	v Boston United	1–2
757	Moor Green	v Tamworth	0–3
250	West Midlands Police	v Burton Albion	0–1
150	Willenhall Town	v Racing Club Warwick	2–1
238	Hinckley Town	v Leicester United	2–0
291	Shepshed Albion	v Stourbridge	2–0
114	Chasetown	v Bilston Town	0–0
107	*Bilston Town*	v *Chasetown*	*0–1*
258	Banbury United	v Hednesford Town	2–1
162	Raunds Town	v Gresley Rovers	1–1
644	*Gresley Rovers*	v *Raunds Town*	*2–0*
550	VS Rugby	v Stamford Town	2–0
47	APV Peterborough City	v Alvechurch	0–0
181	*Alvechurch*	v *APV Peterborough City*	*3–2*
328	Evesham United	v Malvern Town	2–4
250	Chalfont St Peter	v Nuneaton Borough	0–4
287	Corby Town	v Hemel Hempstead	1–0
264	Bedworth United	v Bromsgrove Rovers	0–2
200	Desborough Town	v Rushden Town	2–4
464	Stevenage Borough	v Sutton Coldfield Town	0–2
182	Redditch United	v Edgware Town	5–1
1017	Wisbech Town	v Kettering Town	0–3
256	Bourne Town	v Braintree Town	0–3
102	Aveley	v Heybridge Swifts	0–2
242	Bishop's Stortford	v Mirrlees Blackstone	1–1
204	*Mirrlees Blackstone*	v *Bishop's Stortford*	*2–0*
816	King's Lynn	v Cambridge City	3–3
369	*Cambridge City*	v *King's Lynn*	*1–2**
86	Purfleet	v Collier Row	2–2
164	*Collier Row*	v *Purfleet*	*0–1*
163	Tiptree United	v Dagenham	1–0
61	Harlow Town	v Leyton-Wingate	4–1
230	Clacton Town	v Billericay Town	1–2
504	Sudbury Town	v Histon	1–0
195	Clapton	v Chelmsford City	1–5
412	Enfield	v Walthamstow Pennant	4–0
214	Lowestoft Town	v Boreham Wood	2–1
280	Harwich & Parkeston	v Potton United	2–1
457	East Thurrock United	v Grays Athletic	1–1
503	*Grays Athletic*	v *East Thurrock United*	*2–1*
244	Redbridge Forest	v Haringey Borough	5–0
180	Stowmarket Town	v Hendon	1–4
240	Halstead Town	v Baldock Town	2–3
98	Ford United	v Wivenhoe Town	3–1
631	Dartford	v Ware	5–1
131	Thetford Town	v St Albans City	0–2
74	Biggleswade Town	v Brimsdown Rovers	1–2*
220	Witham Town	v Wealdstone	1–3

Att				Result
564	Chesham United	v	Wolverton	5–1
131	Berkhamsted Town	v	Harrow Borough	3–2
63	Tilbury	v	Leighton Town	1–1
380	*Leighton Town*	v	*Tilbury*	*1–0*
222	Yeading	v	Ruislip Manor	3–1
524	Slough Town	v	Croydon	2–2
246	*Croydon*	v	*Slough Town*	*0–3*
112	Hertford Town	v	Staines Town	2–0
138	Dulwich Hamlet	v	Burnham	1–0
126	Wembley	v	Windsor & Eton	1–2
203	Fisher Athletic	v	Beckenham Town	4–0
121	Banstead Athletic	v	Wokingham Town	1–2
109	Corinthian	v	Erith & Belvedere	1–3
154	Molesey	v	Crawley Town	1–5
146	Hailsham Town	v	Sheppey United	1–1
182	*Sheppey United*	v	*Hailsham Town*	*4–1*
135	Whitehawk	v	Bromley	0–2
112	Whyteleafe	v	Worthing	1–2
208	Faversham Town	v	Carshalton Athletic	3–2
809	Dover Athletic	v	Chipstead	6–0
197	Steyning Town	v	Bognor Regis Town	0–1
74	Cove	v	Burgess Hill Town	1–1
164	*Burgess Hill Town*	v	*Cove*	*4–0*
370	Leatherhead	v	Dorking	1–2
336	Gravesend & Northfleet	v	Canterbury City	2–1
301	Herne Bay	v	Kingstonian	0–2
107	Eastbourne United	v	Lewes	1–4
255	Tooting & Mitcham United	v	Margate	2–1
355	Peacehaven & Telscombe	v	Hastings Town	2–1
247	Walton & Hersham	v	Littlehampton Town	1–1
391	*Littlehampton Town*	v	*Walton & Hersham*	*2–1*
135	Lancing	v	Hampton	1–3
111	Southwick	v	Sittingbourne	1–3
352	Tonbridge	v	Croydon Athletic	2–1
92	Camberley Town	v	Marlow	1–3
160	Portfield	v	Havant Town	1–2
112	Selsey	v	Andover	2–1
120	Romsey Town	v	Newbury Town	2–1
210	Pagham	v	Basingstoke Town	1–3
225	Horsham	v	Buckingham Town	1–0
433	Lymington AFC	v	Bashley	2–4
443	Newport (IOW)	v	Maidenhead United	0–3
118	Swanage Town & Herston	v	Waterlooville	1–1
151	*Waterlooville*	v	*Swanage Town & Herston*	*2–0*
335	Thame United	v	Abingdon Town	2–0
321	Thatcham Town	v	Salisbury	1–1
221	*Salisbury*	v	*Thatcham Town*	*3–0*
169	Poole Town	v	Westbury United	3–1
230	Brockenhurst	v	Dorchester Town	1–2
140	Clevedon Town	v	Witney Town	2–2
176	*Witney Town*	v	*Clevedon Town*	*1–0*
381	*Glastonbury*	v	*Trowbridge Town*	*0–4*

Att				Result
171	Mangotsfield United	v	Cwmbran Town	4–2
302	Wimborne Town	v	Weymouth	1–2
327	Yate Town	v	Barry Town	0–3
110	Bridgend Town	v	Cheltenham Town	3–3
480	*Cheltenham Town*	v	*Bridgend Town*	5–0
237	Taunton Town	v	Devizes Town	2–0
272	Stroud	v	Bath City	1–3
54	Maesteg Park	v	Frome Town	4–0
245	Melksham Town	v	Worcester City	1–8
744	Gloucester City	v	Shortwood United	4–1
122	St Austell	v	Liskeard Athletic	2–3
393	Falmouth Town	v	Minehead	2–0
378	Torrington	v	Tiverton Town	2–2
438	*Tiverton Town*	v	*Torrington*	3–2*
143	Saltash United	v	Ilfracombe Town	6–0

* *after extra time*
† *Match ordered to be replayed due to Seaham Red Star fielding ineligible player*

SECOND QUALIFYING ROUND

Lincoln United 2   Oakham United 0

When Lincoln United were considering their plans for the 1991–92 season the thought of participating in the FA Cup was considered extravagant.

Just where the little club was going to find the £75 entry fee was a mystery, although they were to be thankful for their little indulgence.

Lincoln had never before entered the competition but in the preliminary round they won 4–1 away to Dudley Town and then overcame the first qualifying round hurdle by beating Gainsborough Trinity 3–1.

The city of Lincoln was used to cheering its other team, Lincoln City, but suddenly there were two clubs in search of Cup glory.

United, used to just a handful of spectators, were drawn at home again in the next round and faced a difficult test against Oakham United.

They drew a crowd of 200, won 2–0 and set off for the big time. Subsequent victories over Frickley Athletic and Leek Town sent Lincoln into the first round proper. Hopes that they might draw Lincoln City were dashed when they came out of the velvet bag against Third Division pace-setters Huddersfield Town.

Lincoln lost 7–0 at Leeds Road but left the competition knowing that the £75 'gamble' had brought in enough revenue to build new dressing rooms at their Ashby Avenue ground.

SECOND QUALIFYING ROUND 28 September 1991

(replays in italics)

Att				Result
232	Gateshead	v	Alnwick Town	6–0
188	Netherfield	v	Newcastle Blue Star	2–1
142	North Shields	v	Consett	3–1
257	Bridlington Town	v	Northallerton Town	4–0
101	Gretna	v	Bedlington Terriers	3–1
93	Murton	v	Garforth Town	3–1
131	Dunston FB	v	Penrith	2–2
283	*Penrith*	v	*Dunston FB*	*6–6**
517	*Penrith*	v	*Dunston FB*	*2–1**
213	Durham City	v	Morecambe	1–4
662	Guiseley	v	Shildon	5–1
180	Denaby United	v	Fleetwood Town	1–0
563	Accrington Stanley	v	Knowsley United	2–2
343	*Knowsley United*	v	*Accrington Stanley*	*2–1**
203	Curzon Ashton	v	Buxton	1–0
785	Colwyn Bay	v	Rhyl	2–0
317	Warrington Town	v	Marine	0–0
217	*Marine*	v	*Warrington Town*	*1–0*
342	Mossley	v	Winsford United	1–1
359	*Winsford United*	v	*Mossley*	*6–0*
239	Droylsden	v	Bootle	1–1
212	*Bootle*	v	*Droylsden*	*1–3*
117	Eastwood Hanley	v	Armthorpe Welfare	3–2
417	Southport	v	Stalybridge Celtic	1–2
871	Macclesfield Town	v	Borrowash Victoria	1–2
378	Emley	v	Horwich RMI	4–2
360	Frickley Athletic	v	Alfreton Town	4–1
200	Lincoln United	v	Oakham United	2–0
342	Matlock Town	v	Solihull Borough	2–1
1375	Boston United	v	Tamworth	1–1
1215	*Tamworth*	v	*Boston United*	*1–0**
401	Burton Albion	v	Willenhall Town	4–1
281	Hinckley Town	v	Shepshed Albion	3–3
392	*Shepshed Albion*	v	*Hinckley Town*	*3–2*
147	Chasetown	v	Banbury United	1–1
326	*Banbury United*	v	*Chasetown*	*1–2**
774	Gresley Rovers	v	VS Rugby	3–3
707	*VS Rugby*	v	*Gresley Rovers*	*3–0*
81	Alvechurch	v	Malvern Town	3–0
667	Nuneaton Borough	v	Corby Town	2–2
392	*Corby Town*	v	*Nuneaton Borough*	*1–0**
472	Bromsgrove Rovers	v	Rushden Town	1–0
173	Sutton Coldfield Town	v	Redditch United	1–3
1609	Kettering Town	v	Braintree Town	3–1
142	Heybridge Swifts	v	Mirrlees Blackstone	1–1
350	*Mirrlees Blackstone*	v	*Heybridge Swifts*	*0–1*
749	King's Lynn	v	Purfleet	4–2
79	Tiptree United	v	Harlow Town	0–6
472	Billericay Town	v	Sudbury Town	3–1

39

Att				Result
605	Chelmsford City	v	Enfield	1–1
665	*Enfield*	v	*Chelmsford City*	*2–1*
277	Lowestoft Town	v	Harwich & Parkeston	1–0
344	Grays Athletic	v	Redbridge Forest	3–1
209	Hendon	v	Baldock Town	1–2
323	Ford United	v	Dartford	0–1
338	St Albans City	v	Brimsdown Rovers	1–1
186	*Brimsdown Rovers*	v	*St Albans City*	*2–0*
745	Wealdstone	v	Chesham United	2–4
243	Berkhamsted Town	v	Leighton Town	2–0
475	Yeading	v	Slough Town	0–0
722	*Slough Town*	v	*Yeading*	*1–0*
134	Hertford Town	v	Dulwich Hamlet	2–1
226	Windsor & Eton	v	Fisher Athletic	3–2
277	Wokingham Town	v	Erith & Belvedere	1–2
241	Crawley Town	v	Sheppey United	2–0
413	Bromley	v	Worthing	3–1
1157	Faversham Town	v	Dover Athletic	0–0
1232	*Dover Athletic*	v	*Faversham Town*	*2–1*
211	Bognor Regis Town	v	Burgess Hill Town	1–2
185	Dorking	v	Gravesend & Northfleet	3–4
367	Kingstonian	v	Lewes	3–2
255	Tooting & Mitcham United	v	Peacehaven & Telscombe	2–0
225	Littlehampton Town	v	Hampton	1–3
641	Sittingbourne	v	Tonbridge	1–2
190	Marlow	v	Havant Town	2–1
120	Selsey	v	Romsey Town	1–6
261	Basingstoke Town	v	Horsham	1–1
387	*Horsham*	v	*Basingstoke Town*	*2–1**
205	Bashley	v	Maidenhead United	1–1
252	*Maidenhead United*	v	*Bashley*	*1–0*
147	Waterlooville	v	Thame United	3–3
320	*Thame United*	v	*Waterlooville*	*3–2**
220	Salisbury	v	Poole Town	2–0
458	Dorchester Town	v	Witney Town	3–2
455	Trowbridge Town	v	Mangotsfield United	3–0
584	Weymouth	v	Barry Town	1–1
455	*Barry Town*	v	*Weymouth*	*2–3**
473	Cheltenham Town	v	Taunton Town	8–0
422	Bath City	v	Maesteg Park	5–2
904	Worcester City	v	Gloucester City	2–1
286	Liskeard Athletic	v	Falmouth Town	5–1
278	Tiverton Town	v	Saltash United	0–0
379	*Saltash United*	v	*Tiverton Town*	*1–2*

* after extra time

THIRD QUALIFYING ROUND
North Shields 0 Bridlington Town 2

Most players' preferred preparation routine for a big Cup tie is a quiet night in front of the TV, a cup of cocoa, and off to bed to dream of scoring the winning goal the next day.

For Lee Harvey, the Bridlington midfield player, the pre-match routine was a gruelling six-and-a-quarter-hour shift down the Barnsley Main Colliery pit shaft.

Harvey, like so many players still dreaming of reaching the first round proper of the Cup, has to work outside of football to pay the mortgage.

According to his manager. Garry Watson, in charge at Bridlington, after a playing career with Bradford City and others, 'Professionals just don't know what lifestyle some part-timers have to endure, but we all have mouths to feed. Lee goes home, has a few hours' sleep, puts his boots on and plays as if he has prepared normally.'

This strange routine, endured by Harvey for 10 years, didn't seem to affect his performance when Bridlington, who had made one previous appearance in the first round (in 1960), travelled to North Shields. They won 2–0 and, after beating Barrow 1–0, they drew Fourth Division York City.

Harvey went through his normal routine and helped Bridlington come close, scaring York, before they finally lost 2–1.

THIRD QUALIFYING ROUND   12 October 1991

(replays in italics)

Att				Result
282	Gateshead	v	Netherfield	0–0
867	*Netherfield*	v	*Gateshead*	*0–3*
237	North Shields	v	Bridlington Town	0–2
143	Gretna	v	Murton	3–0
559	Penrith	v	Morecambe	0–3
691	Guiseley	v	Denaby United	1–1
735	*Denaby United*	v	*Guiseley*	*1–2*
329	Knowsley United	v	Curzon Ashton	2–0
651	Colwyn Bay	v	Marine	4–3
681	Winsford United	v	Droylsden	3–2
382	Eastwood Hanley	v	Stalybridge Celtic	1–2
391	Borrowash Victoria	v	Emley	0–3
477	Frickley Athletic	v	Lincoln United	0–0
802	*Lincoln United*	v	*Frickley Athletic*	*3–2*
1149	Matlock Town	v	Tamworth	0–2
704	Burton Albion	v	Shepshed Albion	3–2
492	Chasetown	v	VS Rugby	0–0

Att			Result
605	*VS Rugby*	v *Chasetown*	*3–0*
217	Alvechurch	v Corby Town	2–0
1050	Bromsgrove Rovers	v Redditch United	2–0
1587	Kettering Town	v Heybridge Swifts	3–0
1305	King's Lynn	v Harlow Town	2–3
979	Billericay Town	v Enfield	1–3
679	Lowestoft Town	v Grays Athletic	1–2
628	Baldock Town	v Dartford	2–2
701	*Dartford*	v *Baldock Town*	*1–2**
412	Brimsdown Rovers	v Chesham United	2–2
585	*Chesham United*	v *Brimsdown Rovers*	*2–1*
612	Berkhamsted Town	v Slough Town	1–4
280	Hertford Town	v Windsor & Eton	1–2
400	Erith & Belvedere	v Crawley Town	1–2
1010	Bromley	v Dover Athletic	0–3
341	Burgess Hill Town	v Gravesend & Northfleet	0–1
690	Kingstonian	v Tooting & Mitcham United	0–0
517	*Tooting & Mitcham United*	v *Kingstonian*	*2–3*
529	Hampton	v Tonbridge	2–2
1274	*Tonbridge*	v *Hampton*	*3–0*†*
315	Marlow	v Romsey Town	2–0
535	Horsham	v Maidenhead United	1–1
383	*Maidenhead United*	v *Horsham*	*0–1*
420	Thame United	v Salisbury	0–4
805	Dorchester Town	v Trowbridge Town	1–0
1176	Weymouth	v Cheltenham Town	4–0
813	Bath City	v Worcester City	1–2
341	Liskeard Athletic	v Tiverton Town	1–3

* *after extra time*
† *after abandoned tie, floodlight failure, 2–1 81 mins*

FOURTH QUALIFYING ROUND

Gretna 3   Stalybridge Celtic 2

When Stalybridge Celtic travelled up the M6 and over the Scottish border to face Gretna in the FA Cup fourth qualifying round, they could not have envisaged the culture shock awaiting them at the tiny Raydale Park ground.

Gretna, of the Northern League, were attempting to become the first Scottish team to reach the first round proper since Glasgow Rangers, who had reached the semi-finals in 1887.

The Northern League team had already beaten Cleator Moor Celtic, Bedlington Terriers and Murton when they faced Stalybridge with the chance to reach the furthest stage in their history.

Gretna are fiercely proud of their Scottish roots even though they are based just a quarter of a mile inside the country.

Stalybridge, from Greater Manchester, were greeted by bagpipes and the sight of dozens of Scottish flags as they ran out to do battle.

While Gretna Green carried on the time-honoured tradition of marrying young couples – a dozen couples tied the knot on that October afternoon – Gretna set about beating Stalybridge 3–2.

The reward for their historic victory was another home tie, against Fourth Division Rochdale, and after holding the English side to a goalless draw in front of 2000 spectators, they finally went out of the competition, losing the replay 3–1 at Rochdale.

FOURTH QUALIFYING ROUND   26 October 1991

(replays in italics)

Att				Result
443	Whitley Bay	v	Witton Albion	1–4
964	Guiseley	v	Bishop Auckland	2–1
734	Runcorn	v	Gateshead	1–0
1268	Barrow	v	Bridlington Town	0–1
743	Telford United	v	Knowsley United	1–0
781	Colwyn Bay	v	Morecambe	0–2
664	Chorley	v	Emley	2–2
1151	*Emley*	v	*Chorley*	*1–1†*
1380	*Chorley*	v	*Emley*	*0–1*
730	Leek Town	v	Lincoln United	0–2
449	Gretna	v	Stalybridge Celtic	3–2
1133	Winsford United	v	Altrincham	3–2
704	Welling United	v	Alvechurch	5–1
2147	Colchester United	v	Burton Albion	5–0
1785	Kettering Town	v	Stafford Rangers	0–0
1070	*Stafford Rangers*	v	*Kettering Town*	*0–2*
405	Gravesend & Northfleet	v	Harlow Town	1–1
706	*Harlow Town*	v	*Gravesend & Northfleet*	*1–0*
517	Grays Athletic	v	Atherstone United	0–2
698	Enfield	v	VS Rugby	2–1
1587	Tamworth	v	Bromsgrove Rovers	0–1
927	Baldock Town	v	Halesowen Town	1–1
1219	*Halesowen Town*	v	*Baldock Town*	*1–0*
1288	Aylesbury United	v	Chesham United	1–1
1436	*Chesham United*	v	*Aylesbury United*	*1–3*
756	Tiverton Town	v	Dover Athletic	1–0
521	Merthyr Tydfil	v	Windsor & Eton	1–1
736	*Windsor & Eton*	v	*Merthyr Tydfil*	*1–0*
1483	Tonbridge	v	Yeovil Town	1–2
928	Worcester City	v	Marlow	1–2
808	Salisbury	v	Farnborough Town	1–7
2208	Horsham	v	Crawley Town	0–0
3427	*Crawley Town*	v	*Horsham*	*3–0*
990	Slough Town	v	Kingstonian	2–1
1576	Weymouth	v	Sutton United	1–1
1039	*Sutton United*	v	*Weymouth*	*3–0*
277	Hayes	v	Dorchester Town	1–0

† *abandoned after 90 mins, fog*

FIRST ROUND

West Bromwich Albion 6   Marlow 0

West Bromwich Albion were still trying to come to terms with the shock of being beaten by little Woking a year earlier, when the draw for the first round of the FA Cup was made.

The last thing they wanted was to draw a team of similar status, but that is exactly what happened when Bobby Gould's side came out of the velvet bag against Marlow.

A year earlier Albion, then a Second Division team managed by Brian Talbot, had been humbled 4–2 by Woking. Talbot was sacked and Albion subsequently dropped into the Third Division for the first time in their illustrious history.

Marlow decided against seeking advice from their Diadora League Premier Division rivals, preferring to go to The Hawthorns with their own style and principles.

Dave Russell, the Marlow manager, said: 'I could have asked Geoff Chapple, the Woking manager, for help but we have to accept that Albion are a better team than they were last year and Woking are better than we are.'

Albion may boast a tremendous Cup tradition – 10 finals and five times the winners – but Marlow went to the Midlands with their own little piece of Cup history.

In 1882 Marlow reached the semi-finals before losing 5–0 to Old Etonians, who went on to win the Cup by beating Blackburn Rovers 1–0.

History repeated itself on the afternoon of the first-round tie when Albion laid the ghost of their embarrassing defeat a season earlier by beating Marlow 6–0.

FIRST ROUND   16 November 1991

(replays in italics)

Att				Result
3864	Stockport County	v	Lincoln City	3–1
2864	Hartlepool United	v	Shrewsbury Town	3–2
2002	Witton Albion	v	Halifax Town	1–1*
2182	*Halifax Town*	v	*Witton Albion*	*1–2*
1851	Chester City	v	Guiseley	1–0
6563	Tranmere Rovers	v	Runcorn	3–0
4511	Scunthorpe United	v	Rotherham United	1–1
4816	*Rotherham United*	v	*Scunthorpe United*	*3–3****
9035	Emley	v	Bolton Wanderers	0–3
7509	Mansfield Town	v	Preston North End	0–1†
3805	Bury	v	Bradford City	0–1
3623	Darlington	v	Chesterfield	2–1
1889	Scarborough	v	Wigan Athletic	0–2
2853	Morecambe	v	Hull City	0–1

Att				Result
6763	Huddersfield Town	v	Lincoln United	7–0
2964	Wrexham	v	Winsford United	5–2
1650	Bridlington Town	v	York City	1–2
2037	Gretna	v	Rochdale	0–0
4300	*Rochdale*	v	*Gretna*	*3–1*
4074	Blackpool	v	Grimsby Town	2–1
9974	Stoke City	v	Telford United	0–0
4052	*Telford United*	v	*Stoke City*	*2–1*
7989	Burnley	v	Doncaster Rovers	1–1
4207	*Doncaster Rovers*	v	*Burnley*	*1–3*
3106	Carlisle United	v	Crewe Alexandra	1–1
3733	*Crewe Alexandra*	v	*Carlisle United*	*5–3**
5830	Brentford	v	Gillingham	3–3
7328	*Gillingham*	v	*Brentford*	*1–3*
1866	Halesowen Town	v	Farnborough Town	2–2
1673	*Farnborough Town*	v	*Halesowen Town*	*4–0*
4301	AFC Bournemouth	v	Bromsgrove Rovers	3–1
9315	Swansea City	v	Cardiff City	2–1
1773	Kidderminster Harriers	v	Aylesbury United	0–1
4858	Leyton Orient	v	Welling United	2–1
11082	West Bromwich Albion	v	Marlow	6–0
3370	Crawley Town	v	Northampton Town	4–2
4341	Peterborough United	v	Harlow Town	7–0
2534	Windsor & Eton	v	Woking	2–4††
2008	Maidstone United	v	Sutton United	1–0
6403	Fulham	v	Hayes	0–2
3990	Slough Town	v	Reading	3–3
6363	*Reading*	v	*Slough Town*	*2–1*
2384	Aldershot	v	Enfield	0–1
4635	Yeovil Town	v	Walsall	1–1
3869	*Walsall*	v	*Yeovil Town*	*0–1**
4965	Colchester United	v	Exeter City	0–0
4066	*Exeter City*	v	*Colchester United*	*0–0‡*
2588	Atherstone United	v	Hereford United	0–0
3479	*Hereford United*	v	*Atherstone United*	*3–0*
3317	Kettering Town	v	Wycombe Wanderers	1–1
5299	*Wycombe Wanderers*	v	*Kettering Town*	*0–2*
3964	Barnet	v	Tiverton Town	5–0
4123	Torquay United	v	Birmingham City	3–0

* after extra time
** match won by Rotherham United on penalties
† after abandoned tie, fog, 1–1 32mins, 6422
†† after abandoned tie, fog, 1–1 69 mins 2640
‡ match won by Exeter City on penalties

SECOND ROUND

Hayes 0   Crawley Town 2

Between them, Hayes and Crawley produced two of the shocks of the tournament to date when, in the first round, they saw off Fulham and Northampton respectively.

45

They both had visions of luring Third or Fourth Division sides in the next round. Instead they were stuck with each other.

Hayes had earned their place in the second round (only the second time they had progressed so far) by winning 2–0 at Craven Cottage, while Crawley had overcome Northampton, then managed by Theo Foley, 4–2 at home.

Hayes were given home advantage against Crawley and, despite the lowly status of the two teams, the match attracted a crowd of 4203.

Crawley had never before progressed beyond the first round and had in their team the usual gathering of builders and office workers.

They also had something of an oddity – a prison officer. Cliff Cant, a midfielder, is an officer at Wandsworth Prison in London and he took time off to steer Crawley to a 2–0 win.

Crawley's reward could not have been better – a Sussex derby game against Brighton & Hove Albion. The game attracted a massive crowd of 18,031, but Crawley's joy was short-lived. They were beaten 5–0 and Cant and company had to return to their dreams.

SECOND ROUND   7 December 1991

(replays in italics)

Att				Result
5299	Crewe Alexandra	v	Chester City	2–0
5776	Rochdale	v	Huddersfield Town	1–2
3897	Wrexham	v	Telford United	1–0
9753	Burnley	v	Rotherham United	2–0
4646	York City	v	Tranmere Rovers	1–1
5546	*Tranmere Rovers*	v	*York City*	*2–1*
5509	Darlington	v	Hartlepool United	1–2
7129	Bolton Wanderers	v	Bradford City	3–1
6766	Preston North End	v	Witton Albion	5–1
4554	Blackpool	v	Hull City	0–1
4168	Wigan Athletic	v	Stockport County	2–0
2913	Aylesbury United	v	Hereford United	2–3
6189	Leyton Orient	v	West Bromwich Albion	2–1
5328	Peterborough United	v	Reading	0–0
4373	*Reading*	v	*Peterborough United*	*1–0*
5121	Enfield	v	Barnet	1–4
4250	Woking	v	Yeovil Town	3–0
4186	Exeter City	v	Swansea City	0–0
3159	*Swansea City*	v	*Exeter City*	*1–2*
4203	Hayes	v	Crawley Town	0–2
2765	Maidstone United	v	Kettering Town	1–2
2725	Torquay United	v	Farnborough Town	1–1
2285	*Farnborough Town*	v	*Torquay United*	*4–3*
6538	AFC Bournemouth	v	Brentford	2–1

THIRD ROUND

Wrexham 2   Arsenal 1

Wrexham had finished 92nd and last in the Football League in the previous season. Arsenal had been champions. The gulf could not have been wider, but in the last 10 minutes of a remarkable afternoon at the Racecourse Ground, Wrexham bridged that gap with the help of their veteran captain Mickey Thomas.

Wrexham had been trailing to an Alan Smith goal scored on the stroke of half-time and Arsenal had created enough chances to have ended any hopes that Brian Flynn's side could have had of staging a recovery.

But Vince O'Keefe in the Wrexham goal made a series of excellent saves and when the referee awarded a free-kick to the Robins on the edge of the Arsenal penalty area in the 84th minute, Thomas stepped up to score the goal of his life.

In training, said Gordon Davies, who had delayed his departure for a coaching job in Norway to be a part of the Wrexham Cup adventure, the ball normally flew onto the terracing. This time it flew beyond the diving David Seaman and into the net for a Wrexham equaliser.

Within a minute Arsenal were out of the Cup. Davies crossed and Tony Adams failed to clear. Steve Watkin, one of Wrexham's legion of promising youngsters, forced the ball into the net. It prompted scenes that chairman Pryce Griffiths suggests had not been witnessed at the

Paul Allen just fails to clear from Dwight Yorke as Aston Villa knock Spurs out of the FA Cup in the third round

Racecourse Ground for more than a decade. Flynn and his team became overnight celebrities, but the adventure did not end there.

In the fourth round they were drawn against West Ham at Upton Park after the First Division side had finally overcome the challenge of non-League Farnborough. Twice behind, Wrexham came back to earn a 2–2 draw with goals from Phillips and substitute Jones. There was a crowd of more than 17,000 for the replay – the biggest since Wrexham's Second Division days at the end of the 1970s.

Although Wrexham produced probably their finest display in the Cup so far, they were beaten by a Colin Foster first-half header. 'It was a marvellous experience and we enjoyed the run,' said Flynn afterwards. 'I think that the team and the town has gained some pride from what we have achieved. That is what the FA Cup is all about, isn't it?'

Wrexham were on the wrong end of a giant-killing shock later in the season when they were knocked out of the Allbright's Welsh Cup by non-League Colwyn Bay.

THIRD ROUND   4 January 1992

(replays in italics)

Att				Result
10879	Huddersfield Town	v	Millwall	0–4
6025	Oxford United	v	Tranmere Rovers	3–1
31819	Leeds United	v	Manchester United	0–1
5913	Notts County	v	Wigan Athletic	2–0
12201	Sheffield United	v	Luton Town	4–0
29316	Aston Villa	v	Tottenham Hotspur	0–0
25462	*Tottenham Hotspur*	v	*Aston Villa*	*0–1*
12189	Norwich City	v	Barnsley	1–0
18793	Burnley	v	Derby County	2–2
18374	*Derby County*	v	*Burnley*	*2–0†*
27068	Nottingham Forest	v	Wolverhampton Wanderers	1–0
4753	Woking	v	Hereford United	0–0
8679	*Hereford United*	v	*Woking*	*2–1*
18031	Brighton & Hove Albion	v	Crawley Town	5–0
12220	Ipswich Town	v	Hartlepool United	1–1
8500	*Hartlepool United*	v	*Ipswich Town*	*0–2*
13580	Hull City	v	Chelsea	0–2
7301	Bolton Wanderers	v	Reading	2–0
12679	Bristol City	v	Wimbledon	1–1
3747	*Wimbledon*	v	*Bristol City*	*0–1*
14337	Preston North End	v	Sheffield Wednesday	0–2
10764	Oldham Athletic	v	Leyton Orient	1–1
8500	*Leyton Orient*	v	*Oldham Athletic*	*4–3**
10133	Swindon Town	v	Watford	3–2
12363	Wrexham	v	Arsenal	2–1
6767	Bristol Rovers	v	Plymouth Argyle	5–0
11431	Coventry City	v	Cambridge United	1–1

48

Att				Result
9865	*Cambridge United*	v	*Coventry City*	*1–0*
23499	West Ham United	v	Farnborough Town	1–1‡
23869	*West Ham United*	v	*Farnborough Town*	*1–0*
13710	Southampton	v	Queen's Park Rangers	2–0
19613	Leicester City	v	Crystal Palace	1–0
6765	Exeter City	v	Portsmouth	1–2
9625	Charlton Athletic	v	Barnet	3–1
21174	Middlesbrough	v	Manchester City	2–1
10651	AFC Bournemouth	v	Newcastle United	0–0
25954	*Newcastle United*	v	*AFC Bournemouth*	*2–2**††*
22609	Everton	v	Southend United	1–0
7457	Crewe Alexandra	v	Liverpool	0–4
15578	Sunderland	v	Port Vale	3–0
13821	Blackburn Rovers	v	Kettering Town	4–1

* *after extra time*
** *match won by AFC Bournemouth on penalties*
† *after abandoned tie, fog, 2–0 76 mins, 17621*
†† *after abandoned tie, fog, 0–0 17 mins, 20348*
‡ *Farnborough home tie*

FOURTH ROUND

Bristol Rovers 1   Liverpool 1
Replay: Liverpool 2   Bristol Rovers 1

For Carl Saunders the visit of Liverpool to Twerton Park was the kind of shop window every player outside of the First Division envisages.

He had made a stunning impact on the club, who play on the 'borrowed' ground of Bath City, after his move to the West Country from Stoke for £70,000 in February 1990.

And now the neat little stadium with a capacity of just under 10,000 was packed by an expectant crowd of 9463 hoping to see Rovers emulate the feat of Peterborough in the Rumbelows Cup and knock Liverpool out.

Graeme Souness's team had cruised into the fourth round with a 4–0 victory at Crewe, as John Barnes scored a thrilling hat-trick in his come-back game.

Now there was no Barnes, and Liverpool, their season continuing to splutter along like a car with a faulty spark plug, had just been beaten at home 2–1 by Chelsea.

The apprehension was well placed. The small crowd was generating a fine atmosphere, with one enterprising local resident having erected scaffolding in his garden for his friends to see the game. Whether he charged for the service, no one knows!

What they saw was Dean Saunders, not Carl, open the scoring from a Mike Marsh corner in the first half, the ball hitting the upright and then keeper Brian Parkin before crossing the line.

It was a cruel twist for Rovers who were denied what looked a certain penalty when David Mehew appeared to be clearly tripped by David Burrows. Not a professional foul, said referee Brian Hill. In fact, not a foul at all. Few agreed.

But Rovers were not to be deflected from their lofty ambition and when Mehew moved in from the right to lay the ball back, Carl Saunders grasped his moment of glory.

'We are very happy to be still in the competition,' said a relieved Souness after Carl Saunders had been carried shoulder high like one of the gladiators who once performed in the famous Roman Colosseum.

It seemed that half of Bristol had come to Anfield for the replay on 12 February, the blue and white balloons from their partying followers drifting on the night air.

And they had just cause to celebrate as their hero Saunders put Rovers ahead with a superb 20-yard shot that flew past Bruce Grobbelaar.

For 33 minutes that lead was kept intact, but the fairy tale was brought to its end by Steve McManaman, a precocious young man celebrating his 20th birthday.

Like a willow in the breeze he leaned first one way and then another before planting home the Liverpool equaliser. And then, to illustrate the scope of his promise and talent, he accelerated through the middle to supply Dean Saunders with the pass to provide the winner.

It had been an intriguing tie and the Rovers fans sang their anthem, 'Goodnight Irene', while the Kop applauded. It embodied the spirit of the FA Cup competition.

FOURTH ROUND   25 January 1992

(replays in italics)

Att				Result
12635	Bolton Wanderers	v	Brighton & Hove Albion	2–1
16138	Portsmouth	v	Leyton Orient	2–0
29772	Sheffield Wednesday	v	Middlesbrough	1–2
9968	Oxford United	v	Sunderland	2–3
21152	Chelsea	v	Everton	1–0
11982	Charlton Athletic	v	Sheffield United	0–0
15779	*Sheffield United*	v	*Charlton Athletic*	*3–1*
19313	Leicester City	v	Bristol City	1–2
17010	Norwich City	v	Millwall	2–1
19506	Southampton	v	Manchester United	0–0
33414	*Manchester United*	v	*Southampton*	*2–2***
24712	West Ham United	v	Wrexham	2–2
17995	*Wrexham*	v	*West Ham United*	*0–1*

Att			Result
12173	Notts County	v Blackburn Rovers	2–1
17193	Ipswich Town	v AFC Bournemouth	3–0
24259	Nottingham Forest	v Hereford United	2–0
9463	Bristol Rovers	v Liverpool	1–1
30142	*Liverpool*	v *Bristol Rovers*	*2–1*
7428	Cambridge United	v Swindon Town	0–3
22542	Derby County	v Aston Villa	3–4

** match won 4–2 by Southampton on penalties

Wrexham score an equaliser in their first fourth-round match against West Ham but go out in the replay

FIFTH ROUND

Ipswich 0   Liverpool 0
Replay: Liverpool 3   Ipswich 2*

It had promised to be the tie of the round: the vibrant Ipswich, tutored by John Lyall, the man with purist beliefs, against Liverpool, the team of all talents even if several of them were still injured.

But it was a wild Sunday afternoon in East Anglia, the wind whipping in at almost gale force off the North Sea, and consequently stylish football was almost an impossibility.

Such unpredictability made it a harrowing stage for defenders trying to judge the ball in the air and it was great credit to the ability of Mark Wright and John Wark that they were in such telling command.

For 34-year-old Wark it was a nostalgic occasion since he had once left Ipswich to play for Liverpool and was now back at Portman Road having been converted from marauding midfield star to dependable defender.

'He's an old pal and he played well, the old so-and-so,' said Liverpool manager Graeme Souness affectionately of Wark after the teams had battled through the weather to a goalless draw.

Whether the sentiments would have been quite the same had Wark scored, as he so very nearly did, is another matter. The former Scottish international made a late, perfectly timed run to meet a corner from Neil Thompson and his header thudded against the Liverpool crossbar.

'The ball came across so quickly, I could only run on to it,' Wark recalled after the match. 'I couldn't get direction on it. I wanted to get the ball down but it flew straight. I still thought it was going in.'

That chance and an attempted clearance by Ray Houghton that struck his own upright were evidence enough of just how dangerously Liverpool were living in this campaign.

But they survived, as they had done at Bath against Bristol Rovers in the previous round, and when Souness said, 'I would have settled for that before the game,' you knew he meant it.

The tie, however, was far from over and Anfield was again the stage for another thrilling replay in which Liverpool were obliged to be grateful to young forward Steve McManaman.

Ray Houghton had given Liverpool the lead and they were content to hold it when Ipswich, always trying to play football, made a breakthrough with only seven minutes remaining. Perhaps inevitably it was a John Wark-inspired goal, as he broke up a Liverpool forward move to release Steve Whitton for a dash down the right flank.

* after extra time

The cross was deep enough to elude the Liverpool defence and there was Gavin Johnson beyond the far post to come charging in and drive home the equaliser.

Now we really did have a Cup tie to feast on. Could Ipswich achieve their first-ever victory at Anfield – and would Liverpool lose their first home Cup game since before McManaman was even born?

When Jason Dozzell put Ipswich ahead three minutes into extra time it seemed that history was indeed in the making, until Liverpool's Great Dane was let off the leash. Jan Molby was within his range of goal when he stepped up to take the free-kick awarded for Mick Stockwell's foul on Dean Saunders.

And he struck it from 18 yards with awesome power and accuracy, the ball arching round the Ipswich wall and beyond the grasp of their Canadian international goalkeeper Craig Forrest.

Even then penalties appeared the likely decider of this tie. But McManaman ended all debate – and Ipswich's further involvement in the competition – after Ronny Rosenthal put him through.

It was cruel fortune for Ipswich, but not quite as cruel as that which befell another would-be giant-killer in Bolton Wanderers, replaying at Southampton after fighting back from a 2–0 deficit in the opening game at Burnden Park. They seemed bound for the quarter-finals with just seconds remaining at The Dell after Julian Darby had put them 2–1 in front in the 88th minute.

The Bolton fans were celebrating a famous victory when Barry Horne, with a dipping, swerving shot from fully 30 yards, found the net. The whistle blew almost immediately.

Perhaps it was the desperate disappointment, perhaps tiredness, but in the 107th minute of the match it was Horne again, this time from 20 yards, who drove home Southampton's winner.

FIFTH ROUND 15 February 1992

(replays in italics)

Att				Result
34447	Chelsea	v	Sheffield United	1–0
18138	Portsmouth	v	Middlesbrough	1–1
19479	*Middlesbrough*	v	*Portsmouth*	*2–4*
16402	Swindon Town	v	Aston Villa	1–2
14511	Norwich City	v	Notts County	3–0
20136	Bolton Wanderers.	v	Southampton	2–2
18009	*Southampton*	v	*Bolton Wanderers*	*3–2*
25475	Sunderland	v	West Ham United.	1–1
25830	*West Ham Utd.*	v	*Sunderland*	*2–3*
24615	Nottingham Forest	v	Bristol City	4–1
26140	Ipswich Town	v	Liverpool	0–0
27355	*Liverpool*	v	*Ipswich Town*	*3–2**

* *after extra time*

53

SIXTH ROUND

Southampton 0 Norwich City 0
Replay: Norwich City 2 Southampton 1*

The opening game between Southampton and Norwich for a semi-final place was one of the more eminently forgettable of this season's competition, strangled by a fear of defeat, marred by ragged play and a distinct absence of quality football.

Southampton manager Ian Branfoot blamed the state of the pitch at The Dell for his side's clear intention to by-pass midfield and get the ball into the Norwich penalty area. It turned this into a very physical tie with Norwich defending to such effect that Mark Walton barely had a shot to save throughout the entire match. In a goalless draw it was Southampton keeper Tim Flowers who kept his side in the tie with a series of fine saves from Robert Fleck in particular.

But Norwich got what they wanted and when the replay went to Carrow Road an extra-time winner from Chris Sutton decided the issue but not before the replay had been spoiled by disgraceful scenes.

Jeremy Goss of Norwich beats Southampton's Glenn Cockerill to the ball

*after extra time

It led to two Southampton players, Matthew Le Tissier and Barry Horne being sent off by referee Gerald Ashby, both for aiming wild kicks at Norwich players.

Norwich, semi-finalists three years previously, had been staring at a probable exit when Southampton centre-half Neil Ruddock put Saints into the lead just before half-time.

Even at that stage the two captains had been called together to try and calm the tense atmosphere. Le Tissier seemed to ignore the pleas and was sent off four minutes into the second half for a kick at Robert Fleck while the Norwich striker was on the ground. Yet Norwich still found it difficult against ten men, the equaliser finally coming when Mark Bowen's cross, headed down by Sutton, was fiercely struck home by Rob Newman.

It was Horne's turn to join Le Tissier in disgrace when he aimed a kick at the prostrate Colin Woodthorpe and it was then that Norwich finally made their push for victory.

Southampton, who in the fourth round had beaten Manchester United in a penalty shoot-out, were trying to hang on grimly for another. But in the 116th minute Norwich's semi-final place against Sunderland was at last assured, albeit in rather a fluke fashion.

For there is no doubt that Jeremy Goss was attempting a shot at goal himself when he mis-hit his right-foot effort and 19-year-old Sutton somehow managed to head the ball over the brave Flowers for the vital goal.

They had been two undistinguished games but there could be little argument that over the two of them it was Norwich who merited a place in the last four.

Southampton Flowers, Dodd, Benali, Horne, Moore, Ruddock, Le Tissier, Cockerill, Shearer, Dowie, Hurlock. Subs: Kenna, Maddison.

Norwich Walton, Culverhouse, Woodthorpe, Butterworth, Polston, Goss, Fox, Fleck, Newman, Sutton, Phillips. Subs: Sutch, Crook.

Att 20,088   *Referee* G. R. Ashby (Worcester).

Replay:

Norwich Walton, Culverhouse Woodthorpe (Crook 100), Butterworth, Polston, Goss, Fox, Fleck (Beckford 70), Newman, Sutton, Bowen.

Southampton Flowers, Dodd (Kenna 80), Benali, Horne, Moore, Ruddock, Le Tissier, Cockerill, Shearer, Dowie, Hurlock. Sub: Maddison.

Att 21,017   *Referee* G. R. Ashby (Worcester).

SIXTH ROUND

Portsmouth 1   Nottingham Forest 0

It was the kind of centre that Mark Crossley would catch in his sleep – an easy height, unobstructed view and without a forward climbing to upset his balance. Yet somehow Nottingham Forest's Crossley dropped the ball and for Alan McLoughlin it was like a suitcase full of £50 notes dropping at his feet.

It meant that for 89 minutes at an emotional Fratton Park Pompey were protecting that narrowest of advantages, holding on in the first half and then establishing their control in the second.

It was in 1949 that Portsmouth had last figured in a semi-final, the season in fact in which they became First Division champions.

For their manager Jim Smith it would be a first appearance in the last four, and one perhaps that his pedigree as a coach and manager over 23 seasons justified.

It was ironical, however, that the match-winner for Pompey should be a player on loan to the club. McLoughlin was signed by Southampton from Swindon for £1 million but never settled at The Dell.

Smith had signed him on loan (with a view to a cut-price transfer) at the time of his winning contribution in what was only his third full game of the season. McLoughlin later joined Portsmouth on a permanent basis.

Forest had begun the match as the clear favourites, but their exacting Rumbelows Cup semi-final against Tottenham seven days earlier, with its energy sapping extra time, appeared to have left a mark.

The intricate passing style so typical of a Brian Clough side was disjointed and the cutting edge missing. So Clough's cherished dream of winning the FA Cup just once in his career had eluded him again.

Perhaps typically, however, his thoughts were for the hapless Crossley. 'My heart goes out to him,' said the Forest manager. 'Nobody had to tell him he dropped a clanger. But he then had to watch us for more than 88 minutes trying to get an equaliser. He'll get over it. We'll all get over it even though it was very disappointing to lose a match in that way.'

But Smith, affectionately known as 'Bald Eagle' in football circles, was more concerned about himself than Clough. 'It's all very romantic talking about where Brian missed out. But what about me? I've been in the game for 23 years and anyway Brian knocked me out at Newcastle last season. That defeat hurt and it wasn't long afterwards that I got the sack.'

Smith revealed his belief in superstition. He wore the red silk handkerchief his father had given him as an 18-year-old and in his pocket was a penknife, now broken in two but always carried as a lucky charm.

Portsmouth   Knight, Awford, Beresford, Powell (Aspinall 64), Symons, Burns, Neill, Kuhl, Clarke (Whittingham 75), McLoughlin, Anderton.

Nottingham Forest   Crossley, Laws, Pearce, Walker, Wassall, Keane, Crosby, Gemmill, Clough, Sheringham (Chettle 65), Glover. Sub: Tiler.

Att 25,402   *Referee* S.J. Lodge (Sheffield & Hallamshire).

SIXTH ROUND

Liverpool 1   Aston Villa 0

Michael Thomas had only ever scored one goal at Anfield before this FA Cup quarter-final against Ron Atkinson's Aston Villa. That goal had won the title for Arsenal in 1989.

Now three years later Thomas, who had been signed by Graeme Souness from Arsenal in December 1991, scored his second which gave Liverpool a place in the FA Cup semi-final against Portsmouth.

Thomas, who had been out through injury for the previous three weeks, really should not have even been playing. But the Cup quarter-final, Souness decided, demanded bold managerial decisions.

A few days earlier Liverpool had been to Genoa to play the first leg of the UEFA Cup quarter-final and had lost 2–0. They eventually lost 4–1 on aggregate. The FA Cup was the only realistic target left for Liverpool last season.

So Souness gambled on the fitness of England's John Barnes as well as the Republic of Ireland's Ronnie Whelan, who had not played a first-team game since the Merseyside derby against Everton the ·previous August.

Whelan had suffered a knee injury which had required three operations. Indeed his career had been under serious threat when he was suddenly recalled to the Liverpool side.

His contribution was decisive and Souness was full of praise for the Liverpool captain after a gruelling match which Villa had opportunities to win.

'He is a shining example to any footballer who has been out with injury and feels that his career is threatened. He never gave up and has shown what an asset he can be to Liverpool,' said Souness afterwards.

'People talk about the players that have been out through injury this season, but Ronnie Whelan has been the greatest loss to this football club. It was wonderful to have him back in the side. He had missed 42 games and only played in one and a half reserve matches before this game. He was quite outstanding. I am delighted, and so should every Liverpool supporter be, to see him back.

'It was an enormous gamble to play so many lads who had missed so much football but it was a win or bust situation and thankfully we won.'

The victory kept alive a Liverpool season which had been badly disrupted by injury.

But for all the quality that returned to the Liverpool side they needed time to re-acquaint themselves with the pace and touch required in a Cup tie of this calibre.

That time was bought for them by their colourful goalkeeper Bruce Grobbelaar who made a series of outstanding saves including one spectacular effort from a volley by Villa's £1 million striker Dalian Atkinson.

Although Aston Villa manager Ron Atkinson believed his side, which had struggled to find goals in the previous month, 'had Liverpool on the ropes at that stage' there was always the suspicion that John Barnes would produce something special.

After spending the season overcoming an Achilles' tendon injury Barnes had started just five matches and finished only three in the season. His first come-back attempt had come in the FA Cup third round against Crewe.

There alongside England's most famous railway station, Barnes had scored a splendid hat-trick. He didn't score against Aston Villa but he managed the next best thing.

In the decisive 67th minute he picked up a Whelan clearance and although there was no obvious danger to the Villa defence Barnes soon started the alarm bells ringing when he accelerated away from Kevin Richardson.

He spotted Thomas making a run into the heart of the Villa defence. Barnes delivered the perfect pass and although Dariuz Kubicki, the Villa substitute, came to cover, Thomas had the pace to race clear.

As Spink came off his line Thomas lifted the ball over him and into the empty Villa net. The bold challenge from Ron Atkinson's team was over. They mounted a few more threatening attacks, especially when Steve Froggatt came on as substitute to replace Villa's leading scorer Dwight Yorke.

But once more the much maligned Grobbelaar stood firm even though he damaged his hand making a brave save. He needed hospital treatment after the match.

It had been a productive FA Cup for Villa and for Yorke in particular. The young striker from the Caribbean island of Tobago had scored in each round up to the Anfield game.

Yorke had been spotted by former Villa manager Graham Taylor, who is now England's manager, while the club had been on a mid season tour to Trinidad and Tobago.

After being refused permission by the Tobago team to play for Villa in a match on the island, he persuaded Taylor to offer him a trial at Villa Park. He was signed and took giant strides forward in his first full season in the First Division.

His goal at White Hart Lane – there are those who will argue that it was a Paul Allen own goal – claimed the scalps of FA Cup holders Tottenham and then Yorke scored a hat-trick in Villa's victory over Derby at the Baseball Ground in the fourth round.

They completed a hat-trick of away wins in the fifth round when they beat Swindon 2–1 at the County Ground. Yorke again laid the foundations for the victory with the first goal in that game screened on BBC television.

For Liverpool there was the reward of an FA Cup semi-final against Second Division Portsmouth at Highbury. It produced an historic confrontation surrounded in controversy.

Liverpool   Grobbelaar, Jones, Venison, Nicol, Whelan, Wright, Saunders, Houghton, Thomas (Molby 85), Barnes, McManaman (Rosenthal 77).

Aston Villa   Spink, Blake (Kubicki 45), Staunton, Teale, McGrath, Richardson, Daley, Parker, Regis, Atkinson, Yorke (Froggatt 74).

Att 29,109   *Referee*   P. Don (Middlesex).

Chelsea's Graeme Le Saux and Brian Atkinson of Sunderland tussle for the ball

SIXTH ROUND

Chelsea 1   Sunderland 1
Replay: Sunderland 2   Chelsea 1

Sunderland needed late goals first at Stamford Bridge to stay in this FA Cup quarter-final and then at Roker Park to win a place in the semi-final against Norwich at Hillsborough.

John Byrne maintained his record of scoring in every round to keep Sunderland in the Cup against Chelsea in London on 9 March, after Sunderland were convinced that they had been the victims of a refereeing error.

Chelsea had taken the lead through their bargain signing Clive Allen who had cost Ian Porterfield only £250,000 from Manchester City earlier in the season. Allen had already scored the goal which had accounted for Everton in the fourth round.

Then Allen was described by his former manager at Manchester City, Howard Kendall, as one of the most lethal strikers in the First Division. He offered further evidence to Sunderland's travelling 5,000 fans in this game.

Kerry Dixon, the former England international, appeared to have miscued his shot into the side netting of the goal defended by Welsh international Tony Norman.

To the surprise of Sunderland, not to mention the Chelsea side, Wolverhampton referee Terry Holbrook pointed to the corner flag. He clearly believed the ball had taken a deflection. Television cameras suggested it had not.

From the corner, taken by Wise, Elliott produced a towering header which Stuart, the scorer of the winner against Sheffield United in the previous round, directed towards goal.

Hardyman blocked the ball on the goal line and although the Chelsea players appealed for a penalty, Allen guaranteed there would be no further arguments, with his ninth goal for the club he was to leave on transfer deadline day.

Sunderland manager Malcolm Crosby refused to criticise the referee afterwards. He said simply: 'We did not think that it was a corner in the first place but who would be a referee?'

Until that point Sunderland could have argued, with some justification, that they had controlled most of the game and had it not been for a fine double save by Hitchcock, playing his fiftieth game for the club, the Wearsiders might have been ahead in the 11th minute.

Stung by what they regarded as the injustice of the goal, Sunderland flew forward in the second half putting even greater pressure on the Chelsea goal and they were rewarded with the equaliser eight minutes from the end.

Bracewell, three times a Wembley loser with Everton, launched the ball forward towards the much travelled Byrne. The former York, Queen's Park Rangers, Le Havre and Brighton striker, placed the pass beyond the diving Hitchcock with great skill and deliberation.

Byrne, in his relief, ran to hug the match referee. Maybe the equaliser was a relief to them both. It meant a replay, that was to be as fiercely contested nine days later.

It was another header, even later in the game, that was to decide the replay at Roker Park. This time the goalscorer was Sunderland's Gordon Armstrong.

Chelsea appeared to have performed the late escape act in the North East when Dennis Wise equalised a first-half effort from Davenport with only four minutes remaining in a pulsating Cup tie.

But there was more excitement to come on a bitterly cold night when Atkinson's corner was met by the powerful Armstrong and the ball flew beyond the diving Beasant, an FA Cup winner with Wimbledon in 1988.

It was no more than Sunderland deserved over the two matches. The result was a source of great delight for their fans who poured on to the Roker Park pitch in celebration.

Sunderland had taken the lead in the 20th minute when the promising Sinclair had lost possession to Rush near the half-way line. There was no immediate danger until the youngster spotted the run by the elusive Byrne.

The Republic of Ireland international beat Elliott before shooting from 15 yards. Beasant could not hold the shot and the ball ran into the path of Davenport, the former Nottingham Forest and Manchester United striker, who scored comfortably.

Chelsea responded as spiritedly as Sunderland had in the original match at Stamford Bridge and might have equalised much earlier had it not been for two magnificent saves from Tony Norman. Andy Townsend also had a shot cleared off the line by Paul Bracewell.

It was Vinny Jones who conjured up the equaliser in that frantic finish with a through pass which Wise, another former Don, scrambled into the Sunderland net.

Then came the winner from Armstrong and with it a place for the 1973 FA Cup winners in the semi-final against Dave Stringer's Norwich City.

Chelsea Hitchcock, Hall, Myers, K. Wilson, Elliott, Cundy, Stuart, Townsend, Dixon, Allen, Wise.

Sunderland Norman, Kay, Rogan, Bennett, Hardyman, Rush, Davenport, Bracewell, Armstrong, Byrne, Atkinson.

Att 33,948   *Referee* T. Holbrook (Wolverhampton).

Replay:

Sunderland Norman, Kay, Rogan, Ball, Hardyman (Ord 45), Rush, Bracewell, Davenport, Armstrong, Byrne, Atkinson.

Chelsea Beasant, Clarke, Sinclair, Jones, Elliott, Cundy (Allen 75), Le Saux (Stuart 70), Townsend, Dixon, Cascarino, Wise.

Att 26,039 *Referee* T. Holbrook (Wolverhampton).

SIXTH ROUND (QUARTER-FINAL)   7 March 1992

Att				Result
20088	Southampton	v	Norwich	0–0
25402	Portsmouth	v	Nottingham Forest	1–0
8 March 1992				
29109	Liverpool	v	Aston Villa	1–0
9 March 1992				
33948	Chelsea	v	Sunderland	1–1
Replays	**18 March 1992**			
21017	Norwich	v	Southampton	2–1*
26039	Sunderland	v	Chelsea	2–1

* *after extra time*

SEMI-FINAL

Liverpool 1 Portsmouth 1*
Replay: Liverpool 0 Portsmouth 0**

Portsmouth were not given even a hint of a chance by the pundits. Though Liverpool's season had been a disappointing one compared to their exalted successes of past years they looked to have more than enough to handle Second Division Pompey.

But how differently the story unfolded at Highbury that Sunday afternoon amid a splash of colour from the blue of Hampshire and the red of Merseyside.

Jim Smith's young side had to rise to the occasion. And they did. The cagey 'Bald Eagle' set out to stifle Liverpool's renowned passing game in midfield.

Chris Burns, who 12 months earlier had been playing non-League football at Cheltenham, was now in the thick of the action, breaking up those Liverpool runs from deep positions.

* *after extra time*
** *Liverpool won 3-1 on penalties*

But Graeme Souness's side probed to try and find the weak spots of this proud Pompey team and it was Steve McManaman, their 20-year-old winger who was having the most success down the right flank.

He threatened to win the game almost single-handed and his marker John Beresford, booked in the first 10 minutes, was lucky to stay on the field after the extra-time tackle that put the youngster not only out of the remainder of the match and the replay but also every other League game up to the final.

Portsmouth, much earlier in the match, had lost one of their key players, Mark Chamberlain, with a knee injury but it didn't prevent them creating the best chances.

Bruce Grobbelaar produced a remarkable one-handed save from a shot by Alan McLoughlin and twice Ray Houghton cleared off the line from Colin Clarke.

Pompey's confidence grew visibly but a goal proved elusive. As the game went into the extra half-hour the feeling was that Liverpool would have the greater fitness and lasting power.

Ian Rush missed a sitter in the second minute of extra time, firing over the bar, while Steve Nicol cleared off the line from Colin Clarke at the other end.

Yet after 110 minutes Pompey had their chance. A long ball from Warren Neill at last gave promising young winger Darren Anderton the kind of run at goal that made him such a sought-after player.

It was a test of his nerve as he ran at the experienced Grobbelaar, but he kept cool enough to steer the ball home and give his side a genuine chance of their first Wembley final since 1939.

The celebrations were well advanced when, with three minutes remaining on the big Highbury clock, Andy Awford, a young central defender of vast potential, conceded a free-kick just outside his penalty-area.

Everybody knows of the danger posed by John Barnes' ability to bend the ball in these situations. It was like offering Jimmy White one over the pocket.

Sure enough, Barnes bent his shot almost lazily round the wall, it struck the Portsmouth upright and there was the veteran Irishman Ronnie Whelan following in to clinch the replay.

It was staged eight days later at Villa Park and Portsmouth once again came so very close to creating the biggest Cup upset for many a season.

This time they emerged level from extra-time and were then submerged under the cruel lottery of the penalty shoot-out.

It was another tense and tight meeting, an epic game of football in which Portsmouth won respect and then sympathy for their resilience and organisation.

63

This time it was the flanks Smith concentrated on, introducing Ray Daniel at left-back and playing Beresford just in front of him. That curtailed the attacking instincts of young Jones while on the opposite flank it was Anderton, working backwards, who was prepared to do his share of the defending in front of his right-back Neill. With Awford and Kit Symons producing another heroic and defiant partnership at the heart of defence, Liverpool's surging attacks were repelled.

It was absorbing football, like a game of chess, and such was Pompey's efficiency that it was Jan Molby who was left to fire long-range shots at the excellent Alan Knight.

No one, however, could produce the one shot or header to break the deadlock and the game went to a shoot-out where Pompey's nerve at last snapped.

Three misses by Kuhl, Beresford and Neill while Barnes, Rush and Dean Saunders stroked home their shots, decided the issue. But Portsmouth had contributed richly to two fine matches and it was a pity they didn't get the chance to make it third time lucky.

Liverpool Grobbelaar, Jones, Burrows (Venison 45), Nicol, Whelan, Wright, McManaman, Houghton (Marsh 87), Rush, Barnes, Thomas.

Portsmouth Knight, Awford, Beresford, McLoughlin (Whittingham 109), Symons, Burns, Neill, Kuhl, Clarke, Chamberlain (Aspinall).

Att 41,869 *Referee* M. J. Bodenham (Cornwall).

Replay:

Liverpool Grobbelaar, Jones (Walters 118), Burrows, Nicol, Whelan (Venison 68), Wright, Saunders, Molby, Rush, Barnes, Thomas.

Portsmouth Knight, Awford, Beresford, McLoughlin (Aspinall 116), Symons, Burns, Neill, Kuhl, Clarke (Whittingham 70), Daniel, Anderton.

Att 40,077 *Referee* M. J. Bodenham (Cornwall).

SEMI-FINAL

Sunderland 1   Norwich City 0

The John Byrne and Malcolm Crosby story continued when Sunderland created another FA Cup upset in the semi-final at Hillsborough against First Division Norwich. In an FA Cup campaign masterminded by Crosby, who had been offered the manager's job on a temporary basis after the removal of Denis Smith in December, Sunderland had beaten two other sides from the top flight. Out had gone West Ham, doomed to relegation, and Chelsea. In both matches the goalscoring skills of John Byrne proved decisive. He had scored in every round.

At Hillsborough, staging its first FA Cup semi-final since the tragedy of 1989, Byrne produced the goal that ended Norwich's hopes of reaching a Cup final for the first time in their history. (They had been in the other, understandably overshadowed, semi-final in 1989 when they lost by a single goal to Everton.) This defeat though was to prove the most disappointing in the managerial career of Dave Stringer, who resigned from the Carrow Road job in the last week of the season.

Sunderland had taken the lead at Hillsborough in the 35th minute. Rush's pass sent Atkinson away down the right and he crossed into the heart of the retreating Norwich defence.

Walton, the inexperienced Norwich goalkeeper, who was deputising for the injured Scottish international Gunn, could not cut out the centre and Byrne, who had beaten the offside trap, headed into the net.

His finishing was of the highest order and even Stringer had no doubts that Byrne would score when the ball careered towards the Irish international striker. 'He was the last person I wanted to see waiting for the cross,' said the Norwich manager.

It was a sweet moment for Byrne who had contemplated retiring from the game two years earlier when he had been exiled in the reserves of French League side Le Havre. He spent lonely and frustrating weekends trying to tune his radio into commentaries from English League games, wondering if he would ever return.

He owed his chance to Brighton manager Barry Lloyd and in his only season at the Goldstone Ground, Byrne had formed a profitable partnership with Mike Small, who was to move on to West Ham.

But having scored so early, Sunderland were now forced to endure 55 nerve-racking minutes. It was a measure of the performances of Anton Rogan, twice a Scottish Cup final winner with Celtic, and the combative Kevin Ball, that Norwich failed to equalise.

Fleck, the Scottish international, was recalled to the Norwich side despite the fact that he was still in pain after breaking ribs in the sixth round replay against Southampton. It was his first match back. He created one of Norwich's best chances when he crossed deep to Sutton who missed that and two other outstanding opportunities for the East Anglian side.

Sutton, a gangling young striker whose effectiveness had persuaded Norwich to alter their normal passing style, should have scored from a Bowen cross after only two minutes but shot instead at Norman.

Then, when Norwich were intensifying their search for an equaliser in the second half, Bowen put Sutton through again and although he beat Norman to the pass, the striker's effort drifted a foot wide of the

Chris Sutton (Norwich) gets a toe to the ball before Sunderland's Paul Bracewell

empty net.

Sunderland had their chances as well but both Davenport and Bennett, their substitute, failed to score the second which might have made the final few minutes more comfortable for the watching Crosby.

At the final whistle the Sunderland contingent in the 40,000 crowd stayed for almost half an hour in the hope of seeing their heroes return for a lap of honour. Crosby wanted to grant their wish but the police decided it was inappropriate. It was an outstanding achievement by Sunderland as they reached their first Cup final for 19 years. Bob Stokoe, who had been manager on that memorable day, had no doubts that Crosby's reward should be the manager's job.

'Who ever heard of a caretaker-manager at Wembley?' said Stokoe, who had plotted the downfall of Don Revie's Leeds in 1973. Eventually the Sunderland board, whose reluctance to appoint Crosby on a full-time basis led to speculation that there was another candidate for the job, decided that Crosby was the right man for Roker Park.

He was given the keys to the manager's office a fortnight before the final against Liverpool and the man he replaced, Denis Smith, had no doubts that Sunderland had made the right choice. It had been Smith who had persuaded Crosby, a workmanlike midfield player at York, to take up coaching as his playing career was coming to an end. Crosby, who had watched Sunderland's 1973 Cup success from the terraces, needed some convincing.

But he did take a coaching course and was given a job in Kuwait by the former Fulham, Portsmouth and Chelsea manager Bobby Campbell. Although the money was good in the Middle East, Crosby was looking for a challenge. It came when he bumped into his former manager Smith in Crosby's native North East. He was asked if he would like a chance on the Sunderland coaching staff and accepted the job.

When he moved back to Sunderland he and his wife ran the hostel for young players at their house within a few minutes of Roker Park. 'He is Sunderland through and through,' said Smith. 'He was born in South Shields and has a deep love for Sunderland Football Club.

'If there was anyone who could do a great job for Sunderland and would care about the club then it would be Malcolm Crosby,' he added. The Sunderland directors agreed. It was Malcolm Crosby, Sunderland manager rather than 'caretaker-manager', who led the side out on Cup final day.

Sunderland Norman, Kay, Rogan, Ball (Bennett 60), Hardyman, Rush, Bracewell, Davenport, Armstrong, Byrne, Atkinson. Sub: Brady.

Norwich Walton, Culverhouse, Woodthorpe, Butterworth, Polston, Goss, Fox, Fleck, Newman, Sutton (Sutch 72), Bowen. Sub: Ullathorne.

Att 40,102 *Referee* N. Midgley (Lancashire).

SEMI–FINAL 5 April 1992

	Att			*Result*
Highbury				
	41869 Liverpool (Whelan 117)	v	Portsmouth (Anderton 110)	1–1*
Hillsborough				
	40102 Sunderland (Byrne 34)	v	Norwich City	1–0
Replay Villa Park, 13 April 1992				
	40077 Liverpool	v	Portsmouth	0–0*
	Liverpool won 3–1 on penalties			

after extra time

FA Cup Final Teams 1872–1992

The Football Association Challenge Cup is the most respected club competition in world football. It has become a part of the fabric of English sporting life. The final is seen worldwide. The occasion is cherished by those who are a part of it and seen enviously by those who have tried to repeat its successful but unique formula.

It was the idea of Charles William Alcock back in July 1871. He had been the FA's secretary for less than 12 months – at the tender age of 30 – when he decided that the time had come for a national knock-out competition.

As Bryon Butler's splendid history of The Football Association revealed, the idea was put before six other FA men in the offices of the *Sportsman* newspaper just off Ludgate Hill in London. The plan was accepted and 15 clubs entered the first-ever FA Challenge Cup.

The clubs were Barnes, Civil Service, Crystal Palace, Clapham Rovers, Hitchin, Maidenhead, Marlow, Queen's Park (Glasgow), Donington Grammar School (Spalding), the marvellously named Hampstead Heathens, Harrow Chequers, Reigate Priory, Royal Engineers, Upton Park and the Wanderers.

With the exception of Queen's Park and Donington GS the clubs were all from London. It was not exactly national but it was a start, although the FA had expected a greater entry from their 50-strong membership.

The trophy was known as the 'Little Tin Pot' and cost £20. It was to be the first of four Cups. In the end only 12 teams took part. Harrow, Reigate and Donington all scratched, while Queen's Park were exempted until the semi-final.

The following are those who have made the FA Cup the competition it is today – those who have built legends and lived through tragedy to make it the greatest Cup tournament of them all.

16 March 1872   *Kennington Oval*   *Att 2000*

The Wanderers 1   Royal Engineers 0
(Betts)

The very first FA Cup Final set a pattern that has been often repeated throughout the history of the competition. The favourites lost.

Wanderers found their way to the final, staged in front of a 2000 crowd at Kennington Oval, only because Glasgow side Queen's Park could not afford to travel back to London for a semi-final replay.

A side selected from the public schools and universities, Wanderers were captained by C.W. Alcock, the secretary of The Football Association, whose resolution it was to initiate the competition.

The winning goal was scored by M.P. Betts who actually played in the match under a pseudonym, A.H. Chequer. The Royal Engineers from Chatham lost one of their players, Lieutenant Creswell, after 10 minutes with a broken collar bone – football's first recorded injury.

The Wanderers' side included six future internationals including the Rev. R.W.S. Vidal of Oxford University, nicknamed the 'Prince of Dribblers', who once scored three goals in succession in one match from the kick-offs without an opponent touching the ball.

This first, historic final was played without crossbars or goal-nets, free-kicks or penalties and with no half-way line or centre circle.

Wanderers   de C Welch, Alcock, Betts, Bonsor, Bowen, Crake, Hooman, Lubbock, Thompson, Vidal, Wollaston

Royal Engineers   Merriman, Marindin, Addison, Creswell, Mitchell, Renny-Tailyour, Rich, Goodwyn, Muirhead, Cotter, Boyle.

29 March 1873   Lillie Bridge   Att 3000
Wanderers 2   Oxford University 0
(Wollaston, Kinnaird)

Wanderers   Bowen, Thompson, de C Welch, Kinnaird, Howell, Wollaston, Sturgiss, Stewart, Kenyon-Slaney, Kingsford, Bonsor

Oxford University   Kirke-Smith, Leach, Mackarness, Birley, Longman, Chappell-Maddison, Dixon, Paton, Vidal, Sumner, Ottaway

14 March 1874   *Kennington Oval*   *Att 2500*
Oxford University 2   Royal Engineers 0
(Mackarness, Paton)

Oxford University   Neapean, Mackarness, Birley, Green, Vidal, Ottaway, Benson, Paton, WS Rawson, Chappell-Maddison, Johnson

Royal Engineers   Merriman, Marindin, Addison, Onslow, Oliver, Digby, Renny-Tailyour, HE Rawson, Blackman, Wood, von Donop

13 March 1875   *Kennington Oval*   *Att 3000*
Royal Engineers 1   Old Etonians 1
(Renny-Tailyour)   (Bonsor)

Royal Engineers   Merriman, Sim, Onslow, Ruck, von Donop, Wood, Rawson, Stafford, Renny-Tailyour, Mein, Wingfield-Stratford

Old Etonians   Thompson, Benson, E Lubbock, Wilson, Kinnaird, Stronge, Patton, Farmer, Bonsor, Kenyon-Slaney, Ottaway

*Replay – **16 March 1875***   *Kennington Oval   Att 3000*

Royal Engineers 2   Old Etonians 0
(Renny-Tailyour, Stafford)

Royal Engineers   Merriman, Sim, Onslow, Ruck, von Donop, Wood, Rawson, Stafford, Renny-Tailyour, Mein, Wingfield-Stratford

Old Etonians   Drummond-Moray, Farrer, E Lubbock, Wilson, Kinnaird, Stronge, Patton, Farmer, Bonsor, A Lubbock, Hammond

11 March 1876   *Kennington Oval   Att 3000*

Wanderers 0   Old Etonians 0

Wanderers   Greig, Stratford, Lindsay, Maddison, Birley, Wollaston, F Heron, H Heron, Edwards, Kenrick, Hughes

Old Etonians   Hogg, Meysey, E Lyttleton, Welldon, Kinnaird, Thompson, Kenyon-Slaney, A Lyttleton, Sturgis, Bonsor, Allene

*Replay – **18 March 1876***   *Kennington Oval   Att 3500*

Wanderers 3   Old Etonians 0
(Wollaston, Hughes 2)

Wanderers   Greig, Stratford, Lindsay, Maddison, Birley, Wolaston, H Heron, F Heron, Edwards, Kenrick, Hughes

Old Etonians   Hogg, E Lubbock, E Lyttleton, Faner, Kinnaird, Stronge, Kenyon-Slaney, A Lyttleton, Sturgis, Bonsor, Allene

24 March 1877   *Kennington Oval   Att 3000*

Wanderers 2   Oxford University 0*
(Kenrick, Lindsay)

Wanderers   Birley, Stratford, Lindsay, Green, Kinnaird, Wollaston, F Heron, Hughes, Wace, Denton, Kenrick

Oxford University   Alington, Bain, Dunell, Savory, Todd, Waddington, Fernandez, Hills, Otter, Parry, Rawson

23 March 1878   *Kennington Oval   Att 4500*

Wanderers 3   Royal Engineers 1
(Kenrick 2, og) (Morris)

Wanderers   Kirkpatrick, Stratford, W Lindsay, Kinnaird, Green, Wollaston, H Heron, Wylie, Wace, Denton, Kenrick

Royal Engineers   Friend, Cowan, Morris, Mayne, Heath, Haynes, M Lindsay, Hedley, Bond, Barnet, Ruck

* after extra time

Winning with Style

A Lotto soccer shoe is born from the technology of Lotto's Research and Development Centre and made with all the enthusiasm of those who play the sport themselves. By combining technically innovative features and reflecting the best players' thoughts, Lotto's soccer boots set themselves apart from their rivals.

RUUD GULLIT
LOTTO'S CONSULTANT

The In Stadio shoe is the end result and its characteristics make it a very high quality product to satisfy demands from the World's leading players: Gullit, Hugo, Sanchez, Romario, Clough, Saunders, Thorstedvt, Wright to name just a few.

29 March 1879   *Kennington Oval   Att 5000*

Old Etonians 1   Clapham Rovers 0
(Clerke)

Old Etonians   Hawtrey, Christian, Bury, Kinnaird, E Lubbock, Clerke, Pares, Goodhart, Whitfield, Chevallier, Beaufoy

Clapham   Birkett, Ogilvie, Field, Bailey, Prinsep, Rawson, Stanley, Scott, Bevington, Growse, Keith-Falconer

10 April 1880   *Kennington Oval   Att 6000*

Clapham Rovers 1   Oxford University 0
(Lloyd-Jones)

Clapham   Birkett, Ogilvie, Field, Weston, Bailey, Brougham, Stanley, Barry, Sparks, Lloyd-Jones, Ram

Oxford University   Parr, Wilson, King, Phillips, Rogers, Heygate, Childs, Eyre, Crowdy, Hill, J Lubbock

9 April 1881   *Kennington Oval   Att 4500*

Old Carthusians 3   Old Etonians 0
(Wynyard, Parry, Todd)

Old Carthusians   Gillett, Norris, Colvin, Prinsep, Vintcent, Hansell, Richards, Page, Wynyard, Parry, Todd

Old Etonians   Rawlinson, Foley, French, Kinnaird, Farrer, Chevallier, Anderson, Goodhart, Macaulay, Whitfield, Novelli

25 March 1882   *Kennington Oval   Att 7000*

Old Etonians 1   Blackburn Rovers 0
(Anderson)

Blackburn, one of the Football League's original clubs, became the first provincial club to make the journey to The Oval for the FA Cup Final in its eleventh year.

It proved, however, an abortive visit as Old Etonians won through a goal from W.J. Anderson scored after nine minutes of the game.

Etonians boasted the experience of the Hon. A.F. Kinnaird who was playing in his eighth final, having played first for Wanderers in the second-ever final in 1873 against Oxford University.

He was so elated at this victory that he celebrated by standing on his head in front of the Oval Pavilion.

Blackburn had been upset at having to change their strip because of a colour clash and had been unable to cope with the Old Etonian tactics of counter-attacking charges upfield.

Old Etonians   Rawlinson, French, de Paravicini, Kinnaird, Foley, Novelli, Dunn, Macaulay, Goodhart, Anderson, Chevallier

Blackburn Rovers Howarth, McIntyre, Suter, Sharples, F Hargreaves, Duckworth, Douglas, Strachan, Brown, Avery, J Hargreaves

31 March 1883   Kennington Oval   Att 8000
Blackburn Olympic 2   Old Etonians 1
(Costley, Matthews)   (Goodhart)

Blackburn Olympic Hacking, Ward, Warburton, Gibson, Astley, Hunter, Dewhurst, Matthews, Wilson, Costley, Yates

Old Etonians Rawlinson, French, de Paravicini, Kinnaird, Foley, Chevallier, Anderson, Macaulay, Goodhart, Dunn, Bainbridge

29 March 1884 *Kennington Oval   Att 4000*
Blackburn Rovers 2   Queen's Park 1
(Brown, Forrest)   (Christie)

Blackburn Rovers Arthur, Beverley, Suter, McIntyre, J Hargreaves, Forrest, Lofthouse, Douglas, Sowerbutts, Inglis, Brown

Queen's Park Gillespie, Arnott, MacDonald, Campbell, Gow, Anderson, Watt, Dr Smith, Harrower, Allan, Christie

4 April 1885 *Kennington Oval   Att 12500*
Blackburn Rovers 2   Queen's Park 0
(Forrest, Brown)

Blackburn Rovers Arthur, Turner, Suter, McIntyre, Haworth, Forrest, Lofthouse, Douglas, Brown, Fecitt, Sowerbutts

Queen's Park Gillespie, Arnott, Macleod, Campbell, MacDonald, Hamilton, Anderson, Sellar, Gray, McWhannel, Allan

3 April 1886 *Kennington Oval   Att 15000*
Blackburn Rovers 0   West Bromwich Albion 0

Blackburn Rovers Arthur, Turner, Suter, Douglas, Forrest, McIntyre, Heyes, Strachan, Brown, Fecitt, Sowerbutts

West Bromwich Albion Roberts, H Green, H Bell, Horton, Perry, Timmins, Woodhall, T Green, Bayliss, Loach, G Bell

Replay – **10 April 1886** *Baseball Ground   Att 12000*
Blackburn Rovers 2   West Bromwich Albion 0
(Sowerbutts, Brown)

Blackburn Rovers Arthur, Turner, Suter, Douglas, Forrest, McIntyre, Walton, Strachan, Brown, Fecitt, Sowerbutts

West Bromwich Albion Roberts, H Green, H Bell, Horton, Perry, Timmins, Woodhall, T Green, Bayliss, Loach, G Bell

2 April 1887 *Kennington Oval*   *Att 15500*

Aston Villa 2   West Bromwich Albion 0
(Hodgetts, Hunter)

Aston Villa Warner, Coulton, Simmonds, Yates, Dawson, Burton, Davis, Brown, Hunter, Vaughton, Hodgetts

West Bromwich Roberts, H Green Aldridge, Horton, Perry, Timmins, Woodhall, T Green, Bayliss, Paddock, Pearson

24 March 1888 *Kennington Oval*   *Att 19000*

West Bromwich Albion 2   Preston North End 1
(Bayliss, Woodhall)   (Goodall)

West Bromwich Albion Roberts, Aldridge, Green, Horton, Perry, Timmins, Bassett, Woodhall, Bayliss, Wilson, Pearson

Preston Mills-Roberts, Howarth, N Ross, Holmes, Russell, Graham, Gordon, J Ross, Goodall, Dewhurst, Drummond

30 March 1889 *Kennington Oval*   *Att 22000*

Preston North End 3   Wolverhampton Wanderers 0
(Dewhurst, Ross, Thompson)

Preston Mills-Roberts, Howarth, Holmes, Drummond, Russell, Graham, Gordon, Ross, Goodhall, Dewhurst, Thompson

Wolves Baynton, Baugh, Mason, Fletcher, Allen, Lowder, Hunter, Wykes, Broodie, Wood, Knight

29 March 1890 *Kennington Oval*   *Att 20000*

Blackburn Rovers 6   Sheffield Wednesday 1
(Dewar, John Southworth,   (Bennett)
Lofthouse, Townley 3)

Blackburn Rovers Horne, Jas Southworth, Forbes, Barton, Dewar, Forrest, Lofthouse, Campbell, John Southworth, Walton, Townley

Sheffield Wednesday Smith, Brayshaw, Morley, Dungworth, Betts, Waller, Ingram, Woodhouse, Bennett, Mumford, Cawley

25 March 1891 *Kennington Oval*   *Att 23000*

Blackburn Rovers 3   Notts County 1
(Dewar, John Southworth,   (Oswald)
Townley)

Blackburn Rovers Penninton, Brandon, Forbes, Barton, Dewar, Forrest, Lofthouse, Walton, John Southworth, Hall, Townley

Notts County Thraves, Ferguson, Hendry, Osborne, Calderhead, Shelton, McGregor, McInnes, Oswald, Locker, Daft

19 March 1892   *Kennington Oval   Att 25000*
West Bromwich Albion 3   Aston Villa 0
(Geddes, Nicholls, Reynolds)

This was the last final to be staged at the Kennington Oval because the cricket authorities were increasingly concerned that the huge crowds would damage their pitch.

Ironically it was the first final in which goal-nets were used, and West Bromwich were to hit the net three times as their reputation in the competition increased.

It was a repeat of the final from five years earlier when Villa had been 2–0 winners. They had begun this game as favourites, having eliminated Sunderland, considered a team of great talent and formidable contenders for the cup.

Brilliant approach play by Bassett enabled Geddes to give Albion the lead, with Nicholls again taking advantage of his service to make it 2–0 at half-time.

A third goal from Reynolds in the second half put West Brom's name on the trophy for the second time in their fourth final in a period of six years.

West Bromwich Albion   Reader, Nicholson, McCulloch, Reynolds, Perry, Groves, Bassett, McLeod, Nicholls, Pearson, Geddes

Aston Villa   Warner, Evans, Cox, H Devey, Cowan, Baird, Athersmith, J Devey, Dickson, Campbell, Hodgetts

26 March 1893   *Fallowfield, Manchester   Att 45000*
Wolverhampton Wanderers 1   Everton 0
(Allen)

Wolves   Rose, Baugh, Swift, Malpass, Allen, Kinsey, Topham, Wykes, Butcher, Wood, Griffin

Everton   Williams, Howarth, Kelso, Stewart, Holt, Boyle, Latta, Gordon, Maxwell, Chadwick, Millward

31 March 1894   *Goodison Park, Liverpool   Att 37000*
Notts County 4   Bolton Wanderers 1
(Watson, Logan 3) (Cassidy)

Notts County   Toone, Harper, Hendry, Bramley, Calderhead, Shelton, Watson, Donnelly, Logan, Bruce, Daft

Bolton Wanderers   Sutcliffe, Somerville, Jones, Gardiner, Paton, Hughes, Dickinson, Wilson, Tannahill, Bentley, Cassidy

20 April 1895   *Crystal Palace*   *Att 42560*

Aston Villa 1   West Bromwich Albion 0
(Chatt)

Aston Villa   Wilkes, Spencer, Welford, Reynolds, Cowan, Russell, Athersmith, Chatt, J Devey, Hodgetts, Smith

West Bromwich Albion   Reader, Williams, Horton, Taggart, Higgins, Perry, Bassett, McLeod, Richards, Hutchinson, Banks

18 April 1896   *Crystal Palace*   *Att 48836*

Sheffield Wednesday 2   Wolverhampton Wanderers 1
(Spiksley 2)   (Black)

Sheffield Wednesday   Massey, Earp, Langley, Brandon, Crawshaw, Petrie, Brash, Brady, Bell, Davis, Spiksley

Wolves   Tennant, Baugh, Dunn, Owen, Malpass, Griffiths, Tonks, Henderson, Beats, Wood, Black

10 April 1897   *Crystal Palace*   *Att 65891*

Aston Villa 3   **Everton 2**
(Campbell, Wheldon, Crabtree)   Bell, Boyle)

Aston Villa   Whitehouse, Spencer, Evans, Reynolds, Jas Cowan, Crabtree, Athersmith, J Devey, Campbell, Wheldon, John Cowan

Everton   Menham, Meecham, Storrier, Boyle, Holt, Stewart, Taylor, Bell, Hartley, Chadwick, Milward

16 April 1898   *Crystal Palace*   *Att 62017*

Nottingham Forest 3   Derby County 1
(Capes 2, McPherson)   (Bloomer)

Nottingham Forest   Allsop, Richie, Scott, Forman, McPherson, Wragg, McInnes, Richards, Benbow, Capes, Spouncer

Derby County   Fryer, Methven, Leiper, Cox, A Goodall, Turner, J Goodall, Bloomer, Boag, Stevenson, McQueen

15 April 1899   *Crystal Palace*   *Att 73833*

Sheffield United 4   Derby County 1
(Bennett, Beers,   (Boag)
Almond, Priest)

Sheffield United   Foulke, Thickett, Boyle, Johnson, Morren, Needham, Bennett, Beers, Hedley, Almond, Priest

Derby County   Fryer, Methven, Staley, Cox, Paterson, May, Arkesden, Bloomer, Boag, McDonald, Allen

21 April 1900   *Crystal Palace   Att 68945*

Bury 4   **Southampton 0**
(McLuckie 2, Wood, Plant)

Bury   Thompson, Darrock, Davidson, Pray, Leeming, Ross, Richards, Wood, McLuckie, Sagar, Plant

Southampton   Robinson, Meehan, Durber, Meston, Chadwick, Petrie, Turner, Yates, Farrell, Wood, Milward

20 April 1901   *Crystal Palace   Att 110820*

Tottenham Hotspur 2   Sheffield United 2
(Brown 2)   (Bennett, Priest)

Tottenham   Clawley, Erentz, Tait, Norris, Hughes, Jones, Smith, Cameron, Brown, Copeland, Kirwan

Sheffield United   Foulke, Thickett, Boyle, Johnson, Morren, Needham, Bennett, Field, Hedley, Priest, Lipsham

*Replay – **27 April 1901**   Burnden Park, Bolton   Att 20470*

Tottenham Hotspur 3   Sheffield United 1
(Cameron, Smith, Brown)   (Priest)

Tottenham   Clawley, Erentz, Tait, Norris, Hughes, Jones, Smith, Cameron, Brown, Copeland, Kirwan

Sheffield United   Foulke, Thickett, Boyle, Johnson, Morren, Needham, Bennett, Field, Hedley, Priest, Lipsham

19 April 1902   *Crystal Palace   Att 76914*

Sheffield United 1   Southampton 1
(Common)   (Wood)

Southampton had begun the competition splendidly by knocking out holders Spurs in the very first round after two draws.

Sheffield United, however, were on their third visit to Crystal Palace in four years, having won once and lost once. But their presence made it a real North v South contest.

United were an interesting blend captained by a skilful and tireless player in Ernest Needham who had the delightful nickname of 'Nudger'.

Their goalkeeper, Foulke, was a nimble 22 stone, while in Bennett they had a quality international winger, though he was to miss the replay.

C.B. Fry, who combined intellect with his athletic prowess to make him one of the outstanding personalities of his day, was Southampton's outstanding star but the club's second visit to the final, like their first two seasons earlier, ended in disappointment.

Sheffield United Foulke, Thickett, Boyle, Needham, Wilkinson, Johnson, Bennett, Common, Hedley, Priest, Lipsham

Southampton Robinson, Fry, Molyneux, Meston, Bowman, Lee, A Turner, Wood, Brown, Chadwick, J Turner

*Replay – **26 April 1902** Crystal Palace Att 33068*

Sheffield United 2 Southampton 1
(Hedley, Barnes)   (Brown)

Sheffield United Foulke, Thickett, Boyle, Needham, Wilkinson, Johnson, Barnes, Common, Hedley, Priest, Lipsham

Southampton Robinson, Fry, Molyneux, Meston, Bowman, Lee, A Turner, Wood, Brown, Chadwick, J Turner

18 April 1903 *Crystal Palace Att 63102*

Bury 6   Derby County 0
(Ross, Sagar, Leeming 2,
Wood, Plant)

Bury Monteith, Lindsey, McEwen, Johnson, Thorpe, Ross, Richards, Wood, Sagar, Leeming, Plant

Derby County Fryer, Methven, Morris, Warren, A Goodall, May, Warrington, York, Boag, Richards, Davis

23 April 1904 *Crystal Palace Att 61374*

Manchester City 1 Bolton Wanderers 0
(Meredith)

Manchester City Hillman, McMahon, Burgess, Frost, Hynds, Ashworth, Meredith, Livingstone, Gillespie, Turnbull, Booth

Bolton Wanderers Davies, Brown, Struthers, Clifford, Greenhaigh, Freebairn, Stokes, Marsh, Yenson, White, Taylor

15 April 1905 *Crystal Palace Att 101117*

Aston Villa 2 Newcastle United 0
(Hampton 2)

Aston Villa George, Spencer, Miles, Pearson, Leake, Windmill, Brawn, Garratty, Hampton, Bache, Hall

Newcastle Lawrence, McCombie, Carr, Gardner, Aitken, McWilliam, Rutherford, Howie, Appleyard, Veitch, Gosnell

21 April 1906   *Crystal Palace   Att 75609*
Everton 1   Newcastle United 0
(Young)

Everton   Scott, W Balmer, Crelly, Makepeace, Taylor, Abbott, Sharp, Bolton, Young, Settle, Hardman

Newcastle   Lawrence, McCombie, Carr, Gardner, Aitken, McWilliam, Rutherford, Howie, Veitch, Orr, Gosnell

20 April 1907   *Crystal Palace   Att 84584*
Sheffield Wednesday 2   Everton 1
(Stewart, Simpson)   (Sharp)

Sheffield Wednesday   Lyall, Layton, Burton, Brittleton, Crawshaw, Bartlett, Chapman, Bradshaw, Wilson, Stewart, Simpson

Everton   Scott, W Balmer, R Balmer, Makepeace, Taylor, Abbott, Sharp, Bolton, Young, Settle, Hardman

25 April 1908   *Crystal Palace   Att 74967*
Wolverhampton Wanderers 3   Newcastle United 1
(Hunt, Hedley, Harrison)   (Howie)

Wolves   Lunn, Jones, Collins, Hunt, Wooldridge, Bishop, Harrison, Shelton, Hedley, Radford, Pedley

Newcastle   Lawrence, McCracken, Pudan, Gardner, Veitch, McWilliam, Rutherford, Howie, Appleyard, Speedie, Wilson

26 April 1909   *Crystal Palace   Att 71401*
Manchester United 1   Bristol City 0
(A Turnbull)

Manchester United   Moger, Stacy, Hayes, Duckworth, Roberts, Bell, Meredith, Halse, J Turnbull, A Turnbull, Wall

Bristol City   Clay, Annan, Cottle, Hanlin, Wedlock, Spear, Staniforth, Hardy, Gilligan, Burton, Hilton

23 April 1910   *Crystal Palace   Att 77747*
Newcastle United 1   Barnsley 1
(Rutherford)   (Tuffnell)

Newcastle   Lawrence, McCracken, Whitson, Veitch, Low, McWilliam, Rutherford, Howie, Shepherd, Higgins, Wilson

Barnsley   Mearns, Downs, Ness, Glendinning, Boyle, Utley, Bartrop, Gadsby, Lillycrop, Tuffnell, Forman

*Replay – **28 April 1910**   Goodison Park, Liverpool   Att 69000*
Newcastle United 2   Barnsley 0
(Shepherd 2 (1 pen))

Newcastle   Lawrence, McCracken, Carr, Veitch, Low, McWilliam, Rutherford, Howie, Shepherd, Higgins, Wilson

Barnsley   Mearns, Downs, Ness, Glendinning, Boyle, Utley, Bartrop, Gadsby, Lillycrop, Tuffnell, Forman

22 April 1911   *Crystal Palace   Att 69098*
Bradford City 0   Newcastle United 0

Bradford City   Mellors, Campbell, Taylor, Robinson, Gildea, McDonald, Logan, Spiers, O'Rourke, Devine, Thompson

Newcastle   Lawrence, McCracken, Whitson, Low, Veitch, Willis, Rutherford, Jobey, Stewart, Higgins, Wilson

*Replay – **26 April 1911**   Old Trafford, Manchester   Att 58000*
Bradford City 1   Newcastle United 0
(Spiers)

Bradford City   Mellors, Campbell, Taylor, Robinson, Torrance, McDonald, Logan, Spiers, O'Rourke, Devine, Thompson

Newcastle   Lawrence, McCracken, Whitson, Veitch, Low, Willis, Rutherford, Jobey, Stewart, Higgins, Wilson

20 April 1912   *Crystal Palace   Att 54556*
Barnsley 0   West Bromwich Albion 0

The FA Cup, won the previous year by Bradford City, stayed in Yorkshire as Barnsley, beaten finalists two seasons earlier, won after the first game had ended in a goalless draw.

Ironically it was the third successive season in which the final had been drawn, an event that was not to recur for a further 58 years!

In the second game in Sheffield the score was 0–0 at the end of normal time and it was two minutes into extra-time when Tuffnell climaxed a fine dribbling run with a splendid goal.

Barnsley thus became the third team from the Second Division to lift the trophy, a tribute to their stamina in a long run which included four games against the holders, Bradford, lasting seven hours.

Barnsley   Cooper, Downs, Taylor, Glendinning, Bratley, Utley, Bartrop, Tuffnell, Lillycrop, Travers, Moore

West Bromwich Albion   Pearson, Cook, Pennington, Baddeley, Buck, McNeal, Jephcott, Wright, Pailor, Bowser, Shearman

Replay – **24 April 1912** *Bramall Lane, Sheffield* *Att 38555*
Barnsley 1   West Bromwich Albion 0*
(Tuffnell)

Barnsley Cooper, Downs, Taylor, Glendinning, Bratley, Utley, Bartrop, Tuffnell, Lillycrop, Travers, Moore

West Bromwich Albion Pearson, Cook, Pennington, Baddeley, Buck, McNeal, Jephcott, Wright, Pailor, Bowser, Shearman

19 April 1913   Crystal Palace   Att 120081
Aston Villa 1   Sunderland 0
(Barber)

Aston Villa Hardy, Lyons, Weston, Barber, Harrop, Leach, Wallace, Halse, Hampton, C Stephenson, Bache

Sunderland Butler, Gladwin, Ness, Cuggy, Thompson, Low, Mordue, Buchan, Richardson, Holley, Martin

25 April 1914   Crystal Palace   Att 72778
Burnley 1   Liverpool 0
(Freeman)

Burnley Sewell, Bamford, Taylor, Halley, Boyle, Watson, Nesbit, Lindley, Freeman, Hodgson, Mosscrop

Liverpool Campbell, Longworth, Pursell, Fairfoul, Ferguson, McKinlay, Sheldon, Metcalf, Miller, Lacey, Nicholl

24 April 1915 *Old Trafford, Manchester* *Att 49557*
Sheffield United 3   Chelsea 0
(Simmons, Fazackerley, Kitchen)

Sheffield United Gough, Cook, English, Sturgess, Brelsford, Utley, Simmons, Fazackerley, Kitchen, Masterman, Evans

Chelsea Molyneux, Bettridge, Harrow, Taylor, Logan, Walker, Ford, Halse, Thompson, Croal, McNeil

24 April 1920 *Stamford Bridge, London* *Att 50018*
Aston Villa 1   Huddersfield Town 0*
(Kirton)

Aston Villa Hardy, Smart, Weston, Ducat, Barson, Moss, Wallace, Kirton, Walker, C Stephenson, Dorrell

Huddersfield Mutch, Wood, Bullock, Slade, Wilson, Watson, Richardson, Mann, Taylor, Swan, Islip

* *after extra time*

81

23 April 1921   *Stamford Bridge, London   Att 72805*

Tottenham Hotspur 1   Wolverhampton Wanderers 0
(Dimmock)

Tottenham   Hunter, Clay, McDonald, Smith, Walters, Grimsdell, Banks, Seed, Cantrell, Bliss, Dimmock

Wolves   George, Woodward, Marshall, Gregory, Hodnett, Riley, Lea, Burrill, Edmonds, Potts, Brooks

29 April 1922   *Stamford Bridge, London   Att 53000*

Huddersfield Town 1   Preston North End 0
(WH Smith pen)

Preston reached the final for the first time since 1889 in what was to be the last final at Stamford Bridge before the climax to the competition was transferred to the new Wembley Stadium.

Their opponents, Huddersfield, were now heading for their greatest triumphs. They had terrific strength and quality with players like England internationals Wadsworth, Smith and Clem Stephenson, who had won medals with Aston Villa in 1913 and 1920.

It was a rough and unruly match with a weak referee and it was perhaps a commentary on the game that it was decided by a penalty – and one that was hotly disputed.

Had Billy Smith been pulled down by Preston right-back Hamilton inside or outside the area? The marks on the pitch suggested outside.

Preston's bespectacled goalkeeper Jim Mitchell tried to unsettle penalty-taker Smith by jumping up and down on his line, but Smith stayed cool to collect the winner.

Huddersfield Town   Mutch, Wood, Wadsworth, Slade, Wilson, Watson, Richardson, Mann, Islip, Stephenson, WH Smith

Preston   Mitchell, Hamilton, Doolan, Duxbury, McCall, Williamson, Rawlings, Jefferis, Roberts, Woodhouse, Quinn

28 April 1923   *Wembley Stadium   Att 126047*

Bolton Wanderers 2   West Ham United 0
(Jack, JR Smith)

Bolton Wanderers   Pym, Haworth, Finney, Nuttall, Seddon, Jennings, Butler, Jack, JR Smith, J Smith, Vizard

West Ham   Hufton, Henderson, Young, Bishop, Kay, Tresadern, Richards, Brown, V Watson, Moore, Ruffell

26 April 1924 *Wembley Stadium* *Att 91695*
Newcastle United 2 Aston Villa 0
(Harris, Seymour)

Newcastle Bradley, Hampson, Hudspeth, Mooney, Spencer, Gibson, Low, Cowan, Harris, McDonald, Seymour

Aston Villa Jackson, Smart, Mort, Moss, Milne, Blackburn, York, Kirton, Capewell, Walker, Dorrell

25 April 1925 *Wembley Stadium* *Att 91763*
Sheffield United 1 Cardiff City 0
(Tunstall)

Sheffield United Sutcliffe, Cook, Milton, Pantling, King, Green, Mercer, Boyle, Johnson, Gillespie, Tunstall

Cardiff Farquharson, Nelson, Blair, Wake, Keenor, Hardy, W Davies, Gill, Nicholson, Beadles, J Evans

24 April 1926 *Wembley Stadium* *Att 91447*
Bolton Wanderers 1 Manchester City 0
(Jack)

Bolton Wanderers Pym, Haworth, Greenhalgh, Nuttall, Seddon, Jennings, Butler, Jack, JR Smith, J Smith, Vizard

Manchester City Goodchild, Cookson, McCloy, Pringle, Cowan, McMullan, Austin, Browell, Roberts, Johnson, Hicks

23 April 1927 *Wembley Stadium* *Att 91206*
Cardiff City 1 Arsenal 0
(Ferguson)

Cardiff Farquharson, Nelson, Watson, Keenor, Sloan, Hardy, Curtis, Irving, Ferguson, L Davies, McLachlan

Arsenal Lewis, Parker, Kennedy, Baker, Butler, John, Hulme, Buchan, Brain, Blyth, Hoar

21 April 1928 *Wembley Stadium* *Att 92041*
Blackburn Rovers 3 Huddersfield Town 1
(Roscamp 2, McLean)   (Jackson)

Blackburn Rovers Crawford, Hutton, Jones, Healless, Rankin, Campbell, Thornewell, Puddefoot, Roscamp, McLean, Rigby

Huddersfield Town Mercer, Goodall, Barkas, Redfern, Wilson, Steele, A Jackson, Brown, Stephenson, WH Smith

27 April 1929   *Wembley Stadium   Att 92576*

Bolton Wanderers 2   Portsmouth 0
(Butler, Blackmore)

Bolton Wanderers   Pym, Haworth, Finney, Kean, Seddon, Nuttall, Butler, McClelland, Blackmore, Gibson, W Cook

Portsmouth   Gilfillan, Mackie, Bell, Nichol, McIlwaine, Thackeray, Forward, J Smith, Weddle, Watson, F Cook

26 April 1930   *Wembley Stadium   Att 92488*

Arsenal 2   Huddersfield Town 0
(James, Lambert)

Arsenal   Preedy, Parker, Hapgood, Baker, Seddon, John, Hulme, Jack, Lambert, James, Bastin

Huddersfield Town   Turner, Goodall, Spence, Naylor, Wilson, Campbell, A Jackson, Kelly, Davies, Raw, WH Smith

25 April 1931   *Wembley Stadium   Att 92406*

West Bromwich Albion 2   Birmingham City 1
(WG Richardson 2)   (Bradford)

West Bromwich Albion   Pearson, Shaw, Trentham, Magee, W Richardson, Edwards, Glidden, Carter, WG Richardson, Sandford, Wood

Birmingham   Hibbs, Liddell, Barkas, Cringan, Morrall, Leslie, Briggs, Crosbie, Bradford, Gregg, Curtis

23 April 1932   *Wembley Stadium   Att 92298*

Newcastle United 2   Arsenal 1
(Allen 2)   (John)

This was the great Arsenal side of the 1930s including Male, Hapgood, Bastin and Hulme, but on this Wembley occasion they were without the great Alex James.

It seemed an easy passage for Arsenal, when 'Police Constable' Roberts instigated the move which enabled John to put Arsenal ahead from Hulme's cross.

Allen's header just before half-time, however, enabled Newcastle to level the scores, though it was a goal that was to be disputed for years.

Photographs seemed clearly to indicate that the ball had crossed the dead-ball line before it was centred by Richardson, and the Arsenal defenders had lost concentration in believing it had.

Allen snatched the winner for Newcastle in the 72nd minute and Arsenal thus became the first side to lose a Wembley final after scoring first.

Queen Mary presenting the medals to the victorious Newcastle side after the 1932 FA Cup Final

Newcastle McInroy, Nelson, Fairhurst, McKenzie, Davidson, Weaver, Boyd, Richardson, Allen, McMenemy, Lang

Arsenal Moss, Parker, Hapgood, C Jones, Roberts, Male, Hulme, Jack, Lambert, Bastin, John

29 April 1933 *Wembley Stadium* *Att 92950*

Everton 3　　　　**Manchester City 0**
(Stein, Dean, Dunn)

Everton Sagar, Cook, Cresswell, Britton, White, Thomson, Geldard, Dunn, Dean, Johnson, Stein

Manchester City Langford, Cann, Dale, Busby, Cowan, Bray, Toseland, Marshall, Herd, McMullan, Brook

28 April 1934 *Wembley Stadium* *Att 93548*

Manchester City 2　**Portsmouth 1**
(Tilson 2)　　　　　　　(Rutherford)

Manchester City Swift, Barnett, Dale, Busby, Cowan, Bray, Toseland, Marshall, Tilson, Herd, Brook

Portsmouth Gilfillan, Mackie, W Smith, Nichol, Allen, Thackeray, Worrall, J Smith, Weddle, Easson, Rutherford

27 April 1935   *Wembley Stadium   Att 93204*
Sheffield Wednesday 4   West Bromwich Albion 2
(Rimmer 2, Palethorpe,   (Boyes, Sandford)
Hooper)

Sheffield Wednesday   Brown, Nibloe, Cattlin, Sharp, Millership, Burrows, Hooper, Surtees, Palethorpe, Starling, Rimmer

West Bromwich Albion   Pearson, Shaw, Trentham, Murphy, W Richardson, Edwards, Glidden, Carter, WG Richardson, Sandford, Boyes

25 April 1936   *Wembley Stadium   Att 93384*
Arsenal 1   Sheffield United 0
(Drake)

Arsenal   Wilson, Male, Hapgood, Crayston, Roberts, Copping, Hulme, Bowden, Drake, James, Bastin

Sheffield United   Smith, Hooper, Wilkinson, Jackson, Johnson, McPherson, Barton, Barclay, Dodds, Pickering, Williams

1 May 1937   *Wembley Stadium   Att 93495*
Sunderland 3   Preston North End 1
(Gurney, Carter, Burbanks)   (F O'Donnell)

Sunderland   Mapson, Gorman, Hall, Thomson, Johnson, McNab, Duns, Carter, Gurney, Gallacher, Burbanks

Preston   Burns, Gallimore, A Beattie, Shankly, Tremelling, Milne, Dougal, Beresford, F O'Donnell, Fagan, H O'Donnell

30 April 1938   *Wembley Stadium   Att 93357*
Preston North End 1   Huddersfield Town 0*
(Mutch)

Preston   Holdcroft, Gallimore, A Beattie, Shankly, Smith, Batey, Watmough, Mutch, Maxwell, R Beattie, H O'Donnell

Huddersfield Town   Hesford, Craig, Mountford, Willingham, Young, Boot, Hulme, Isaac, McFadyen, Barclay, Beasley

29 April 1939   *Wembley Stadium   Att 99370*
Portsmouth 4   Wolverhampton Wanderers 1
(Parker 2, Barlow, Anderson)   (Dorsett)

Portsmouth   Walker, Rochford, Morgan, Guthrie, Rowe, Wharton, Worrall, McAlinden, Anderson, Barlow, Parker

Wolves   Scott, Morris, Taylor, Galley, Cullis, Gardiner, Burton, McIntosh, Westcott, Dorsett, Maguire

* *after extra time*

27 April 1946   *Wembley Stadium*   *Att 98215*

Derby County 4   **Charlton Athletic 1**
(H Turner og, Stamps 2, Doherty)   (H Turner)

Derby County   Woodley, Nicholas, Howe, Bullions, Leuty, Musson, Harrison, Carter, Stamps, Doherty, Duncan

Charlton   Bartram, Phipps, Shreeve, H Turner, Oakes, Johnson, Fell, Brown, AA Turner, Welsh, Duffy

26 April 1947   *Wembley Stadium*   *Att 99000*

Charlton Athletic 1   Burnley 0*
(Duffy)

Charlton   Bartram, Croker, Shreeve, Johnson, Phipps, Whittaker, Hurst, Dawson, W Robinson, Welsh, Duffy

Burnley   Strong, Woodruff, Mather, Attwell, Brown, Bray, Chew, Morris, Harrison, Potts, FP Kippax

24 April 1948   *Wembley Stadium*   *Att 99000*

Manchester United 4   **Blackpool 2**
(Rowley 2, Pearson, Anderson)   (Shimwell pen, Mortensen)

Manchester United   Crompton, Carey, Aston, Anderson, Chilton, Cockburn, Delaney, Morris, Rowley, Pearson, Mitten

Blackpool   Robinson, Shimwell, Crossland, Johnston, Hayward, Kelly, Matthews, Munro, Mortensen, Dick, Rickett

30 April 1949   *Wembley Stadium*   *Att 99500*

Wolverhampton Wanderers 3   Leicester City 1
(Pye 2, Smyth)   (Griffiths)

Wolves   Williams, Pritchard, Springthorpe, W Crook, Shorthouse, Wright, Hancocks, Smyth, Pye, Dunn, Mullen

Leicester   Bradley, Jelly, Scott, W Harrison, Plummer, King, Griffiths, Lee, J Harrison, Chisholm, Adam

29 April 1950   *Wembley Stadium*   *Att 100000*

Arsenal 2   Liverpool 0
(Lewis 2)

Arsenal   Swindin, Scott, Barnes, Forbes, L Compton, Mercer, Cox, Logie, Goring, Lewis, D Compton

Liverpool   Sidlow, Lambert, Spicer, Taylor, Hughes, Jones, Payne, Baron, Stubbins, Fagan, Liddell

* after extra time

28 April 1951   *Wembley Stadium*   *Att 100000*

Newcastle United 2   Blackpool 0
(Milburn 2)

Newcastle   Fairbrother, Cowell, Corbett, Harvey, Brennan, Crowe, Walker, Taylor, Milburn, G Robledo, Mitchell

Blackpool   Farm, Shimwell, Garrett, Johnston, Hayward, Kelly, Matthews, Mudie, Mortensen, W Slater, Perry

3 May 1952   *Wembley Stadium*   *Att 100000*

Newcastle United 1   Arsenal 0
(G Robledo)

A repeat of the 1932 final, with the outcome again disappointment for Arsenal.

The London side were handicapped from the first half when their full-back Walley Barnes had to leave the field after damaging knee ligaments, and in the days before substitutions the Gunners had to play on with ten men.

They made a valiant effort at holding out, having won the sympathy of the Wembley crowd, and almost pulled off a remarkable victory

Newcastle win again – 1952, Joe Harvey with the Cup

when Doug Lishman's header 11 minutes from time struck the cross-bar.

But then in the 84th minute their brave resistance was ended when George Robledo headed the winner.

Newcastle Simpson, Cowell, McMichael, Harvey, Brennan, E Robledo, Walker, Foulkes, Milburn, G Robledo, Mitchell

Arsenal Swindin, Barnes, L Smith, Forbes, Daniel, Mercer, Cox, Logie, Holton, Lishman, Roper

2 May 1953 *Wembley Stadium Att 100000*

Blackpool 4 **Bolton Wanderers 3**
(Mortensen 3, Perry) (Lofthouse, Moir, Bell)

Blackpool Farm, Shimwell, Garrett, Fenton, Johnston, Robinson, Matthews, Taylor, Mortensen, Mudie, Perry

Bolton Wanderers Hanson, Ball, R Banks, Wheeler, Barrass, Bell, Holden, Moir, Lofthouse, Hassall, Langton

1 May 1954 *Wembley Stadium Att 100000*

West Bromwich Albion 3 **Preston North End 2**
(Allen 2 (1 pen), Griffin) (Morrison, Wayman)

West Bromwich Albion Sanders, Kennedy, Millard, Dudley, Dugdale, Barlow, Griffin, Ryan, Allen, Nicholls, Lee

Preston Thompson, Cunningham, Walton, Docherty, Marston, Forbes, Finney, Foster, Wayman, Baxter, Morrison

7 May 1955 *Wembley Stadium Att 100000*

Newcastle United 3 **Manchester City 1**
(Milburn, Mitchell, Hannah) (Johnstone)

Newcastle Simpson, Cowell, Batty, Scoular, Stokoe, Casey, White, Milburn, Keeble, Hannah, Mitchell

Manchester City Trautmann, Meadows, Little, Barnes, Ewing, Paul, Spurdle, Hayes, Revie, Johnstone, Fagan

5 May 1956 *Wembley Stadium Att 100000*

Manchester City 3 **Birmingham City 1**
(Hayes, Dyson, Johnstone) (Kinsey)

Manchester City Trautmann, Leivers, Little, Barnes, Ewing, Paul, Johnstone, Hayes, Revie, Dyson, Clarke

Birmingham Merrick, Hall, Green, Newman, Smith, Boyd, Astall, Kinsey, Brown, Murphy, Govan

4 May 1957   *Wembley Stadium   Att 100000*

Aston Villa 2   Manchester United 1
(McParland 2)   (Taylor)

Aston Villa   Sims, Lynn, Aldis, Crowther, Dugdale, Saward, Smith, Sewell, Myerscough, Dixon, McParland

Manchester United   Woods, Foulkes, Byrne, Colman, J Blanchflower, Edwards, Berry, Whelan, T Taylor, Charlton, Pegg

3 May 1958   *Wembley Stadium   Att 100000*

Bolton Wanderers 2   Manchester United 0
(Lofthouse 2)

Bolton Wanderers   Hopkinson, Hartle, Banks, Hennin, Higgins, Edwards, Birch, Stevens, Lofthouse, Parry, Holden

Manchester United   Gregg, Foulkes, Greaves, Goodwin, Cope, Crowther, Dawson, E Taylor, Charlton, Viollet, Webster

2 May 1959   *Wembley Stadium   Att 100000*

Nottingham Forest 2   Luton Town 1
(Dwight, Wilson)   (Pacey)

Nottingham Forest   Thomson, Whare, McDonald, Whitefoot, McKinlay, Burkitt, Dwight, Quigley, Wilson, Gray, Imlach

Luton   Baynham, McNally, Hawkes, Groves, Owen, Pacey, Bingham, Brown, Morton, Cummins, Gregory

7 May 1960   *Wembley Stadium   Att 100000*

Wolverhampton Wanderers 3   Blackburn Rovers 0
(McGrath og, Deeley 2)

Wolves   Finlayson, Showell, Harris, Clamp, Slater, Flowers, Deeley, Stobart, Murray, Broadbent, Horne

Blackburn Rovers   Leyland, Bray, Whelan, Clayton, Woods, McGrath, Bimpson, Dobing, Dougan, Douglas, McLeod

6 May 1961   *Wembley Stadium   Att 100000*

Tottenham Hotspur 2   Leicester City 0
(Smith, Dyson)

Tottenham Hotspur   Brown, Baker, Henry, D Blanchflower, Norman, Mackay, Jones, White, Smith, Allen, Dyson

Leicester   Banks, Chalmers, Norman, McLintock, King, Appleton, Riley, Walsh, McIlmoyle, Keyworth, Cheesebrough

Danny Blanchflower scores in Spurs' victory over Burnley, 1962

5 May 1962   *Wembley Stadium*   *Att 100000*

Tottenham Hotspur 3   **Burnley 1**
(Greaves, Smith, Blanchflower, pen)   (Robson)

A final between two of the country's best passing sides earned the label 'the chessboard final' and many felt it was a match lacking the fervour and feeling worthy of the occasion.

Spurs, of course, had won the 'double' 12 months earlier and had the reassurance that no side making a return in consecutive seasons had lost.

When Jimmy Greaves gave them the lead in the third minute there was no suggestion that the sequence was about to be broken.

Burnley, however, did equalise early in the second half and Jimmy Robson claimed the distinction of scoring the 100th goal in a Wembley final.

It took Tottenham only a minute to regain the lead through Bobby Smith and though there was some controversy about a challenge by Smith on Adam Blacklaw that produced a penalty incident, Danny Blanchflower stroked the ball home to collect the trophy for a second successive season.

Tottenham Hotspur   Brown, Baker, Henry, D Blanchflower, Norman, Mackay, Medwin, White, Smith, Greaves, Jones

Burnley   Blacklaw, Angus, Elder, Adamson, Cummings, Miller, Connelly, McIlroy, Pointer, Robson, Harris

25 May 1963   *Wembley Stadium   Att 100000*

Manchester United 3   Leicester City 1
(Law, Herd 2)   (Keyworth)

Manchester United   Gaskell, Dunne, Cantwell, Crerand, Foulkes, Setters, Giles, Quixall, Herd, Law, Charlton

Leicester   Banks, Sjoberg, Norman, McLintock, King, Appleton, Riley, Cross, Keyworth, Gibson, Stringfellow

2 May 1964   *Wembley Stadium   Att 100000*

West Ham United 3   Preston North End 2
(Sissons, Hurst, Boyce)   (Holden, Dawson)

West Ham   Standen, Bond, Burkett, Bovington, Brown, Moore, Brabrook, Boyce, Byrne, Hurst, Sissons

Preston   Kelly, Ross, Smith, Lawton, Singleton, Kendall, Wilson, Ashworth, Dawson, Spavin, Holden

1 May 1965   *Wembley Stadium   Att 100000*

Liverpool 2   Leeds United 1*
(Hunt, St John)   (Bremner)

Liverpool   Lawrence, Lawler, Byrne, Strong, Yeats, Stevenson, Callaghan, Hunt, St John, Smith, Thompson

Leeds   Sprake, Reaney, Bell, Bremner, Charlton, Hunter, Giles, Storrie, Peacock, Collins, Johanneson

14 May 1966   *Wembley Stadium   Att 100000*

Everton 3   Sheffield Wednesday 2
(Trebilcock 2, Temple)   (McCalliog, Ford)

Everton   West, Wright, Wilson, Gabriel, Labone, Harris, Scott, Trebilcock, Young, Harvey, Temple

Sheffield Wednesday   Springett, Smith, Megson, Eustace, Ellis, Young, Pugh, Fantham, McCalliog, Ford, Quinn

20 May 1967   *Wembley Stadium   Att 100000*

Tottenham Hotspur 2   Chelsea 1
(Robertson, Saul)   (Tambling)

Tottenham Hotspur   Jennings, Kinnear, Knowles, Mullery, England, Mackay, Robertson, Greaves, Gilzean, Venables, Saul (sub: Jones)

Chelsea   Bonetti, A Harris, McCreadie, Hollins, Hinton, R Harris, Cooke, Baldwin, Hateley, Tambling, Boyle

* after extra time

18 May 1968 *Wembley Stadium* *Att 100000*

West Bromwich Albion 1 Everton 0*
(Astle)

West Bromwich Albion Osborne, Frazer, Williams, Brown, Talbot, Kaye, (Clarke), Lovett, Collard, Astle, Hope, Clark

Everton West, Wright, Wilson, Kendall, Labone, Harvey, Husband, Ball, Royle, Hurst, Morrisey (sub: Kenyon)

26 April 1969 *Wembley Stadium* *Att 100000*

Manchester City 1 Leicester City 0
(Young)

Manchester City Dowd, Book, Pardoe, Doyle, Booth, Oakes, Summerbee, Bell, Lee, Young, Coleman (sub: Connor)

Leicester Shilton, Rodrigues, Nish, Roberts, Woollett, Cross, Fern, Gibson, Lochhead, Clarke, Glover (sub: Manley)

11 April 1970 *Wembley Stadium* *Att 100000*

Chelsea 2   **Leeds United 2***
(Houseman, Hutchinson)   (Charlton, Jones)

Chelsea Bonetti, Webb, McCreadie, Hollins, Dempsey, Harris (Hinton), Baldwin, Houseman, Osgood, Hutchinson, Cooke

Leeds Sprake, Madeley, Cooper, Bremner, Charlton, Hunter, Lorimer, Clarke, Jones, Giles, E Gray

Replay – 29 April 1970 *Old Trafford, Manchester* *Att 62078*

Chelsea 2   **Leeds United 1***
(Osgood, Webb)   (Jones)

Chelsea Bonetti, Harris, McCreadie, Hollins, Dempsey, Webb, Baldwin, Cooke, Osgood (Hinton), Hutchinson, Houseman

Leeds Harvey, Madeley, Cooper, Bremner, Charlton, Hunter, Lorimer, Clarke, Jones, Giles, E Gray

8 May 1971 *Wembley Stadium* *Att 100000*

Arsenal 2   **Liverpool 1***
(Kelly, George) (Heighway)

Arsenal Wilson, Rice, McNab, Storey (Kelly), McLintock, Simpson, Armstrong, Graham, Radford, Kennedy, George

Liverpool Clemence, Lawler, Lindsay, Smith, Lloyd, Hughes, Callaghan, Evans (Thompson), Heighway, Toshack, Hall

* *after extra time*

93

6 May 1972   *Wembley Stadium   Att 100000*

Leeds United 1   Arsenal 0
(Clarke)

Arsenal's desire to emulate their north London neighbours Tottenham in returning to win at Wembley twelve months after winning the 'double' was to remain unfulfilled.

It was a final that turned into a defensive battle involving Leeds' renowned back four which centred around the towering Jack Charlton.

This was far from a classic final, with tempers often frayed. Indeed, Allan Clarke was booked after only five seconds for a foul on Alan Ball and that set the tone for the match.

It was decided by a 53rd-minute goal, with Mick Jones providing the centre which Clarke headed decisively home. Leeds further hit the woodwork twice and undoubtedly deserved their victory.

However, the celebrations were marred slightly by a last-minute injury to Jones, who damaged his shoulder and had to be helped up the steps to receive his winner's medal.

Leeds   Harvey, Reaney, Madeley, Bremner, Charlton, Hunter, Lorimer, Clarke, Jones, Giles, E Gray

Arsenal   Barnett, Rice, McNab, Storey, McLintock, Simpson, Armstrong, Ball, George, Radford (Kennedy), Graham

5 May 1973   *Wembley Stadium   Att 100000*

Sunderland 1   Leeds United 0
(Porterfield)

Sunderland   Montgomery, Malone, Guthrie, Horswill, Watson, Pitt, Kerr, Hughes, Halom, Porterfield, Tueart

Leeds   Harvey, Reaney, Cherry, Bremner, Madeley, Hunter, Lorimer, Clarke, Jones, Giles, E Gray (Yorath)

May 4 1974   *Wembley Stadium   Att 100000*

Liverpool 3   Newcastle United 0
(Keegan 2, Heighway)

Liverpool   Clemence, Smith, Lindsay, Thompson, Cormack, Hughes, Keegan, Hall, Heighway, Toshack, Callaghan

Newcastle   McFaul, Clark, Kennedy, McDermott, Howard, Moncur, Smith (Gibb), Cassidy, Macdonald, Tudor, Hibbitt

Allan Clarke, Leeds United, 1972

3 May 1975 *Wembley Stadium* *Att 100000*

West Ham United 2 Fulham 0
(A Taylor 2)

West Ham Day, McDowell, T Taylor, Lock, Lampard, Bonds, Paddon, Brooking, Jennings, A Taylor, Holland

Fulham Mellor, Cutbush, Lacy, Moore, Fraser, Mullery, Conway, Slough, Mitchell, Busby, Barrett

1 May 1976 *Wembley Stadium* *Att 100000*

Southampton 1 Manchester United 0
(Stokes)

Southampton Turner, Rodrigues, Peach, Holmes, Blyth, Steele, Gilchrist, Channon, Osgood, McCalliog, Stokes

Manchester United Stepney, Forsyth, Houston, Daly, B Greenhoff, Buchan, Coppell, McIlroy, Pearson, Macari, Hill (McCreery)

21 May 1977 *Wembley Stadium* *Att 100000*

Manchester United 2 Liverpool 1
(Pearson, J Greenhoff) (Case)

Manchester United Stepney, Nicholl, Albiston, McIlroy, B Greenhoff, Buchan, Coppell, J Greenhoff, Pearson, Macari, Hill (McCreery)

Liverpool Clemence, Neal, Jones, Smith, Kennedy, Hughes, Keegan, Case, Johnson (Callaghan), Heighway, McDermott

6 May 1978 *Wembley Stadium* *Att 100000*

Ipswich Town 1 Arsenal 0
(Osborne)

Ipswich Cooper, Burley, Mills, Osborne (Lambert), Hunter, Beattie, Talbot, Wark, Mariner, Geddis, Woods

Arsenal Jennings, Rice, Nelson, Price, Young, O'Leary, Brady (Rix), Hudson, Macdonald, Stapleton, Sunderland

12 May 1979 *Wembley Stadium* *Att 100000*

Arsenal 3 **Manchester United 2**
(Talbot, Stapleton, Sunderland) (McQueen, McIlroy)

Arsenal Jennings, Rice, Nelson, Talbot, O'Leary, Young, Brady, Sunderland, Stapleton, Price (Walford), Rix

Manchester United Bailey, Nicholl, Albiston, McIlroy, McQueen, Buchan, Coppell, J Greenhoff, Jordan, Macari, Thomas

10 May 1980   *Wembley Stadium   Att 100000*

West Ham 1   Arsenal 0
(Brooking)

West Ham   Parkes, Stewart, Lampard, Bonds, Martin, Devonshire, Allen, Pearson, Cross, Brooking, Pike

Arsenal   Jennings, Rice, Devine (Nelson), Talbot, O'Leary, Young, Brady, Sunderland, Stapleton, Price, Rix

9 May 1981   *Wembley Stadium   Att 99500*

Tottenham Hotspur 1   Manchester City 1*
(Hutchison og)   (Hutchison)

Tottenham Hotspur   Aleksic, Hughton, Miller, Roberts, Villa (Brooke), Perryman, Ardiles, Archibald, Galvin, Hoddle, Crooks

Manchester City   Corrigan, Ranson, McDonald, Reid, Power, Caton, Bennett, Gow, Mackenzie, Hutchison (Henry), Reeves

Replay – **14 May 1981**   *Wembley Stadium   Att 92000*

Tottenham Hotspur 3   Manchester City 2
(Villa 2, Crooks)   (Mackenzie, Reeves, pen)

Tottenham Hotspur   Aleksic, Hughton, Miller, Roberts, Villa, Perryman, Ardiles, Archibald, Galvin, Hoddle, Crooks

Manchester City   Corrigan, Ranson, McDonald (Tueart), Caton, Reid, Gow, Power, Mackenzie, Reeves, Bennett, Hutchison

22 May 1982   *Wembley Stadium   Att 100000*

Tottenham Hotspur 1   Queen's Park Rangers 1*
(Hoddle)   (Fenwick)

This was the fourth all-London final and in the first match looked as if it might be the first Wembley final to end as a 0–0 draw.

That changed in extra-time, however, with Glenn Hoddle putting Spurs ahead and Terry Fenwick equalising later.

Rangers were handicapped in the replay the following Thursday by the loss of Glenn Roeder, the first captain to miss a final through suspension. They were also without their principal goalscorer, Clive Allen, through injury.

Yet the match was still decided on a penalty conceded in the sixth minute, Rangers skipper Tony Currie chopping down Graham Roberts as he burst into the penalty area at the end of a 30-yard run.

* after extra time

Glen Hoddle, Spurs, v Clive Allen, QPR, 1982

Glenn Hoddle stroked the penalty past Peter Hucker, the sixth penalty to be awarded in an FA Cup Final at Wembley – every one of them successfully converted.

Rangers made a spirited attempt to recover and John Gregory hit the crossbar, but this was not to be another success for a Second Division side like the one achieved by West Ham two years earlier.

Tottenham Hotspur   Clemence, Hughton, Miller, Price, Hazard (Brooke), Perryman, Roberts, Archibald, Galvin, Hoddle, Crooks

Queen's Park Rangers   Hucker, Fenwick, Gillard, Waddock, Hazell, Roeder, Currie, Flanagan, Allen (Micklewhite), Stainrod, Gregory

*Replay – **27 May 1982***   *Wembley Stadium*   *Att 90000*

Tottenham Hotspur 1   Queen's Park Rangers 0
(Hoddle, pen)

Tottenham Hotspur   Clemence, Hughton, Miller, Price, Hazard (Brooke), Perryman, Roberts, Archibald, Galvin, Hoddle, Crooks

Queen's Park Rangers   Hucker, Fenwick, Gillard, Waddock, Hazell, Neill, Currie, Flanagan, Micklewhite (Burke), Stainrod, Gregory

21 May 1983   *Wembley Stadium*   *Att 100000*

Manchester United 2   **Brighton 2***
(Stapleton, Wilkins)   (Smith, Stevens)

Manchester United   Bailey, Duxbury, Albiston, Wilkins, Moran, McQueen, Robson, Muhren, Stapleton, Whiteside, Davies

Brighton   Moseley, Ramsey (Ryan), Pearce, Grealish, Stevens, Gatting, Case, Howlett, Robinson, Smith, Smillie

Replay – 26 May 1983   *Wembley Stadium*   *Att 92000*

Manchester United 4   **Brighton 0**
(Robson 2, Whiteside, Muhren pen)

Manchester United   Bailey, Duxbury, Albiston, Wilkins, Moran, McQueen, Robson, Muhren, Stapleton, Whiteside, Davies

Brighton   Moseley, Gatting, Pearce, Grealish, Foster, Stevens, Case, Howlett (Ryan), Robinson, Smith, Smillie

19 May 1984   *Wembley Stadium*   *Att 100000*

Everton 2   Watford 0
(Sharp, Gray)

Everton   Southall, Stevens, Bailey, Ratcliffe, Mountfield, Reid, Steven, Heath, Sharp, Gray, Richardson

Watford   Sherwood, Bardsley, Price (Atkinson), Taylor, Terry, Sinnott, Callaghan, Johnston, Reilly, Jackett, Barnes

18 May 1985   *Wembley Stadium*   *Att 100000*

Manchester United 1   Everton 0*
(Whiteside)

Manchester United   Bailey, Gidman, Albiston (Duxbury), Whiteside, McGrath, Moran, Robson, Strachan, Hughes, Stapleton, Olsen

Everton   Southall, Stevens, Van den Hauwe, Ratcliffe, Mountfield, Reid, Steven, Gray, Sharp, Bracewell, Sheedy

10 May 1986   *Wembley Stadium*   *Att 98000*

Liverpool 3   **Everton 1**
(Rush 2, Johnston)   (Lineker)

Liverpool   Grobbelaar, Lawrenson, Beglin, Nicol, Whelan, Hansen, Dalglish, Johnston, Rush, Molby, MacDonald

Everton   Mimms, Stevens (Heath), Van den Hauwe, Ratcliffe, Mountfield, Reid, Steven, Lineker, Sharp, Bracewell, Sheedy

* after extra time

16 May 1987   *Wembley Stadium   Att 98000*

Coventry 3   **Tottenham Hotspur 2***
(Bennett, Houchen, Mabbutt og)   (C Allen, Mabbutt)

Coventry   Ogrizovic, Phillips, Downs, McGrath, Kilcline (Rodger), Peake, Bennett, Gynn, Regis, Houchen, Pickering

Tottenham Hotspur   Clemence, Hughton (Claesen), M Thomas, Hodge, Gough, Mabbutt, C Allen, P Allen, Waddle, Hoddle, Ardiles (Stevens)

14 May 1988   *Wembley Stadium   Att 98203*

Wimbledon 1   Liverpool 0
(Sanchez)

Wimbledon   Beasant, Goodyear, Phelan, Jones, Young, Thorn, Gibson (Scales), Cork (Cunningham), Fashanu, Sanchez, Wise

Liverpool   Grobbelaar, Gillespie, Ablett, Nicol, Spackman (Molby), Hansen, Beardsley, Aldridge (Johnston), Houghton, Barnes, McMahon

20 May 1989   *Wembley Stadium   Att 82500*

Liverpool 3   **Everton 2***
(Aldridge, Rush 2)   (McCall 2)

Liverpool   Grobbelaar, Ablett, Staunton (Venison), Nicol, Whelan, Hansen, Beardsley, Aldridge (Rush), Houghton, Barnes, McMahon

Everton   Southall, McDonald, Van den Hauwe, Ratcliffe, Watson, Bracewell (McCall), Nevin, Steven, Sharp, Cottee, Sheedy (Wilson)

12 May 1990   *Wembley Stadium   Att 80000*

Manchester United 3   Crystal Palace 3*
(Robson, Hughes 2)   (O'Reilly, Wright 2)

Manchester United   Leighton, Ince, Martin (Blackmore), Bruce, Phelan, Pallister (Robins), Robson, Webb, McClair, Hughes, Wallace

Crystal Palace   Martyn, Pemberton, Shaw, Gray (Madden), O'Reilly, Thorn, Barber (Wright), Thomas, Bright, Salako, Pardew

*Replay – **17 May 1990**   Wembley Stadium   Att 80000*

Manchester United 1   Crystal Palace 0
(Martin)

Manchester United   Sealey, Ince, Martin, Bruce, Phelan, Pallister, Robson, Webb, McClair, Hughes, Wallace

Crystal Palace   Martyn, Pemberton, Shaw, Gray, O'Reilly, Thorn, Barber (Wright), Thomas, Bright, Salako (Madden), Pardew

* *after extra time*

Lee Martin scores the only goal of the game, 1990 FA Cup Final replay

18 May 1991   *Wembley Stadium*   *Att 80000*

Tottenham Hotspur 2   **Nottingham Forest 1***
(Stewart, Walker og)   (Pearce)

Tottenham Hotspur   Thortsvedt, Edinburgh, Van den Hauwe, Sedgley, Howells, Mabbutt, Stewart, Gascoigne (Nayim), Samways (Walsh), Lineker, Allen

Nottingham Forest   Crossley, Charles, Pearce, Walker, Chettle, Keane, Crosby, Parker, Clough, Glover (Laws), Woan (Hodge)

9 May 1992   *Wembley Stadium*   *Att 79544*

Liverpool 2   Sunderland 0
(Thomas, Rush)

Liverpool   Grobbelaar, Jones, Burrows, Nicol, Molby, Wright, Saunders, Houghton, Rush, McManaman, Thomas

Sunderland   Norman, Owers, Ball, Bennett, Rogan, D Rush (Hardyman), Bracewell, Davenport, Armstrong (Hawke), Byrne, Atkinson

* *after extra time*

FA Cup Winners 1872–1992

Final venues:

1872 & 1874-92	Kennington Oval	1895-1914	Crystal Palace
1873	Lillie Bridge, London	1915	Old Trafford, Manchester
1893	Fallowfield, Manchester	1920–22	Stamford Bridge, London
1894	Goodison Park, Liverpool	1923 to date	Wembley Stadium

Year	Winners		Runners–up	Result
1872	Wanderers	v	Royal Engineers	1–0
1873	Wanderers	v	Oxford University	2–0
1874	Oxford University	v	Royal Engineers	2–0
1875	Royal Engineers	v	Old Etonians	2–0 after 1–1 draw
1876	Wanderers	v	Old Etonians	3–0 after 0–0 draw
1877	Wanderers	v	Oxford University	2–0 after extra time
1878	†Wanderers	v	Royal Engineers	3–1
1879	Old Etonians	v	Clapham Rovers	1–0
1880	Clapham Rovers	v	Oxford University	1–0
1881	Old Carthusians	v	Old Etonians	3–0
1882	Old Etonians	v	Blackburn Rovers	1–0
1883	Blackburn Olympic	v	Old Etonians	2–1 after extra time
1884	Blackburn Rovers	v	Queen's Park, Glasgow	2–1
1885	Blackburn Rovers	v	Queen's Park, Glasgow	2–0
1886	††Blackburn Rovers	v	West Bromwich Albion	2–0 after 0–0 draw
1887	Aston Villa	v	West Bromwich Albion	2–0
1888	West Bromwich Albion	v	Preston North End	2–1
1889	Preston North End	v	Wolverhampton Wanderers	3–0
1890	Blackburn Rovers	v	Sheffield Wednesday	6–1
1891	Blackburn Rovers	v	Notts. County	3–1
1892	West Bromwich Albion	v	Aston Villa	3–0
1893	Wolverhampton Wanderers	v	Everton	1–0
1894	Notts. County	v	Bolton Wanderers	4–1
1895	Aston Villa	v	West Bromwich Albion	1–0
1896	Sheffield Wednesday	v	Wolverhampton Wanderers	2–1
1897	Aston Villa	v	Everton	3–2
1898	Nottingham Forest	v	Derby County	3–1
1899	Sheffield United	v	Derby County	4–1
1900	Bury	v	Southampton	4–0
1901	Tottenham Hotspur	v	Sheffield United	3–1 after 2–2 draw
1902	Sheffield United	v	Southampton	2–1 after 1–1 draw
1903	Bury	v	Derby County	6–0
1904	Manchester City	v	Bolton Wanderers	1–0
1905	Aston Villa	v	Newcastle United	2–0
1906	Everton	v	Newcastle United	1–0
1907	Sheffield Wednesday	v	Everton	2–1
1908	Wolverhampton Wanderers	v	Newcastle United	3–1
1909	Manchester United	v	Bristol City	1–0
1910	Newcastle United	v	Barnsley	2–0 after 1–1 draw
1911	Bradford City	v	Newcastle United	1–0 after 0–0 draw
1912	Barnsley	v	West Bromwich Albion	1–0 after 0–0 draw
1913	Aston Villa	v	Sunderland	1–0
1914	Burnley	v	Liverpool	1–0
1915	Sheffield United	v	Chelsea	3–0
1920	Aston Villa	v	Huddersfield Town	1–0 after extra time
1921	Tottenham Hotspur	v	Wolverhampton Wanderers	1–0

† *Won outright but restored to the Association*
†† *A special trophy was awarded for third consecutive win*

Year	Winners		Runners–up	Result
1922	Huddersfield Town	v	Preston North End	1–0
1923	Bolton Wanderers	v	West Ham United	2–0
1924	Newcastle United	v	Aston Villa	2–0
1925	Sheffield United	v	Cardiff City	1–0
1926	Bolton Wanderers	v	Manchester City	1–0
1927	Cardiff City	v	Arsenal	1–0
1928	Blackburn Rovers	v	Huddersfield Town	3–1
1929	Bolton Wanderers	v	Portsmouth	2–0
1930	Arsenal	v	Huddersfield Town	2–0
1931	West Bromwich Albion	v	Birmingham	2–1
1932	Newcastle United	v	Arsenal	2–1
1933	Everton	v	Manchester City	3–0
1934	Manchester City	v	Portsmouth	2–1
1935	Sheffield Wednesday	v	West Bromwich Albion	4–2
1936	Arsenal	v	Sheffield United	1–0
1937	Sunderland	v	Preston North End	3–1
1938	Preston North End	v	Huddersfield Town	1–0 after extra time
1939	Portsmouth	v	Wolverhampton Wanderers	4–1
1946	Derby County	v	Charlton Athletic	4–1 after extra time
1947	Charlton Athletic	v	Burnley	1–0 after extra time
1948	Manchester United	v	Blackpool	4–2
1949	Wolverhampton Wanderers	v	Leicester City	3–1
1950	Arsenal	v	Liverpool	2–0
1951	Newcastle United	v	Blackpool	2–0
1952	Newcastle United	v	Arsenal	1–0
1953	Blackpool	v	Bolton Wanderers	4–3
1954	West Bromwich Albion	v	Preston North End	3–2
1955	Newcastle United	v	Manchester City	3–1
1956	Manchester City	v	Birmingham City	3–1
1957	Aston Villa	v	Manchester United	2–1
1958	Bolton Wanderers	v	Manchester United	2–0
1959	Nottingham Forest	v	Luton Town	2–1
1960	Wolverhampton Wanderers	v	Blackburn Rovers	3–0
1961	Tottenham Hotspur	v	Leicester City	2–0
1962	Tottenham Hotspur	v	Burnley	3–1
1963	Manchester United	v	Leicester City	3–1
1964	West Ham United	v	Preston North End	3–2
1965	Liverpool	v	Leeds United	2–1 after extra time
1966	Everton	v	Sheffield Wednesday	3–2
1967	Tottenham Hotspur	v	Chelsea	2–1
1968	West Bromwich Albion	v	Everton	1–0 after extra time
1969	Manchester City	v	Leicester City	1–0
1970	Chelsea	v	Leeds United	2–1 after 2–2 draw both games extra time
1971	Arsenal	v	Liverpool	2–1 after extra time
1972	Leeds United	v	Arsenal	1–0
1973	Sunderland	v	Leeds United	1–0
1974	Liverpool	v	Newcastle United	3–0
1975	West Ham United	v	Fulham	2–0
1976	Southampton	v	Manchester United	1–0
1977	Manchester United	v	Liverpool	2–1
1978	Ipswich Town	v	Arsenal	1–0
1979	Arsenal	v	Manchester United	3–2
1980	West Ham United	v	Arsenal	1–0
1981	Tottenham Hotspur	v	Manchester City	3–2 after 1–1 draw after extra time
1982	Tottenham Hotspur	v	Queen's Park Rangers	1–0 after 1–1 draw after extra time

FA Cup Trivia

TEAMS

Tottenham Hotspur hold the record for FA Cup wins. Their defeat of Nottingham Forest in the 1991 final was their eighth FA Cup success. Manchester United, the 1990 winners, are next with seven wins along with Aston Villa.

The Wanderers and **Blackburn Rovers** are the only teams to have won the FA Cup in three successive seasons. The Wanderers won in 1876, '77 and '78 while Blackburn Rovers won the Cup in 1884, '85 and '86.

Wimbledon were the last new name on the FA Cup when they beat Liverpool in 1988. A total of 42 different teams have won the competition.

Arsenal have the most FA Cup Final appearances at Wembley with 11 but they have won only five of their finals, the last being in 1979 against Manchester United.

Blackburn Rovers have won six Cup Finals but only one of those wins was at Wembley – against Huddersfield in 1928.

Cardiff City in 1927 are the only team to have taken the FA Cup outside England when they beat Arsenal. They had only one Englishman in their side.

Old Carthusians and **Wimbledon** are the only clubs to have won both the FA Amateur Cup and the FA Cup. Old Carthusians won the FA Cup in 1881 and the FA Amateur Cup thirteen years later. Wimbledon took the Amateur Cup at Wembley in 1963 and 25 years later beat Liverpool in the FA Cup Final.

Tottenham Hotspur were the last non-League side to win the Cup. They were in the Southern League when they beat Sheffield United in the 1901 final replay.

West Ham United were the last of seven Second Division sides to win the FA Cup when they beat Arsenal in 1980. The other Second Division winners were: **Notts County** in 1894, **Wolverhampton Wanderers** in 1908, **Barnsley** in 1912, **West Bromwich Albion** in 1931, **Sunderland** in 1973 and **Southampton** in 1976.

West Bromwich Albion are the only team to complete the double of FA Cup success and promotion in the same season. Preston, Aston Villa, Tottenham, Arsenal and Liverpool have all managed the League and Cup 'double'.

Leicester City have been to four FA Cup Finals at Wembley and have lost them all. Three were in the 1960s.

West Bromwich Albion and **Blackburn Rovers** were the teams in the first all-professional final in 1886 which Blackburn won in a replay at the Baseball Ground, Derby.

Tranmere Rovers and **Grimsby Town** were the first teams from the First or Second Division to appear in the first round of the FA Cup since Newport County in 1945-46. They both played in the first round in 1991-92 to balance up the competition after the expansion of the Football League.

Shrewsbury (1950-51) and **Hull** (1945-46) are the only League teams to have missed out on the FA Cup competition since the War.

Chester City, Hartlepool United, Southend United and **Torquay United** have never beaten a First Division side in the FA Cup. Gillingham achieved the feat as New Brompton back in 1907-08 when they beat Sunderland.

Derby County hold the record number of wins in one FA Cup season but that was in the 1945-46 competition which was played on a home and away basis. They won nine matches.

Tottenham Hotspur are the only club to have retained the FA Cup twice, in 1961 and '62 and again in 1981 and '82.

Millwall, in 1937, when they were beaten by Sunderland; **Port Vale**, who lost to West Brom in 1954; **York City**, who lost to Newcastle in 1955; **Norwich**, who lost to Luton in 1959; **Crystal Palace**, who lost to Southampton in 1976 and **Plymouth,** beaten by Watford in 1984 are the only Third Division sides to reach the semi-finals of the FA Cup.

GOALS

There have been only three hat-tricks in FA Cup Finals. The first was in 1890 by **Billy Townley** for Blackburn Rovers against Sheffield Wednesday. **Jimmy Logan** scored three for Notts County against Bolton in 1894 and **Stan Mortensen** claimed three in the 'Matthews Final' of 1953 for Blackpool, also against Bolton.

Jackie Milburn of Newcastle is *credited* with the fastest Wembley Cup Final goal. It came after 45 seconds in the 1955 final against Manchester City, although Jack Roscamp scored in 'less than a minute' for Blackburn Rovers against Huddersfield in 1928.

John Devey of Aston Villa scored a goal in the 1895 final against West Bromwich Albion which was timed at between 30 and 40 seconds, although there are suggestions that Bob Chatt actually scored the goal.

Norman Whiteside of Manchester United was the youngest-ever goalscorer in a Wembley final. He was 18 years 18 days old when he scored against Brighton in the FA Cup Final replay of 1983.

Denis Law holds the record for the number of FA Cup goals scored in a career. He scored 41 during his career with Huddersfield, Manchester United and Manchester City.

Bury hold the record for the highest Cup Final score when they beat Derby 6–0 in 1903. The highest score at Wembley was Manchester United's 4–0 replay defeat of Brighton in 1983.

Blackburn Rovers and **Blackpool** have the highest winning aggregate score in an FA Cup Final. Blackburn beat Sheffield Wednesday 6–1 in 1890 and Blackpool beat Bolton Wanderers 4–3 in 1953.

Ian Rush of Liverpool and **Stuart McCall** of Everton were the first players to come on as substitutes in an FA Cup Final and score two goals. They both achieved the feat in the 1989 final, which Liverpool won 3–2 against Everton. Ian Wright of Crystal Palace did the same thing the following season against Manchester United in the 3–3 draw.

Eddie Kelly was the first substitute to score in an FA Cup Final, for Arsenal against Liverpool in 1971.

Aston Villa have scored the most goals in an FA Cup campaign, – 40 in the 1886-87 season – a sequence that included four matches against Wolverhampton Wanderers. Derby scored 37 in the 1945-46 season but the ties were played on a home and away basis.

Jimmy Brown scored in three consecutive Cup Finals for Blackburn Rovers from 1884 to 1886 but he scored only in the 1886 final replay. Four players have scored in successive finals and three are from Blackburn.

John Aldridge (1988) and **Gary Lineker** (1991) are the only players to miss a penalty at Wembley, although Charlie Wallace of Aston Villa was the first to miss in a Cup Final when he shot wide in the 1913 match at Crystal Palace which Villa won against Sunderland.

Preston North End hold the scoring record for a single match. They scored 26 to beat Hyde in the first round of the 1887-88 competition.

Nottingham Forest's 14–0 win at Clapton in the first round in 1890-91 stands as the biggest away win in the competition.

Ted MacDougall, then with Bournemouth, holds the record for the highest number of goals in one match in the FA Cup proper. He scored nine in Bournemouth's 11–0 win over Margate in the first round in 1971.

Peter Osgood of Chelsea was the last player to score in every round from the third round. The seven other players to equal that were: **Ellis Rimmer** (Sheffield Wednesday) 1935; **Frank O'Donnell** (Preston) 1937; **Stan Mortensen** (Blackpool) 1948; **Jackie Milburn** (Newcastle) 1951; **Nat Lofthouse** (Bolton) 1953; **Charlie Wayman** (Preston) 1954; **Jeff Astle** (West Bromwich Albion) 1968.

Sandy Brown of Tottenham is credited with scoring in *every* round in the Cup-winning run of 1901. He scored 15 goals in that season which is still an FA Cup record.

PLAYERS

Paul Allen is the youngest player to appear in an FA Cup Final when he was picked for West Ham at 17 years 256 days to face Arsenal in the 1980 Cup Final.

Billy Hampson of Newcastle was the oldest when he played in the 1924 final against Aston Villa at the age of 41 years 8 months.

Arsenal had the oldest average age for their team in the 1950 final, which they won against Liverpool at Wembley. The average age of the team was more than 31.

Scott Endersby was the youngest player to appear in the FA Cup first round when he played for Kettering against Tilbury in the 1977-78 competition at the age of 15 years 279 days.

Billy Meredith was the oldest player to appear in the FA Cup proper when he was 49 years 8 months in the 1924 semi-final for Manchester City against Newcastle United.

David Nish was the youngest FA Cup Final captain when he led Leicester City in the 1969 final. He was 21 years and 7 months old, while **Peter Shilton**, in the same Leicester side, was the youngest-ever FA Cup Final goalkeeper at 19 years 7 months.

Stan Cullis was the youngest FA Cup Final manager. He was still only 33 as he took Wolverhampton Wanderers to the final in 1949 where they beat Leicester 3–1.

Ernie Taylor is the only player to have played in three different finals for different teams. He was in the Newcastle line-up in 1951, the Blackpool side in 1953, and his only loss was with Manchester United in 1958.

Ray Clemence, with Liverpool and Tottenham, was the last of five players to appear in five finals. **Joe Hulme** (Arsenal), **Johnny Giles** (Manchester United and Leeds), **Pat Rice** (Arsenal) and **Frank Stapleton** (Arsenal and Manchester United) were the others.

Lord Kinnaird, C.H.R. Wollaston and **James Forrest** are the only three players to win five FA Cup winners' medals. Lord Kinnaird's came in 1873, '77, '78 (Wanderers) and 1879, '82 (Old Etonians). Wollaston's were with the Wanderers in 1872, '73,'76, '77 and '78 and Forrest's were with Blackburn Rovers in 1884, '85, '86, '90 and '91.

Ian Callaghan, with Liverpool, Swansea and Crewe holds the appearance record in the FA Cup with 88. Stanley Matthews played 86 times and Bobby Charlton 84.

Jimmy and **Brian Greenhoff** are the last brothers to have appeared in an FA Cup Final. They were in the Manchester United side that won the Cup in 1977. They were the third set of brothers – the others were Denis and Leslie Compton (Arsenal 1950) and Ted and George Robledo (Newcastle 1952).

Kevin Moran is the only player to be sent off in an FA Cup Final. He was dismissed while playing for Manchester United against Everton in 1985. In 1913 there was a fracas involving Harry Hampton of Aston Villa and Charlie Thompson of Sunderland and although neither was sent off they were both suspended for a month afterwards.

Kevin Howley was the youngest referee, for Wolves' final against Blackburn in 1960. He was 35.

OTHER FA CUP FACTS

Floodlights

The first FA Cup tie to be played under floodlights was in 1955 when Kidderminster Harriers replayed Brierley Hill Alliance, in a preliminary round tie on 14 September. The first floodlit match between two League sides in the FA Cup was the first round second replay between Carlisle and Darlington at St James's Park, Newcastle, on 28 November 1955.

Substitutes

The first FA Cup Final substitute was Dennis Clarke of West Bromwich Albion who replaced John Kaye in the 1968 final. Marvin Hinton of Chelsea was the first man to be a substitute in both the final and replay. He came on for Ron Harris in the 1970 final and then for Peter Osgood in the replay at Old Trafford as Chelsea finally beat Leeds.

Television

The first FA Cup Final to be screened was the 1937 game between Sunderland and Preston. The first final broadcast on radio was the 1927 match between Cardiff and Arsenal. The first FA Cup tie to be televised – other than the final – was Charlton against Blackburn in the fifth round on 8 February 1947.

Equipment

The crossbar replaced a tape in 1875, and a whistle was used by the referee for the first time in 1878. Nets were invented and patented by J. A. Brodie of Liverpool in 1890 and were used for the first time in the 1892 Cup Final between West Bromwich Albion and Aston Villa.

The Cup

This is the fourth FA Cup trophy that has been played for. The original, made in 1872 by Martin, Hall & Co, was stolen on 11 September 1895 from a shop window in Newton Row, Birmingham. Even a reward of £10 failed to recover it. Aston Villa, who had been Cup holders and had loaned it out for exhibition, were fined £25 by the FA.

The new Cup was made by Vaughton's & Co of Birmingham and was played for until 1910 when the FA discovered that their design was being copied. The Cup was presented to Lord Kinnaird, upon completing 21 years as President of the FA. Fattorini & Sons of Bradford were selected to manufacture the new trophy. The Cup is 19 inches high and weighs 175 ounces. It has been played for since 1911 when Bradford won it. A duplicate trophy was kept in the FA vaults and then used for the first time in 1992.

Leeds United secure the First Division Championship against Sheffield United

CHAPTER TWO

The Premier League

The Search for Excellence

RICK PARRY

Chief Executive of The FA Premier League

In the last twelve months much has been written and said about the formation of the new Football Association Premier League. It has provoked argument and discussion. There has been approval and criticism. In the midst of this moving landscape though, there has been one clear objective. The FA Premier League which kicks off in August 1992 has tried to focus its energies on providing excellence in all aspects of the national sport.

From the moment the Premier League idea was conceived the aim has been to provide quality both on and off the playing fields of England. We believe the best players must be kept in England and in order to do that, we must be able to compete with the big continental clubs in terms of wages and transfer fees.

It cannot be good for the English game that players like Des Walker and David Platt, both members of England's European Championship squad, are now playing their football in the Italian League. If they are the best players that England possesses we want them to be leading the charge towards outstanding achievement at Old Trafford, Anfield, Highbury and the other great English stadia. Instead, next season they will be playing in Genoa and Turin and exciting fans in Rome, Naples, Venice and Milan. We feel the time has come to reverse that trend and re-establish the English game as the best in Europe.

But to achieve that aim there is a need for refinancing. Football cannot produce the miracles without the financial resources and this has meant a maximising of commercial income. The revenue will not be used purely for the purchasing or retention of the best players but also for refurbishment of our grounds to provide spectators with comfortable and safe surroundings. If we want English football to be a super power again then this is the route we must take.

The £304 million generated by the television contract which was signed in late May with BSkyB and the BBC is the sort of giant com-

mercial stride that is needed to speed up improvements in the English game.

The guidelines to be followed when negotiating the television contract were as clear as the terms of reference for the whole League. There was a need to be visionary rather than mercenary. We wanted to establish more control of our own destiny so that the fans, especially those in the grounds while not forgetting those at home, had a fairer deal. We had to make sure that this time we were not just handing over the television rights to a broadcasting company. We needed to create a partnership.

There was also a gap in the market for programmes that promote the game to the full rather than trivialise and ridicule the product on which they survive.

We had to balance the need for short-term revenue with the prospect of a longer and more lucrative future. It was significant that short-term cash came last on the list of priorities.

Above all the deal had to be fair. It had to be fair to the clubs, the fans and the game in general. We think this is something that we managed to guarantee with the BSkyB and BBC contract.

There are other changes next season. There will be no loan deals between Premier League clubs, with the exception of goalkeepers, and there will also be three substitutes allowed, one a goalkeeper. These may not seem radical shifts in the direction of the game, but what we have achieved in bringing the Premier League to the starting line is the most dramatic change in English football for 100 years.

People tend to forget the enormity of the achievement in creating the Premier League, looking rather instant differences. In the past, football has been guilty of making decisions in haste and reflecting and regretting at leisure. That is not the intention of the Premier League.

We now have a streamlined competition in tune with football for the 21st rather than the 19th century. In the coming years there will be further steps forward as we strive to establish firm and proven foundations on which the sport can prosper.

SIR JOHN QUINTON

Sir John Quinton, the former chairman of Barclays Bank, accepted the job as Premier League non-executive chairman in early December 1991. In this honorary capacity he supported chief executive Rick Parry in negotiations with the Professional Footballers' Association and the television companies, combining the job with his role as Barclays chairman until the spring of 1992 when he stepped down at the Bank.

Sir John, 61, is a keen football fan, holding a season ticket at Tottenham Hotspur. He was also a fervent supporter of the Barclays sponsorship of the Football League, one of the most lucrative and successful sponsorships of its era.

The Role of the LMA

HOWARD WILKINSON

Chairman of the League Managers' Association

Howard Wilkinson of Leeds United will manage the 1991-92 champion club in the first season of the FA Premier League. He also chairs the new League Managers' Association (LMA), inaugurated last season to give football managers a greater say in the running of the game.

He spoke of the new role of the LMA in his acceptance speech at the Barclay's Manager of the Year luncheon at the Savoy Hotel on 8 May. Below are extracts from his speech.

'As managers we have a vested interest in the future of the game, largely because it is the hobby we love as well as being our job.

'I have to admit, also, that our prosperity and well being are directly linked to the prosperity and well being of the game. That is why, nine months ago, a few of us decided to form the League Managers' Association. It gives me great pleasure to announce that the confinement has gone its full term and hopefully the birth will be even more successful.

'We have finally realised that fighting each other on a Saturday afternoon should be enough and for the rest of the week we should be pulling together.

'If we suffer, football suffers, because, in my opinion, we offer potentially the most informed views in the football debate. In recent weeks representatives of the Premier League and the LMA have sat down to discuss matters which will have a crucial effect on the development of the game.

'During the summer we are committed to further meetings to sort out the game's most pressing issues: law changes on offsides and pass backs, the transfer system, the registration of contracts and the removal of the fear element from the game.

'Quality has to be the watchword. We think it is crucial that we sit down with the players, referees, The Football Association and the leagues.

'For years clubs have sought salvation through quantity and many, including myself, believe this road will eventually lead us into the cul-de-sac of mediocrity, both on and off the field.

'Whilst we at Elland Road are delighted to be champions, our sympathy extends to Alex Ferguson and his Manchester United players who were forced, through their success, to play four games in six days at a critical time of the season.

Howard Wilkinson with the Championship trophy

'No sensible person can condone a system that forces that on to a club. Our top players are not machines. Football is not essentially a marathon but we have turned it into one and, as a result, produced players who can cope with the demands of that type of race.

'But for international management in this country that must be a nightmare.

'There are other areas of concern that seriously damage our product image. Red and yellow cards have been used with depressing frequency this season at a time when most observers see the game as cleaner than at any time.

'Referees, players, managers and administrators are often not on the same wavelength. This has to change and mechanisms for change have to be sought.

'If the "Blueprint for Soccer" offered anything, it seemed to offer the chance for change. Quality at every level seemed to be the watchword for the future.

'Supporters do not want, and neither can we afford to give them, a poor product. The vision is in danger of disappearing without trace.

'Someone out there has to listen. We cannot afford to let vested interest be the basis for decisions that dramatically affect the game we love.'

FOOTBALL MANAGERS OF THE YEAR

1965/66	Jock Stein, *Celtic.*
1966/67	Jock Stein, *Celtic.*
1967/68	Matt Busby, *Manchester United.*
1968/69	Don Revie, *Leeds United.*
1969/70	Don Revie, *Leeds United.*
1970/71	Bertie Mee, *Arsenal.*
1971/72	Don Revie, *Leeds United.*
1972/73	Bill Shankly, *Liverpool.*
1973/74	Jack Charlton, *Middlesbrough.*
1974/75	Ron Saunders, *Aston Villa.*
1975/76	Bob Paisley, *Liverpool.*
1976/77	Bob Paisley, *Liverpool.*
1977/78	Brian Clough, *Nottingham Forest.*
1978/79	Bob Paisley, *Liverpool.*
1979/80	Bob Paisley, *Liverpool.*
1980/81	Ron Saunders, *Aston Villa.*
1981/82	Bob Paisley, *Liverpool.*
1982/83	Bob Paisley, *Liverpool.*
1983/84	Joe Fagan, *Liverpool.*
1984/85	Howard Kendall, *Everton.*
1985/86	Kenny Dalglish, *Liverpool.*
1986/87	Howard Kendall, *Everton.*
1987/88	Kenny Dalglish, *Liverpool.*
1988/89	George Graham, *Arsenal.*
1989/90	Kenny Dalglish, *Liverpool.*
1990/91	George Graham, *Arsenal.*
1991/92	Howard Wilkinson, *Leeds United.*

PREMIER LEAGUE OFFICERS

Chairman: Sir John Quinton
Chief Executive: Rick Parry
Secretary: Mike Foster
Assistant Secretary: Adrian Cook

The Twenty-two Clubs in The Premier League

ARSENAL
Arsenal Stadium, Avenell Road,
    Highbury, London N5 1BU
Telephone 071-226 0304
Capacity 30,000 (reconstruction
    work underway)
Chairman P Hill-Wood
Manager George Graham

ASTON VILLA
Villa Park, Trinity Road,
    Birmingham B6 6HE
Telephone 021-327 2299
Capacity 40,312
Chairman H D Ellis
Manager Ron Atkinson

BLACKBURN ROVERS
Ewood Park, Blackburn BB2
    4JF
Telephone 0254-55432
Capacity 20,000
Chairman J Walker
Manager Kenny Dalglish

CHELSEA
Stamford Bridge, Fulham Road,
    London SW6 1HS
Telephone 071-385 5545
Capacity 37,000
Chairman K Bates
Manager Ian Porterfield

COVENTRY CITY
Highfield Road Stadium, King
    Richard Street, Coventry
    CV2 4FW
Telephone 0203-223535
Capacity 25,000
Chairman J Robbins
Manager Bobby Gould

CRYSTAL PALACE
Selhurst Park, London SE25
    6PU
Telephone 081-653 4462
Capacity 30,000
Chairman R Noades
Manager Steve Coppell

EVERTON
Goodison Park, Liverpool L4
    4EL
Telephone 051-521 2020
Capacity 39,000
Chairman Dr D Marsh
Manager Howard Kendall

IPSWICH TOWN
Portman Road, Ipswich, Suffolk
    IP1 2DA
Telephone 0473-219211
Capacity 23,000
Chairman P Cobbold
Manager John Lyall

LEEDS UNITED
Elland Road, Leeds LS11 0ES
Telephone 0532-716037
Capacity 31,000
Chairman L Silver OBE
Manager Howard Wilkinson

LIVERPOOL
Anfield Road, Anfield, Liverpool
    L4 0TH
Telephone 051-263 2361
Capacity 44,600
Chairman D Moores
Manager Graeme Souness

MANCHESTER CITY
Maine Road, Moss Side,
    Manchester M14 7WN
Telephone 061-226 1191
Capacity 34,000
Chairman P Swales
Manager Peter Reid

MANCHESTER UNITED
Old Trafford, Manchester
    M16 0RA
Telephone 061-872 1661
Capacity 34,000 (building work
    underway)
Chairman M Edwards
Manager Alex Ferguson

MIDDLESBROUGH
Ayresome Park, Middlesbrough,
    Cleveland TS1 4PB
Telephone 0642-819659
Capacity 27,000
Chairman M Henderson
Manager Lennie Lawrence

NORWICH CITY
Carrow Road, Norwich NR1 1JE
Telephone 0603-612131
Capacity 20,559
Chairman R Chase
Manager Mike Walker

NOTTINGHAM FOREST
City Ground, Nottingham NG2
    5FJ
Telephone 0602-822202
Capacity 28,000
Chairman F Reacher
Manager Brian Çlough

OLDHAM ATHLETIC
Boundary Park, Sheepfoot Lane,
    Oldham, Lancashire OL1 2PA
Telephone 061-624 4972
Capacity 16,500
Chairman I Stott
Manager Joe Royle

QUEEN'S PARK RANGERS
Rangers Stadium (Loftus Rd),
    South Africa Road, Shepherds
    Bush, London W12 7PA
Telephone 081-743 0262
Capacity 23,000
Chairman R Thompson
Manager Gerry Francis

SHEFFIELD UNITED
Bramall Lane, Sheffield S2 4SU
Telephone 0742-738955
Capacity 32,000
Chairman P Woolhouse
Manager Dave Bassett

SHEFFIELD WEDNESDAY
Hillsborough, Sheffield S6 1SW
Telephone 0742-343122
Capacity 41,000
Chairman D Richards
Manager Trevor Francis

SOUTHAMPTON
The Dell, Milton Road,
    Southampton SO9 4XX
Telephone 0703-220505
Capacity 22,000
Chairman G Askham
Manager Ian Branfoot

TOTTENHAM HOTSPUR
748 High Road, Tottenham,
    London N17 0AP
Telephone 081-808 6666
Capacity 33,500
Chairman A Sugar
Manager Doug Livermore

WIMBLEDON
Selhurst Park, London SE25
    6PU
Telephone 081-771 2233
Capacity 30,000
Chairman/Owner S Hammam
Manager Joe Kinnear

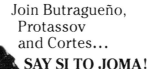

CHAPTER THREE

The FA Youth Cup

FA Youth Cup Final 1992

Manchester United 6   Crystal Palace 3   (aggregate)

The 1991-92 season for Manchester United was to be a significant one for many reasons. Rumbelows Cup victory apart, the main objective for Alex Ferguson's team was to banish once and for all the ghosts of the 1960s who still haunted the club, as impatient fans awaited their first championship triumph for 25 years.

It was even longer, 28 years, since United had clinched the FA Youth Cup, the trophy they had virtually made their own in the twelve years after its inception in 1953. In those years United won the competition no fewer than six times, a record which is second to none.

But the trophy had eluded them ever since the waif-like skill and mesmerising pace of George Best had guided them to a 5–2 defeat of Swindon Town, 28 long seasons ago.

Hopes of an end to that particular bogey were raised during the 1991-92 season with the emergence of yet another wing wonder. This time the boy prodigy was an 18-year-old Welshman called Ryan Giggs, whose irresistible talent had propelled him dramatically into the senior side's arduous, but ultimately doomed, campaign for the First Division crown. Giggs' contribution to the youth team, albeit sporadic, added to the general consensus of opinion that this was one of the greatest youth teams Old Trafford had ever nurtured. Manager Alex Ferguson definitely agreed, and Luton manager David Pleat noted with some envy, that Mr Ferguson was sitting on a proverbial goldmine. There has never been any doubting the pedigree of the youth team structure at Old Trafford. Current first-team players such as Clayton Blackmore, Mark Hughes, a former PFA Player of the Year, Mark Robins, Russell Beardsmore, Darren Ferguson and of course Giggs, who this year clinched the PFA Young Player of the Year award, have all graduated from the youth team in recent seasons, as well as last year's PFA Young Player of the Year Lee Sharpe, who was ushered into the youth team ranks following his move from Torquay as a 17-year-old.

United started their long journey to the final with a 4–2 defeat of Sunderland at Roker Park. Victories over Walsall, Manchester City,

Tranmere Rovers and the fancied Tottenham Hotspur, confirmed the potential of Eric Harrison's side and set up the prospect of a final between United and Crystal Palace.

The first leg between the two sides took place at the beginning of April on a rain-soaked night at Selhurst Park. Despite the torrent, almost 8,000 fans turned up to watch the contest, which began in the best possible way for United when they scored after just 17 minutes. Another promising winger Ben Thornley instigated the move with a tantalising cross from the left which striker Nicky Butt swept first time past a bemused Jimmy Glass.

The visitors extended their lead on 25 minutes when a suicidal back-pass from defender Andrew McPherson let in the busy Thornley, who rode a clumsy challenge from the advancing Glass before slipping the ball intelligently to David Beckham, who rifled home a shot from the edge of the area.

It was all United now, as they swept forward in droves, clearly not suffering too much from the enforced absence of Giggs. But as the game progressed Palace at last began to find their feet. Willowy winger George Ndah went close with a mazy run and shot before substitute Stuart McCall looped home a magnificent header after 86 minutes to give his side a glimmer of hope for the return leg. But no sooner had the cheers of the Palace crowd died away, than United recaptured their two-goal advantage when Butt slid home another tantalising centre from Thornley with just 60 seconds of the match to go, to leave the final score **Crystal Palace 1 Manchester United 3**.

The return leg at Old Trafford was scheduled for 15 May, just long enough perhaps for the Manchester faithful to have recovered from the desperate shock of seeing the championship slip away from Alex Ferguson and his men, when it had seemed to be firmly in their grasp.

The United youth side had been forced to encounter similar disappointments in their league programme, missing out on the title in both the Lancashire League Divisions One and Two, when they finished as runners-up in both. But when news hummed around the Old Trafford crowd that Giggs would be playing in the second leg, there suddenly seemed little doubt that the trophy would be making a long overdue return trip to Old Trafford.

So it proved with the inspirational Giggs and Thornley setting up a thrilling 3–2 victory in front of more than 14,000 fans. Thornley scored one of the goals and Simon Davies and Colin McKee found the net for the others, as United turned on a super show. To their credit Crystal Palace kept trying for the entire 90 minutes, and were rewarded with two consolation goals, but it was not enough to prevent the ceremonial laying to rest of at least some of the spectres that have continued to haunt Old Trafford.

FA Youth Cup Winners – Manchester United

All Manchester United Youth Team Coach Eric Harrison would say directly about his side of talented young individuals, was that they were exactly that – talented. The experienced Mr Harrison was very sensibly and astutely refusing to jump headlong on to the media bandwagon that implored him aboard, as the press praise and hype continued to ring deafeningly in his ears. Indeed, despite even the assessment of manager Alex Ferguson, which stated quite simply that the current youth side were as good as any ever assembled at the Old Trafford club, Mr Harrison preferred instead to underplay the significance of individual performances, highlighting more the importance of the side's team ethic.

'They are a very good side,' he confessed. 'The most pleasing thing is that most are only first year apprentices and will be available again next season. 'But when they went out to play Crystal Palace for the second leg of the FA Youth Cup, I just told them to do what they always try to do, play their very best.

'I know it sounds like a huge cliché, but as far as we're ever concerned it is just another game of football. The good thing about that particular game was that by the time the second leg came around, the lads had already forgotten how Crystal Palace had played, so they had to go out there with a more relaxed view.

'The secret with kids is not to put pressure on them, by telling them to be careful in what they do all the time. Whilst they have to have discipline, they must also be allowed to express themselves.'

Expression doesn't seem to have been a problem with more recent youth team graduates such as the emerging Lee Sharpe, already capped by England at senior level, and the breathtaking Ryan Giggs, who this season became the youngest player ever to wear a senior Wales shirt.

What with winning the FA Youth Cup again for the first time in 28 years, and producing a selection of players who look set to burst as dramatically into the First Division spotlight as Sharpe and Giggs have done, the long-term prospects for success at Old Trafford look encouraging, particularly for a side for whom championship success has been painfully long overdue.

Ryan Giggs, Manchester United's Young Player of the Year

FA Youth Cup 1991–92

PRELIMINARY ROUND

Scarborough 0 Atherton Laburnham Rovers 2

The charmingly named Atherton Laburnham Rovers from Greater Manchester had never beaten a League side in the FA Youth Cup. Their achievements in the competition had been little more than modest, until the 1991–92 season that is.

An unsuspecting Scarborough played host to Atherton in the preliminary round of the competition, with high hopes of progressing through to the qualifying stages themselves. But it was not to be their year. Atherton began the tie in subdued mood, having to defend with alarming regularity as their hosts swarmed dangerously around the penalty area. But Scarborough's inability to convert their territorial advantage into goals was to be Atherton's gain. Phillip Whittaker scored the visitors' first goal against the run of play, and it was soon followed by a second from Craig Mulaney.

With ten of the Atherton team having played together since the age of nine, the Bolton Boys' Federation League side successfully thwarted all attempts by their more illustrious League hosts to get back into the game, and Atherton held on for a 2–0 win.

However, Rovers' romance with the FA Youth Cup was to prove a short-lived affair. Their next Cup match, a first qualifying round tie against Rotherham United, was a much more one-sided encounter, with the more experienced League side running out 7–1 winners.

Craig Mulaney scored Atherton's only goal of the tie, and the enterprising youngsters returned to Crilly Park to dream of next season and another Cup run.

PRELIMINARY ROUND 7 September 1991

(replays in italics)			*Result*
South Bank	v	Marske United	0–2
Billingham Synthonia	v	Hartlepool United	0–2
Guisborough Town	v	Stockton	3–1
Accrington Stanley	v	Flixton	5–1
Huddersfield Town	v	Lancaster City	8–0
Barrow	v	Bootle	†
Rochdale	v	Preston North End	1–4
Blackpool (Wren) Rovers	v	Rotherham United	1–4
Scarborough	v	Atherton LR	0–2
Chadderton	v	Halifax Town	1–4
Wrexham	v	Stockport County	3–0

† *walkover for Barrow, Bootle withdrawn*

(replays in italics)			Result
Warrington Town	v	Chester City	1–1††
Yorkshire Amateurs	v	Bolton Wanderers	1–2
Marine	v	Shrewsbury Town	1–1
Shrewsbury Town	v	*Marine*	*3–0*
Telford United	v	Leek Town	7–3
Willenhall Town	v	Hednesford Town	5–1
Hinckley Town	v	Leicester United	3–3
Leicester United	v	*Hinckley Town*	*3–2*
Burton Albion	v	Chasetown	4–0
Mile Oak Rovers	v	Kidderminster Harriers	0–6
Nuneaton Borough	v	Sutton Coldfield Town	5–0
Tamworth	v	Corby Town	3–1
Redditch United	v	Rothwell Town	0–3
Wisbech Town	v	Lye Town	2–1
Cambridge City	v	Stowmarket Town	5–1
Witham Town	v	Brantham Athletic	1–4
Eynesbury Rovers	v	Norwich City	1–6
Stevenage Borough	v	Wivenhoe Town	1–2
Bishop's Stortford	v	Hitchin Town	0–4
Letchworth Garden City	v	Barkingside	6–2
East Thurrock United	v	Hertford Town	4–1
Tiptree United	v	Royston Town	1–0
Braintree Town	v	Welwyn Garden City	2–1
St Albans City	v	Billericay Town	4–1
Canvey Island	v	Eton Manor	1–6
Enfield	v	Clapton	1–3
Buckingham Town	v	Maidenhead United	2–4
Marlow	v	Bedfont	1–1
Bedfont	v	*Marlow*	*3–1*
Feltham & Hounslow Borough	v	Harefield United	2–5
Staines Town	v	Northwood	4–1
Hendon	v	Leyton-Wingate	1–2
Cheshunt	v	Thamesmead Town	1–0
Hillingdon Borough	v	Kingsbury Town	2–2
Kingsbury Town	v	*Hillingdon Borough*	*4–3*
Ruislip Manor	v	Wembley	3–3
Wembley	v	*Ruislip Manor*	*2–1*
Banstead Athletic	v	Wingate & Finchley	†††
Uxbridge	v	Southall	2–4
Bracknell Town	v	Chertsey Town	1–0
Wycombe Wanderers	v	Molesey	5–0
Chatham Town	v	Herne Bay	1–0
Bromley	v	Maidstone United	4–1
Fisher Athletic	v	Dulwich Hamlet	0–2
Three Bridges	v	Whitehawk	1–0
Farnborough Town	v	Redhill	10–1
Shoreham	v	Chipstead	1–1
Chipstead	v	*Shoreham*	*3–6*
Horsham	v	Kingstonian	2–10

†† *walkover for Warrington Town, Chester City withdrawn*
††† *walkover for Wingate & Finchley, Banstead Athletic withdrawn*

125

FIRST QUALIFYING ROUND

Bashley 5 Bristol Rovers 1 (replay)

Nestling deep in the heart of the New Forest midway between the southern coastal port of Southampton and the holiday resort of Bournemouth lies a slumbering football giant by the name of Bashley.

The quiet country village with a population of just over 400 were every bit as surprised as the rest of the football world when Bashley, up until 12 years ago a modest Bournemouth Junior League side, swept aside the challenge of three League sides on their way to a place in FA Youth Cup folklore, before finally capitulating to the might of Wimbledon in round three.

Their first and perhaps most surprised opponents were an unsuspecting Bristol Rovers youth side in the first qualifying round. Bashley had clearly signalled their intent by holding the League side to a 3–3 draw in the first match at Twerton Park, with Mark Jones, Spencer Batty and Paul Sales scoring for the visitors.

In the replay Bristol Rovers were bludgeoned into submission by a rampant Bashley, who romped home 5–1 winners. Ian Quirk, Mark Jones, Paul Sales (2) and Spencer Batty supplied the goals to the delight and astonishment of a mere 74 spectators and the beginnings of a growing cluster of League scouts.

Bashley required another replay to dispose of Dorchester Town in the second qualifying round when, following a 1–1 stalemate at home, Bashley exacted a 1–0 victory thanks to a Quirk strike.

This set up the mouthwatering prospect of a first-round home tie against First Division neighbours Southampton. The first tie again could produce no winner and no goals, but the replay at The Dell saw Jones and Sales, with his fifth goal of the campaign, overturn a disbelieving Saints team 2–1.

Neighbours Portsmouth got the same treatment in round two when they underestimated the steely resolve of their Hampshire Youth League opponents, as the prolific Sales hit the winner in a 1–0 victory at Fratton Park.

But the romantic voyage of discovery for Bashley ended abruptly in round three when Wimbledon, themselves no strangers to Cup and League tales of the unexpected, produced a professional display to demolish Bashley 6–0.

But there was no disgrace in defeat for the Hampshire side who, in their first season in the FA Youth Cup and only their second as a team, had captured the attention of youth football.

FIRST QUALIFYING ROUND 28 September 1991

(replays in italics)

			Result
Guisborough Town	v	Netherfield	1–3
Hartlepool United	v	Marske United	3–1
Barrow	v	Preston North End	3–5
Accrington Stanley	v	Huddersfield Town	0–3
Halifax Town	v	Wrexham	0–3
Rotherham United	v	Atherton LR	7–1
Shrewsbury Town	v	Telford United	4–0
Warrington Town	v	Bolton Wanderers	0–2
Burton Albion	v	Kidderminster Harriers	0–1
Willenhall Town	v	Leicester United	3–0
Rothwell Town	v	Wisbech Town	6–0
Nuneaton Borough	v	Tamworth	0–0
Tamworth	v	*Nuneaton Borough*	*2–0*
Norwich City	v	Wivenhoe Town	9–0
Cambridge City	v	Brantham Athletic	6–2
East Thurrock United	v	Tiptree United	6–3
Hitchin Town	v	Letchworth Garden City	6–3
Eton Manor	v	Clapton	0–1
Braintree Town	v	St Albans City	1–1
St Albans City	v	*Braintree Town*	*8–2*
Harefield United	v	Staines Town	5–1
Maidenhead United	v	Bedfont	0–1
Kingsbury Town	v	Wembley	4–4
Wembley	v	*Kingsbury Town*	*3–1**

* after extra time

127

			Result
Leyton-Wingate	v	Cheshunt	0–2
Bracknell Town	v	Wycombe Wanderers	2–2
Wycombe Wanderers	v	*Bracknell Town*	*6–4*
Wingate & Finchley	v	Southall	4–2
Dulwich Hamlet	v	Three Bridges	6–0
Chatham Town	v	Bromley	1–4
Kingstonian	v	Walton & Hersham	1–3
Farnborough Town	v	Shoreham	5–2
Malden Vale	v	Havant Town	0–3
Slough Town	v	Sutton United	2–3
Petersfield United	v	Basingstoke Town	1–6
Thatcham Town	v	Witney Town	0–2
Newport AFC	v	Abingdon United	0–0
Abingdon United	v	*Newport AFC*	*4–1*
Evesham United	v	Cheltenham Town	2–4
Bristol Rovers	v	Bashley	3–3
Bashley	v	*Bristol Rovers*	*5–1*
Dorchester Town	v	Odd Down	0–0
Odd Down	v	*Dorchester Town*	*0–1**

* after extra time

SECOND QUALIFYING ROUND

Havant Town 2 Sutton United 3

To many people, the mere mention of the name Sutton United will always conjure up the enduring memory of a smiling Barrie Williams wandering dazed but delirious on to the Gander Green Lane pitch as manager of a Sutton side that had minutes earlier defeated First Division Coventry City 2–1 in the 1988–89 FA Cup third round.

Since those heady days life has become a little more sedate for the Surrey side, who have had to endure the disappointment of relegation to the Diadora League Premier Division as their footballing fortunes have dipped.

But their youth side evoked memories of great Cup days gone by when they enjoyed an impressive run in the 1991–92 FA Youth Cup.

Having disposed of nearby Croydon 2–1 in the preliminary round, Sutton buckled down to the business of qualifying for the first round proper when they defeated Slough Town 3–2 in the first qualifying round.

Their next task in the second and final qualifying round was to overcome Havant Town, down on the South Coast. Their task was made no easier when Havant went in front midway through the first half. But Sutton replied with a 25-yard free-kick from Richard Baum to make it 1–1. Havant then swept back into the lead and continued to outplay their Surrey visitors.

However, Sutton capitalised on Havant's inability to convert possession into goals, and levelled through Robert Scott with only ten minutes remaining. The scene was set for a grand finale and so it proved, with Sutton snatching victory in the 88th minute, courtesy of Scott's second goal of the match.

The first round produced another thriller as Sutton defeated Wembley 4–3, Scott scoring all four. But the Southern Youth League side came unstuck against Third Division Bournemouth where they were finally ousted from the competition 5–1.

SECOND QUALIFYING ROUND   12 October 1991

(replays in italics)			*Result*
Netherfield	v	Hartlepool United	0–3
Preston North End	v	Huddersfield Town	4–1
Wrexham	v	Rotherham United	0–4
Shrewsbury Town	v	Bolton Wanderers	1–0
Kidderminster Harriers	v	Willenhall Town	3–0
Rothwell Town	v	Tamworth	2–2†
Tamworth	v	*Rothwell Town*	*2–1*
Norwich City	v	Cambridge City	5–0
East Thurrock United	v	Hitchin Town	3–2
Clapton	v	St Albans City	1–3
Harefield United	v	Bedfont	0–0
Bedfont	v	*Harefield United*	*1–2*
Wembley	v	Cheshunt	1–1*
Cheshunt	v	*Wembley*	*3–4*
Wycombe Wanderers	v	Wingate & Finchley	3–0
Dulwich Hamlet	v	Bromley	0–1
Walton & Hersham	v	Farnborough Town	2–1
Havant Town	v	Sutton United	2–3
Basingstoke Town	v	Witney Town	0–2
Cheltenham Town	v	Abingdon United	9–1
Bashley	v	Dorchester Town	1–1
Dorchester Town	v	*Bashley*	*0–3*

* *after extra time*
† *after abandoned tie, floodlight failure, 0–0   87 mins*

FIRST ROUND

Aldershot 3 Carshalton Athletic 4

The Southern Youth League champions of 1990–91, Carshalton Athletic, had reached the second round of the FA Youth Cup for the last three successive seasons, although they have never progressed beyond that stage.

This season's competition presented them with the difficult task of overcoming beleaguered Fourth Division Aldershot before they could even contemplate the second round.

Aldershot, for all the financial worries and speculation surrounding the future of the club, were certainly no walkover. They took the game to their opponents with an intricate passing game which provided a deserved 2–1 half-time advantage, with Robbie Williams scoring for Carshalton.

But the Surrey side equalised early in the second half, with Williams again finding the back of the net. Mark Withers put the home side under intense pressure when he put Carshalton 3–2 in front and, despite a third Aldershot goal, the visitors clinched a fine victory when substitute Tony Abajo finished excellently to make it 4–3.

One of Carshalton's most recent youth team exports has been former Arsenal, Bristol City and Cambridge defender Gus Caesar, and Carshalton could certainly have benefited from his experience against a skilful Reading side in round two. The Third Division side's superior fitness was the telling factor as their part-time Carshalton opponents struggled to keep pace with the game.

The end result was a 2–0 victory for Reading, to leave the Surrey side with the memory of another second round FA Youth Cup exit, and the opportunity to concentrate on their League aspirations.

FIRST ROUND   9 November 1991

(replays in italics)   *Result*

York City	v	Blackburn Rovers	1–1
Blackburn Rovers	v	*York City*	*4–3*
Carlisle United	v	Rotherham United	0–1
Blackpool	v	Bradford City	2–2
Bradford City	v	*Blackpool*	*0–3*
Barnsley	v	Darlington	3–2
Bury	v	Sunderland	3–3
Sunderland	v	*Bury*	*2–0*
Burnley	v	Sheffield United	0–2
Oldham Athletic	v	Wigan Athletic	3–2
Tranmere Rovers	v	Preston North End	4–1
Shrewsbury Town	v	Hartlepool United	2–0
Nottingham Forest	v	Wolverhampton Wanderers	0–0
Wolverhampton Wanderers	v	*Nottingham Forest*	*0–0*
Nottingham Forest	v	*Wolverhampton Wanderers*	*0–1*
Scunthorpe United	v	Norwich City	0–2
Northampton Town	v	Stoke City	1–0
Crewe Alexandra	v	Port Vale	1–0
Mansfield Town	v	Aston Villa	0–1
Peterborough United	v	Derby County	1–3
Tamworth	v	Kidderminster Harriers	1–2
Fulham	v	Bromley	5–0
Walton & Hersham	v	Cambridge United	2–2*

* after extra time

130

SECOND ROUND

Liverpool 1 Tranmere Rovers 2

It is often forgotten that Merseyside boasts a third football team of no little quality, in Second Division Tranmere Rovers. While Liverpool and Everton have grabbed the traditional headlines with their perennial tussles for Merseyside superiority, Tranmere have been moving stealthily through the divisions, navigating a course from the Fourth to their Second Division stronghold in just three years.

But last season, while the senior side were enjoying their first season back in the Second Division since 1939, the youth side offered Liverpool a reminder of their developing potential with a surprise FA Youth Cup victory. Worst of all for mighty Liverpool, Tranmere Youth's most famous moment was inflicted on an unsuspecting Liverpool crowd of almost a thousand, at Anfield itself.

Having safely negotiated the first round of the competition with a 4–1 defeat of Preston North End, Tranmere approached their second-round trip to Anfield with some confidence. Promising 17-year-old striker Ian Cooke who, like many of the new breed of up-and-coming footballers, has resisted the temptation to leave school at 16 to join a club, preferring instead to continue his education and take his 'A' Levels, gave Tranmere a dream start with two goals in the opening 20 minutes.

But having squandered several fine opportunities to go even further in front, Tranmere were forced to defend valiantly in the face of a ferocious Liverpool fight-back in the second half, which produced one goal but was unable to provide an equaliser.

Suitably inspired by their defeat of Liverpool, Tranmere swept aside the challenge of Oldham in round three, 3–1 at the third attempt, before disposing of Rotherham 1–0 in round four. Their reward was a fifth-round trip to Old Trafford to face a crowd of 8000 and the skill and pace of Ryan Giggs, making his first appearance in the competition for the 'Red Devils' this season.

It was an inspired choice. Giggs got both goals in a 2–0 win, and Tranmere were left to reflect on their best-ever showing in the FA Youth Cup and the prospect of the emergence from their youth ranks of players to match the calibre of Tranmere graduates such as Roy McFarland, Derek Mountfield, Steve Coppell, and five of the current Tranmere first team.

SECOND ROUND   7 December 1991

(replays in italics)   *Result*

Barnsley	v	Everton	1–2
Doncaster Rovers	v	Manchester City	1–1
Manchester City	v	*Doncaster Rovers*	*4–0*
Hull City	v	Crewe Alexandra	1–1
Crewe Alexandra	v	*Hull City*	*3–0*
Middlesbrough	v	Newcastle United	4–0
Sunderland	v	Manchester United	2–4
Liverpool	v	Tranmere Rovers	1–2
Blackburn Rovers	v	Rotherham United	0–2
Sheffield United	v	Blackpool	5–3
Leeds United	v	Oldham Athletic	3–3
Oldham Athletic	v	*Leeds United*	*3–2*
Shrewsbury Town	v	Sheffield Wednesday	3–0
West Ham United	v	Kidderminster Harriers	3–0
Northampton Town	v	Birmingham City	3–0
Notts County	v	Derby County	0–0
Derby County	v	*Notts County*	*1–0†*
Tottenham Hotspur	v	Coventry City	6–1
West Bromwich Albion	v	Wolverhampton Wanderers	3–1
Witney Town	v	Southend United	0–3
Luton Town	v	Aston Villa	1–0
Watford	v	Leicester City	2–1
Cambridge United	v	Colchester United	2–3
Norwich City	v	Leyton Orient	6–3
Walsall††	v	Ipswich Town	1–0
Sutton United	v	AFC Bournemouth	1–5
Brighton & Hove Albion	v	Arsenal	2–5
Portsmouth	v	Bashley	0–1
Fulham	v	Brentford	2–2
Brentford	v	*Fulham*	*2–0*

† after abandoned tie, fog, 1–2 80 mins
†† Walsall received a bye into the second round

		Result
Reading	v Carshalton Athletic	3–0
Cardiff City	v Queen's Park Rangers	0–1
Bristol City	v Epsom & Ewell	3–2
Wimbledon	v Millwall	2–0
Exeter City	v Chelsea	0–4
St Albans City	v Plymouth Argyle	0–4
Charlton Athletic	v Crystal Palace	0–2

THIRD ROUND

Crewe Alexandra 3 Middlesbrough 2

Rob Jones, Liverpool's brilliant and precocious young talent and recent England debutant, is just the latest in an impressive list of international exports from Gresty Road, the home of Fourth Division Crewe. Following in the hallowed footsteps of the likes of David Platt and Geoff Thomas, Jones is yet another feather in the cap of Crewe manager Dario Gradi, who has transformed interest in the town from trains to football.

In a bid to capitalise on the club's reputation for producing young players of extraordinary talent, Crewe's youth side, formed only six years ago, have been making modest strides in their League and Cup competitions. In the 1991–92 FA Youth Cup, their progress through to the fourth round and elimination at Crystal Palace, prompted great interest, and raised hopes and expectations surrounding their current selection of young stars.

Crewe's FA Youth Cup voyage began in relatively subdued fashion with a 1–0 defeat of Port Vale, thanks to a lone strike by Anthony Hughes. Hull City were their next victims, swept out of the competition in round two 3–0, following a 1–1 draw in their first meeting.

But it was Crewe's third round performance which really set their competition alight, a home tie against mighty Middlesbrough who, despite their Second Division status, have provided the football world with ample evidence this season alone of their enormous cup pedigree. In a thrilling match watched by a crowd of 871, Crewe took the game to their visitors and eventually ran out 3–2 winners, thanks to goals from Hughes, Francis Turney and Ryan Keen.

It was a victory that set up a fourth round excursion to Selhurst Park, where the young side's cup ambitions finally perished in a 2–0 defeat. But there was much to admire and digest from Crewe's progress last season, and with the memory of a certain Rob Jones exploding into first team action at the age of just 16, there is plenty to aim for next season.

THIRD ROUND   11 January 1992

(replays in italics)   *Result*

Tranmere Rovers	v	Oldham Athletic	0–0
Oldham Athletic	v	*Tranmere Rovers*	*1–1*
Oldham Athletic	v	*Tranmere Rovers*	*1–3*
Rotherham United	v	Shrewsbury Town	3–1
Northampton Town	v	Derby County	1–7
Manchester United	v	Walsall	2–1
Crewe Alexandra	v	Middlesbrough	3–2
Manchester City	v	West Bromwich Albion	1–1
West Bromwich Albion	v	*Manchester City*	*0–2*
Everton	v	Sheffield United	1–1
Sheffield United	v	*Everton*	*2–3*
Reading	v	West Ham United	2–6
Chelsea	v	Crystal Palace	0–2
Colchester United	v	Brentford	1–3
Arsenal	v	Watford	4–0
Tottenham Hotspur	v	AFC Bournemouth	7–0
Luton Town	v	Norwich City	1–1
Norwich City	v	*Luton Town*	*4–1*
Wimbledon	v	Bashley	6–0
Southend United	v	Bristol City	3–0
Plymouth Argyle	v	Queen's Park Rangers	1–3

FOURTH ROUND

Manchester City 1 Manchester United 3

A Manchester derby, at any level, is always bound to be a special occasion and this season's FA Youth Cup fourth round tie between the two sides was no exception. United brought to the encounter a Youth Cup pedigree that is difficult to match. They have won the competition six times, with their most successful period coinciding with the tournament's first five years. The team that was to nurture many of Sir Matt Busby's tragic Babes won the first ever Youth Cup in 1953 and then went on to win the next four finals.

Manchester City have a more modest record, lifting the trophy on only the one occasion, in 1986, when they completed a sweet 3–1 victory over their for once vanquished Manchester rivals.

A crowd of 5421 braved the elements to peruse the latest selection of Manchester talent, with United fans in particular surveying their side's cherished ranks for a glimpse of the next Lee Sharpe or Ryan Giggs. They weren't to be disappointed. Having safely negotiated the second and third rounds with wins over Sunderland and Walsall, United maintained their momentum with a comfortable victory over City at Maine Road thanks to two goals from the emerging new wing talent Ben Thornley, and another from John O'Kane.

City did manage to conjure one goal to give their side a glimmer of hope, but it was United's collection of young talent, most are just 16, who marched into round five. There, with just a little assistance from Giggs, they disposed of Tranmere 2–0, with the young Welshman producing both goals to beguile an ecstatic Old Trafford gathering of 8708.

FOURTH ROUND   on or before 8 February 1992

(replays in italics)

Att				Result
379	Queen's Park Rangers	v	Brentford (27.1.92)	5–1
166	Wimbledon	v	Norwich City (28.1.92)	1–1
300	*Norwich City*	v	*Wimbledon* (11.2.92)	*3–4*
629	Southend United	v	West Ham United (3.2.92)	3–3
629	*West Ham United*	v	*Southend United* (10.2.92)	*1–1*
283	*West Ham United*	v	*Southend United* (15.2.92)	*3–2*
217	Arsenal	v	Everton (28.1.92)	1–2
204	Crystal Palace	v	Crewe Alexandra (5.2.92)	2–0
5421	Manchester City	v	Manchester United (6.2.92)	1–3
851	Derby County	v	Tottenham Hotspur (10.2.92)	0–1
443	Rotherham United	v	Tranmere Rovers (3.2.92)	0–1

FIFTH ROUND

Tottenham Hotspur 4 Everton 0

Tottenham's cup tradition in any competition is second to none. Having clinched the FA Cup a record eight times, Spurs' ambitions in the FA Youth Cup have regularly been realised, winning the trophy on three occasions, a record that is only surpassed by Manchester United. And as well as picking up trophies, Tottenham's Youth side has nurtured the developing talents of the likes of Graeme Souness, who played in the victorious 1970 FA Youth Cup winning side, Steve Perryman, Glenn Hoddle and Des Walker.

The team of 1991–92 began the tournament with devastating effect, sweeping aside the challenge of Coventry in round two with a crushing 6–1 victory. The goals continued to flow in round three when it was Bournemouth who felt the sharp end of Tottenham's lethal attack, succumbing 7–0, with Lee Hodges and Kevin Watson both scoring twice.

Goalscoring opportunities were at a premium in round four when a resilient Derby were finally breached by a Hodges piece of magic to give the north London side passage into the last eight and a home tie against Everton. Amidst the familiar surroundings of White Hart Lane, the world famous home of the Spurs, the Youth side regained their rhythm and their Merseyside visitors were demolished by a 4–0 margin. Lee

Hodges was again amongst the goals, with Neil Young, Nick Barnby and Andrew Turner scoring the others to take Tottenham through to a semi-final date with the form team of the competition, and hot favourites, Manchester United.

FIFTH ROUND   on or before 7 March 1992

Att				Result
468	Wimbledon	v	Queen's Park Rangers (26.2.92)	2–0
479	Tottenham Hotspur	v	Everton (26.2.92)	4–0
437	Crystal Palace	v	West Ham United (4.3.92)	2–0
8708	Manchester United	v	Tranmere Rovers (13.2.92)	2–0

SEMI-FINAL

Crystal Palace 5 Wimbledon 4 (aggregate)

The fortunes of Crystal Palace and Wimbledon have become entwined in recent seasons as the financial realities of life in the First Division have bitten hard into the pockets of both clubs. Wimbledon abandoned the dilapidated surroundings of Plough Lane to share the more luxurious facilities of their south London neighbours at Selhurst Park at the beginning of the season, although their youth team's and some reserve matches have been played at their former ground.

Indeed it was to Plough Lane that an optimistic Crystal Palace Youth side travelled for the first leg of their FA Youth Cup semi-final against the Dons, with an impressive series of victories over Charlton, Chelsea, Crewe and West Ham, all behind them. It was a run that sparked flickering memories of the Palace youth sides of 1977 and 1978, which won the competition two years running and spawned the talents of Jim Cannon, Vince Hilaire, Billy Gilbert and Jerry Murphy, all of whom went on to star in Terry Venables' team of the 80s. However the mid-80s saw a decline in youth football at Palace, with the youth team scrapped completely for four years, only to be re-activated in 1984. Wimbledon have never won the trophy, although a 1991–92 run which produced wins over Millwall, Bashley, Norwich and Queen's Park Rangers, suggested that the semi-final would be a close fought affair.

And so it proved, with Crystal Palace taking the honours in the first leg with a 2–1 win thanks to goals from Niall Thompson and Grant Watts, both of whom have been offered professional contracts for next season. The second leg was an even closer contest. Wimbledon refused to lie down and accept defeat and the lead changed hands on several occasions before Watts, Thompson and Mark Holman earned Palace a 3–3 draw and a 5–4 aggregate win.

Their objective now, as well as attempting to emulate the success of this year's youth team graduates such as Gareth Southgate, Jamie Moralee, Simon Rodger, David Whyte, John Salako and Richard Shaw, all of whom have broken into the first team, was to try to overcome a Manchester United side in the final, whose progress through the latter stages of the competition had been nothing short of relentless.

SEMI-FINAL First leg   17 March 1992

Att				Result
2031	Wimbledon	v	Crystal Palace	1–2
7633	Manchester United	v	Tottenham Hotspur	3–0

Second leg

2630	Crystal Palace	v	Wimbledon (24.3.92)	3–3
967	Tottenham Hotspur	v	Manchester United (25.3.92)	1–3

(Crystal Palace won 5–4, Manchester United 6–1 on aggregate)

FINAL First leg   14 April 1992

7825	Crystal Palace	v	Manchester United	1–3

Second leg   15 May 1992

14681	Manchester United	v	Crystal Palace	3–2

[Manchester United beat Crystal Palace 6–3 on aggregate]

History of the FA Youth Cup

Discussions surrounding the competition that is now the FA Youth Cup were first initiated by the committee of the Northern Intermediate League, led by Joe Richards in 1951. Meetings and further discussions followed the next year and by the beginning of the 1952–53 season a set of rules and regulations had been decided and a total of 93 clubs had entered what became known as the FA Youth Cup.

Manchester United dominated the first competition, hammering Nantwich 23–0 in an early round before defeating Wolves 9–3 on aggregate in a two-legged final.

Indeed United were to win the competition for the next four seasons as well, as the team that was to develop into the astonishingly talented Busby Babes, swept aside their rivals. But after 1957, when United beat West Ham 8–2, the Red Devils had to wait until 1964 for their next success, and since then they hadn't lifted the trophy again, until last season.

However the only teams even to begin to threaten United's record of six wins, are the north London giants Tottenham and Arsenal, who have both clinched the trophy three times.

In the 1991-91 season a total of 222 clubs, including 89 from the Football League, entered the FA Youth Cup. The only League clubs to decline an invitation were Barnet, Chesterfield, Grimsby Town and Lincoln City. Eligibility for the competition requires that all competing clubs hold membership, either full or associate, of the FA, or other such membership as the FA should approve. The participating teams should also play in a youth league or equivalent competition and the actual youth team must be officially affiliated into the structure of the club. Members of the youth teams must also be under 18.

Famous players to have emerged following FA Youth Cup success include Paul Gascoigne, who was a member of Newcastle's successful 1985 side that beat Watford 4–1, and members of the Crystal Palace 'team of the 80s', orchestrated by Terry Venables, such as Jim Cannon and Vince Hilaire.

FA YOUTH CUP WINNERS

The FA Youth Cup Final is played on a two-leg basis but the 1978 final between Crystal Palace and Aston Villa was a single match. The only final which needed a replay was the 1983 final between Norwich and Everton.

Year	Winner		Runner-up	Result
1953	Manchester United	v	Wolverhampton Wanderers	9–3
1954	Manchester United	v	Wolverhampton Wanderers	5–4
1955	Manchester United	v	West Bromwich Albion	7–1
1956	Manchester United	v	Chesterfield	4–3
1957	Manchester United	v	West Ham United	8–2
1958	Wolverhampton Wanderers	v	Chelsea	7–6
1959	Blackburn Rovers	v	West Ham United	2–1
1960	Chelsea	v	Preston North End	5–2
1961	Chelsea	v	Everton	5–3
1962	Newcastle United	v	Wolverhampton Wanderers	2–1
1963	West Ham United	v	Liverpool	6–5
1964	Manchester United	v	Swindon Town	5–2
1965	Everton	v	Arsenal	3–2
1966	Arsenal	v	Sunderland	5–3
1967	Sunderland	v	Birmingham City	2–0

Year	Winner		Runner-up	Result
1968	Burnley	v	Coventry City	3–2
1969	Sunderland	v	West Bromwich Albion	6–3
1970	Tottenham Hotspur	v	Coventry City	4–3
1971	Arsenal	v	Cardiff City	2–0
1972	Aston Villa	v	Liverpool	5–2
1973	Ipswich Town	v	Bristol City	4–1
1974	Tottenham Hotspur	v	Huddersfield	2–1
1975	Ipswich	v	West Ham United	5–1
1976	West Bromwich Albion	v	Wolverhampton Wanderers	5–0
1977	Crystal Palace	v	Everton	1–0
1978	Crystal Palace	v	Aston Villa	1–0
1979	Millwall	v	Manchester City	2–0
1980	Aston Villa	v	Manchester City	3–2
1981	West Ham United	v	Tottenham Hotspur	2–1
1982	Watford	v	Manchester United	7–6
1983	Norwich City	v	Everton	6–5*
1984	Everton	v	Stoke City	4–2
1985	Newcastle United	v	Watford	4–1
1986	Manchester City	v	Manchester United	3–1
1987	Coventry City	v	Charlton Athletic	2–1
1988	Arsenal	v	Doncaster Rovers	6–1
1989	Watford	v	Manchester City	2–1
1990	Tottenham Hotspur	v	Middlesbrough	3–2
1991	Millwall	v	Sheffield Wednesday	3–0
1992	Manchester United	v	Crystal Palace	6–3

* aggregate score after replay

CHAPTER FOUR

The FA Trophy

VAUXHALL FA CHALLENGE TROPHY FINAL 1992

Colchester United 3   Witton Albion 1

1992 was to prove a history-making year for the FA Trophy competition in more ways than one. For the first time ever the traditional non-League football showpiece was held on a Sunday, coming just 24 hours after Liverpool had hoisted aloft the FA Cup following their 2–0 defeat of Sunderland, in front of a capacity 80,000 fans.

Whilst there may not have been a full house at Wembley for the Trophy Final, the crowd of 27,806 was swelled significantly by the presence of a television audience, as BSkyB became the first television company ever to screen the competition final live.

Interest in the final had been spurred by the remarkable progress of Colchester United, who only a week before had finally secured promotion back to the Fourth Division at the second attempt. The U's return followed a nail-biting contest with Wycombe Wanderers which had seen Colchester eventually clinch the coveted Vauxhall Conference title by virtue of a superior goal difference.

As Colchester player-manager Roy McDonough led his side out of the Wembley tunnel, to become only the second ever player-manager to lead a side out at Wembley for an FA final, following in the footsteps of Kenny Dalglish in 1986, the 20,000 U's fans in the ground were hoping to see their side complete the League and Trophy 'double'.

The odds though were certainly against it. Only Wealdstone, back in the 1984-85 season, had successfully completed the Pyramid Double, winning the FA Trophy in 1985 by beating Boston United 2–1, just a week after they had won the Gola League title.

In addition, Witton Albion were no walkovers. The Vauxhall Conference side had deposed last year's holders Wycombe *en route* to Wembley, with a thrilling 2–1 victory at Adams Park in round four. As if that wasn't enough, Colchester needed no reminding that their only other appearance in the competition, the year before, had finished abruptly in the quarter-finals, when Witton over-turned the form book to exact a 2–0 victory over the U's at Layer Road. But the 1991 semi-final appearance which was to be their reward for such a fine result, was the farthest Witton had ever progressed in the competition, so whatever happened, there was going to be a new name on the FA Trophy at the final whistle on 10 May.

Colchester soon gave the Wembley crowd the earliest possible indication of their intent, when they took the lead in the fifth minute. The Witton Albion defence had hardly had the chance to organise their positions when a long, looping throw from left-back Paul Roberts was flicked-on at the near post by McDonough, to give the giant 6' 4" US striker Mike Masters the easiest of glancing headers, to become the first American to score at Wembley.

Colchester keeper Scott Barrett, whose last-minute excursion into the Kingstonian penalty area for a corner-kick had set up a last-gasp equaliser for skipper Tony English in round one, was immediately forced into action when Colin Rose tested him with an angled shot.

But Witton could find little to trouble a composed and well-organised Colchester defence, which merely absorbed Albion's probing attacks and turned rearguard action into attack with almost effortless ease. It was from one such moment that Colchester extended their lead in the 19th minute. As a Witton attack broke down on the left, a long ball out of defence released Mark Kinsella down the Colchester right, and although his cross to the far post just evaded the desperate lunge of top-scorer Steve McGavin, the ball fell invitingly for the incoming Nicky Smith, who shot first-time into the unguarded net to make it 2–0.

Witton's best chance of a goal fell to Karl Thomas on the half-hour, but the rangy Albion striker could only direct his header wide of the far post following Rose's cross. Indeed Witton's main contribution to the first of 45 increasingly bad-tempered minutes, was to offer three names for referee Keren Barratt's notebook. Stewart Anderson, Lee Coathup and Andy Grimshaw all had their names taken for niggling fouls, as did Colchester's McGavin and McDonough, as the half shuddered to a close.

141

To make matters worse, Witton were without striker Mike Lutkevitch for the closing moments of the half. The Albion player was forced to leave the field to have stitches in a cut over the left eye. Fortunately his sight was not seriously impaired and he returned for the second half to make an almost immediate and telling contribution. As Witton pressed forward, an accurate cross from left-back Coathup curled invitingly across the Colchester box and found the head of the lurking Lutkevitch at the near post, and his header left Barrett with no chance on 57 minutes.

Colchester, who had lapsed into a lethargic and lazy pattern of play, were galvanised into action and the elusive McGavin almost set up a third goal for his side when his mazy run into the penalty area gave Masters a glorious chance to score, but he swept his shot against the outside of the post.

Substitute Gary Bennett, on in place of the tiring McDonough, shot straight at keeper Mason when well placed minutes later, and Colchester were forced to suffer an uneasy final 10 minutes when fiery midfielder Jason Cook was given his marching orders in the 81st minute when he directed a flurry of punches at Witton substitute Jim McCluskie following an unnecessary off-the-ball incident. But despite a moment of complete panic in the Colchester defence in the 90th minute when the usually unflappable English fluffed a clearing header and almost gifted Rose an equaliser, Witton were unable to exploit their one-man advantage. Indeed it was Colchester who finished the stronger, with the ubiquitous McGavin poaching a third and decisive goal deep into injury time when he pounced on a momentary lapse in the Witton defence to seize upon a through ball and beat the advancing Mason with ease and style.

Colchester United Barrett, Donald, Roberts, Kinsella, English, Martin, Cook, Masters, McDonough (Bennett 64), McGavin, Smith. Sub not used: Collins.

Witton Albion Mason, Halliday, Coathup, McNeilis, Connor, Anderson, Thomas, Rose, Alford, Grimshaw (Connor 66), Lutkevitch (McCluskie 79).

Vauxhall FA Trophy 1991–92

FIRST QUALIFYING ROUND

Stevenage Borough 2 Wembley 3

For Diadora League Division One side Wembley, the journey to the national stadium would not be an arduous one. Just two miles separate the Lions' modest Sudbury Vale Farm ground from the gleaming twin towers and magical surroundings of Wembley Way.

Unfortunately for Wembley, apart from a Middlesex Charity Cup appearance in 1988, the Lions have never made it to the final of a major trophy competition, and when the draw for the first qualifying round of the Trophy was made for 1991–92, the national stadium seemed as far away as ever.

Fellow Diadora Division One members Stevenage Borough were to be the Lions' opponents in what looked likely to be an extremely difficult task, especially given Borough's exceptional home record.

The visitors' job was made no easier when they conceded an early goal and then lost defender Andy O'Brien, dismissed for a professional foul. But the Lions responded in suitably robust Cup tradition. Steve Graham hammered a well-deserved equaliser and then, to the astonishment of the home supporters, 10-man Wembley went in front with goals from Kenny Page and Steve Lawrence. Despite a late consolation goal from Stevenage to make it 3–2, Wembley held on for a tremendous victory.

Their prize was another potentially hazardous trip to Diadora Division One opposition Harlow Town. Following a goalless draw in Essex, Wembley won the replay 1–0 and progressed to the third qualifying round, where they encountered Chalfont St. Peter. The Lions again demonstrated a rich vein of Cup form when they triumphed 2–0 to book a place in the first round proper.

But that was where their Trophy ambitions evaporated for another year. Mighty Woking, of the Diadora Premier Division, proved too powerful for their Middlesex visitors, and ran out 4–2 winners.

FIRST QUALIFYING ROUND   21 September 1991

(replays in italics)   *Result*

Whitby Town	v Newcastle Blue Star	2–1
Ferryhill Athletic	v Whitley Bay	0–2
Alnwick Town	v Southport	0–5
Peterlee Newtown	v Murton	0–2
Workington	v Northallerton Town	2–2
Northallerton Town	v *Workington*	*4–0*
Consett	v Shildon	0–3

144

Brandon United	v	Spennymoor United	1–1
Spennymoor United	v	*Brandon United*	*1–0*
Whickham	v	North Shields	1–2
Willenhall Town	v	Colwyn Bay	3–1
Rhyl	v	Halesowen Town	1–1
Halesowen Town	v	*Rhyl*	*1–2*
Moor Green	v	Radcliffe Borough	5–2
Goole Town	v	Warrington Town	2–1
Alvechurch	v	Gainsborough Trinity	0–1
Winsford United	v	Newtown	3–0
Dudley Town	v	Redditch United	5–3
Bromsgrove Rovers	v	Bedworth United	1–1
Bedworth United	v	*Bromsgrove Rovers*	*1–2*
Nuneaton Borough	v	Marine	0–0
Marine	v	*Nuneaton Borough*	*2–2*
Nuneaton Borough	v	*Marine*	*0–1*
Eastwood Town	v	Caernarfon Town	5–1
Worksop Town	v	Matlock Town	1–1
Matlock Town	v	*Worksop Town*	*3–3*
Matlock Town	v	*Worksop Town*	*2–0*
Grantham Town	v	Buxton	0–2
Congleton Town	v	Atherstone United	0–3
Mossley	v	Alfreton Town	2–3
Corby Town	v	Leyton–Wingate	1–3
Stevenage Borough	v	Wembley	2–3
Chelmsford City	v	St Albans City	0–1
Vauxhall Motors	v	Staines Town	†
Barking	v	Rushden Town	4–2
Hitchin Town	v	Grays Athletic	2–1
Chalfont St Peter	v	Stourbridge	3–2
Boreham Wood	v	Aveley	4–1
Hayes	v	Baldock Town	3–1
Chesham United	v	Tamworth	1–0
Yeading	v	Fareham Town	2–1
Uxbridge	v	Tooting & Mitcham United	1–2
Molesey	v	Marlow	2–3
Andover	v	Bashley	1–2
Bromley	v	Basingstoke Town	3–0
Gosport Borough	v	Croydon	4–1
Maidenhead United	v	Canterbury City	4–0
Erith & Belvedere	v	Walton & Hersham	3–3
Walton & Hersham	v	*Erith & Belvedere*	*2–1*
Margate	v	Abingdon Town	1–1
Abingdon Town	v	*Margate*	*0–1*
Dorking	v	Bognor Regis Town	2–1
Waterlooville	v	Crawley Town	3–2
Trowbridge Town	v	Dorchester Town	1–1
Dorchester Town	v	*Trowbridge Town*	*3–2*
Ton Pentre	v	Barry Town	2–3
Taunton Town	v	Maesteg Park	6–2

† *walkover for Staines Town, Vauxhall Motors withdrawn*

(replays in italics)			*Result*
Bideford	v	Newport AFC	0–1
Bridgend Town	v	Poole Town	3–1
Salisbury	v	Cwmbran Town	1–0
Weston–super–Mare	v	Saltash United	2–2
Saltash United	v	*Weston-super-Mare*	*5–3*

SECOND QUALIFYING ROUND

Newport AFC 5 Saltash United 4

Despite their protestations to the contrary, Newport AFC will always be synonymous with the much-lamented but now deceased Newport County FC. The famous old Welsh club finally disppeared from view at the end of the 1980s, beneath an avalanche of debt and confusion.

Newport AFC were formed a year later in 1989 and play at County's old stadium, Somerton Park. They have a handful of ex-County players, as well as boasting former County servant of over 400 League appearances, John Relish, who also managed the club for a brief spell. But the Beazer Homes Midlands Division side are keen to preserve their own identity and insist they are not a phoenix risen from the ashes of Newport County.

The season of 1991-92 was only the second Newport had ever experienced in the FA Trophy competition, but the Welsh side negotiated their first qualifying round with a 1–0 defeat of Bideford. In the second qualifying round they faced another Great Mills Western League side in the form of Saltash United. The visitors quickly seized the initiative to take a 1–0 lead, but Newport striker Paul Green, whose goal had ousted Bideford from the competition in the previous round, stole two quick goals to make it 2–1.

Saltash levelled before Paul Sanderson rattled the back of the net twice in quick succession to make it 4–2. Saltash then responded with two well-taken goals to draw level at 4–4, before Green completed his hat-trick to give the home side a narrow win.

Green was on the mark again in the next round when Newport disposed of Stroud 3–1 to slip quietly into the first round proper. But that was where the Welsh club's luck ran out. They allowed Diadora League Premier Division Aylesbury a 3–0 lead, and despite a superb fight-back which produced goals from Price and Sanderson, Newport were out of the reckoning for another year, with only the satisfaction of a best-ever performance in reaching the first round to cherish.

146

SECOND QUALIFYING ROUND 19 October 1991

(replays in italics)   *Result*

Southport	v	North Shields	4–1
Accrington Stanley	v	Shildon	5–2
Northallerton Town	v	Whitley Bay	0–0
Whitley Bay	v	*Northallerton Town*	*2–3**
Whitby Town	v	Murton	5–1
Spennymoor United	v	Easington Colliery	1–2
Bromsgrove Rovers	v	Hednesford Town	1–0
Goole Town	v	Marine	1–3
Alfreton Town	v	Atherstone United	0–3
Dudley Town	v	Shepshed Albion	2–1
Eastwood Town	v	Rhyl	1–2
Droylsden	v	Winsford United	1–1
Winsford United	v	*Droylsden*	*1–3*
Willenhall Town	v	Matlock Town	2–3
Leicester United	v	Gainsborough Trinity	1–0
Buxton	v	Moor Green	1–3
Chesham United	v	Leyton-Wingate	1–0
Barking	v	Chalfont St Peter	0–2
Staines Town	v	Heybridge Swifts	0–1
Sutton Coldfield Town	v	Hayes	2–0
Bishop's Stortford	v	Boreham Wood	1–1
Boreham Wood	v	*Bishop's Stortford*	*0–1*
Hitchin Town	v	St Albans City	2–3
Wembley	v	Harlow Town	0–0
Harlow Town	v	*Wembley*	*0–1*
Dorking	v	Yeading	2–1
Bromley	v	Maidenhead United	2–0
Bashley	v	Ashford Town	3–1
Whyteleafe	v	Margate	1–2
Waterlooville	v	Walton & Hersham	1–1
Walton & Hersham	v	*Waterlooville*	*4–0*
Gosport Borough	v	Marlow	0–2
Tooting & Mitcham United	v	Dulwich Hamlet	3–0
Barry Town	v	Bridgend Town	2–0
Newport AFC	v	Saltash United	5–4
Llanelli	v	Dorchester Town	1–3
Salisbury	v	Taunton Town	4–1

* after extra time

THIRD QUALIFYING ROUND

Blyth Spartans 4 Accrington Stanley 0

Football in the North-East has always been viewed as something akin
to religion, the love affair with the game permeating down through
every level of competitive football.

Blyth Spartans of the Northern League are certainly no exception.
The First Division outfit can boast a set of supporters as passionate as

the next club's, and brandishing an FA Amateur Cup record that makes impressive reading, the Spartans prepared for the 1991–92 FA Trophy with some optimism.

The Spartans also had some much-needed comic relief along the way when, as debts of some several thousand pounds were announced, their unlikely saviour came in the form of two of the pioneering forces behind *Viz* magazine. The adult comic bailed the club out with a five-figure shirt sponsorship deal.

Back on the pitch, Blyth's hopes of emulating their best-ever display in the competition were boosted when Spartans swept aside their very first opponents, Accrington Stanley, one of the great names of non-League football. Accrington, once a mighty League force but now reduced to HFS Loans Premier Division status, were the visitors to an expectant Croft Park.

Blyth destroyed their opponents with a display of intricate football which deservedly brought four goals, from Richard Bond (a hat-trick) and Mark Cameron, who has since been snapped up by Blackpool.

The luck of the first-round draw saw Spartans pitted against bitter rivals Gateshead. The first match ended goalless and the first 90 minutes of the replay, which was again hosted by Blyth because of their floodlights, also produced few goal-scoring opportunities. But in extra time Gateshead romped away with the tie, as they plundered three swift goals to end the Spartans' Trophy ambitions.

THIRD QUALIFYING ROUND   30 November 1991

(replays in italics)			*Result*
Chorley	v	Frickley Athletic	0–2
Fleetwood Town	v	Seaham Red Star	4–0
Morecambe	v	Emley	2–2
Emley	v	*Morecambe*	*2–4*
Northallerton Town	v	Matlock Town	4–2
Tow Law Town	v	Bishop Auckland	0–3
Whitby Town	v	Easington Colliery	1–0
Rhyl	v	Southport	0–3
Horwich RMI	v	Marine	1–3
Billingham Synthonia	v	Droylsden	4–1
South Bank	v	Bangor City	1–1
Bangor City	v	*South Bank*	*1–0*
Blyth Spartans	v	Accrington Stanley	4–0
Fisher Athletic	v	Bromsgrove Rovers	1–1
Bromsgrove Rovers	v	*Fisher Athletic*	*2–0*
VS Rugby	v	Leicester United	2–1
Dudley Town	v	Worcester City	2–3
Wembley	v	Chalfont St Peter	2–0
Sutton Coldfield Town	v	Cambridge City	2–1

Hendon	v	Wealdstone	0–0
Wealdstone	v	*Hendon*	*4–1*
Harrow Borough	v	Bishop's Stortford	2–1
Atherstone United	v	Heybridge Swifts	1–1
Heybridge Swifts	v	*Atherstone United*	*0–1*
Burton Albion	v	Chesham United	0–0
Chesham United	v	*Burton Albion*	*4–0*
Moor Green	v	Boston United	1–3
Dagenham	v	St Albans City	3–2
Tooting & Mitcham United	v	Walton & Hersham	0–0
Walton & Hersham	v	*Tooting & Mitcham United*	*2–1*
Dorking	v	Barry Town	2–1
Stroud	v	Newport AFC	1–3
Windsor & Eton	v	Sutton United	2–2
Sutton United	v	*Windsor & Eton*	*4–2*
Gravesend & Northfleet	v	Marlow	1–3
Bromley	v	Weymouth	1–0
Wokingham Town	v	Salisbury	0–0
Salisbury	v	*Wokingham Town*	*1–0*
Slough Town	v	Margate	0–0
Margate	v	*Slough Town*	*1–2*
Bashley	v	Carshalton Athletic	2–0
Kingstonian	v	Dorchester Town	3–0

FIRST ROUND

Northallerton Town 1 Frickley Athletic 0 (replay)*

To the inhabitants of the North Yorkshire town of Northallerton, the FA Trophy has largely been something of an unknown quantity. Its football club has seen barely a decade of semi-professional football, although a burgeoning reputation as a side of the future was confirmed when they gained promotion to the Northern League First Division in the 1990–91 season.

However, the Town were forced to wait until the 1991–92 season to make their long-awaited debut in the Trophy, and there was little sign of nerves as the Yorkshire side disposed of former League side Workington Town 4–2 in a replay, following a 2–2 draw.

Under the guidance of manager Geoff Cane, who had assumed command of Northallerton after the departure of former Leeds and Arsenal star Ray Hankin three years earlier, Northallerton required another replay to deal with Whitley Bay, whom they finally dispatched 3–2 after extra time.

Matlock were swept aside in the third qualifying round 4–2, to set up a first-round tie with Frickley Athletic, their third successive HFS Loans Premier Division opposition.

* *after extra time*

149

But Northallerton rose to the occasion splendidly, with Lee Wasden and Paul Kennedy scoring vital goals to take the tie to a replay. Again the first 90 minutes failed to separate the sides, but extra time gave striker Jimmy Lagan the opportunity to steal victory for Northallerton and send his side into round two.

However, the Yorkshire side were brought down to earth with an almighty crash in the second round when they were crushed 3–0 by GM Vauxhall Conference Telford United, skilfully organised by manager Gerry Daly, the former Manchester United and Northern Ireland star.

FIRST ROUND   11 January 1992

(replays in italics)			*Result*
Witton Albion	v	Billingham Synthonia	2–2
Billingham Synthonia	v	*Witton Albion*	*1–2**
Macclesfield Town	v	Boston United	0–0
Boston United	v	*Macclesfield Town*	*0–2*
Southport	v	Bishop Auckland	1–0
Northwich Victoria	v	Hyde United	1–0
Whitby Town	v	Barrow	0–2
Altrincham	v	Stalybridge Celtic	1–2
Blyth Spartans	v	Gateshead	0–0
Blyth Spartans	v	*Gateshead*	*0–3**
Telford United	v	Guisborough Town	2–0
Frickley Athletic	v	Northallerton Town	2–2
Frickley Athletic	v	*Northallerton Town*	*0–1**
Fleetwood Town	v	Morecambe	1–1
Morecambe	v	*Fleetwood Town*	*1–0*
Bangor City	v	Gretna	0–0
Gretna	v	*Bangor City*	*1–2*
Stafford Rangers	v	Marine	0–1
Leek Town	v	Runcorn	3–3
Runcorn	v	*Leek Town*	*3–1*
Welling United	v	Dover Athletic	3–2
Wycombe Wanderers	v	Salisbury	2–0
Woking	v	Wembley	4–2
Redbridge Forest	v	Bromsgrove Rovers	1–1
Bromsgrove Rovers	v	*Redbridge Forest*	*0–1*
Gloucester City	v	Harrow Borough	1–2
Wivenhoe Town	v	Marlow	1–0
Sutton Coldfield Town	v	Farnborough Town	0–3
Colchester United	v	Kingstonian	2–2
Kingstonian	v	*Colchester United*	*2–3*
VS Rugby	v	Kettering Town	0–1
Bromley	v	Worcester City	1–0
Atherstone United	v	Dorking	1–3
Yeovil Town	v	Chesham United	3–1
Walton & Hersham	v	Kidderminster Harriers	0–2
Merthyr Tydfil	v	Dartford	1–1

* *after extra time*

SECOND ROUND

Kidderminster Harriers 5 Runcorn 2 (replay)*

Kidderminster Harriers last lifted the FA Trophy back in 1987 when, in a replay at The Hawthorns following a goalless draw at Wembley, they disposed of Burton Albion 2–1.

In 1991 they again appeared in the final at Wembley, sharing a record attendance of 34,842 with Wycombe Wanderers, although Wycombe spoiled the Kidderminster party by taking the Trophy with a 2–1 win.

The 1991–92 competition started for the Harriers with a lengthy trip to Walton & Hersham in Surrey, where a 2–0 triumph for the visitors was enough to book a second-round place against Runcorn.

The first encounter between the two sides saw Runcorn hold the lead for long periods of the match, until Kidderminster, in true Cup tradition, equalised in the last minute through longest-serving player Paul Davies to take the tie to a replay.

Davies was on target again for Kidderminster in the replay when he hoisted a two-goal lead for the Harriers in the early stages of the match. Runcorn hit back to draw level and send the tie spinning into extra time. Peter Howell gave the home side an immediate boost when he scored in the 91st minute to make it 3–2.

When youngsters David Benton and Mark Wolsey added to the score, to the delight of the assembled 1189 crowd, the Harriers were safely through to round three and another Wembley adventure seemed likely.

However, their next opponents were none other than Yeovil Town, the Somerset Cup giants whose FA Cup exploits are rather better known than their Trophy antics. On the day it was Yeovil who provided the better football and despite a consolation goal from Forsythe, Graham Allner's Harriers were sent tumbling out of the competition 3–1.

* after extra time

SECOND ROUND   1 February 1992

(replays in italics)   *Result*

Telford United	v Northallerton Town	3–0
Morecambe	v Welling United	2–1
Runcorn	v Kidderminster Harriers	1–1
Kidderminster Harriers	v *Runcorn*	*5–2**
Gateshead	v Barrow	1–0
Bromley	v Yeovil Town	1–3
Macclesfield Town	v Bangor City	1–0
Witton Albion	v Aylesbury United	1–0
Northwich Victoria	v Cheltenham Town	4–2
Bashley	v Kettering Town	2–3
Bath City	v Dorking	2–0
Harrow Borough	v Stalybridge Celtic	1–3
Marine	v Wivenhoe Town	3–0
Farnborough Town	v Southport	5–0
Merthyr Tydfil	v Colchester United	0–0
Colchester United	v *Merthyr Tydfil*	*1–0*
Wycombe Wanderers	v Woking	1–0
Redbridge Forest	v Enfield	2–0

* *after extra time*

THIRD ROUND
Yeovil Town 3 Kidderminster Harriers 1

The Somerset town of Yeovil is without doubt one of the great names in
FA Cup folklore. The club's famous Huish slope was the graveyard of
many a Football League side, especially in 1949 when the Southern
League outfit defeated First Division Sunderland in front of a crowd of
17,000.

These days the club has moved to the more modern and luxurious
surroundings of Huish Park. A Tesco superstore stands on what re-
mains of the old Huish, but the appetite in the town for the Cup, indeed,
any trophy competition is just as fierce as ever.

Yeovil have never won the FA Trophy, nor figured in any of its 22
finals, but the 1991–92 season saw the Glovers at last begin to show
some real promise in the competition.

Goals from Mickey Spencer (2) and former Arsenal, Norrköping, Fulham, Oxford, Huddersfield, Cardiff and Exeter City striker Brian
McDermott were enough to give Yeovil safe passage past Chesham in
round one, and Spencer added another brace in round two, along with a
goal from Robbie Carroll, to defeat Bromley 3–1.

And so it came to a home tie against Kidderminster Harriers, winners of the Trophy in 1987 and the previous year's beaten finalists at
Wembley where they succumbed 2–1 to Wycombe Wanderers.

But any lingering hopes Harriers may have had of reaching the final for a second successive season were blasted into small pieces by a robust Yeovil performance in the first half which saw the home side 2–0 up. David Robinson gave Yeovil the lead in the 14th minute, and Carroll added a second just before half-time.

When McDermott added a third with a penalty two minutes into the second period, there was no way back for Kidderminster who could only add a late consolation goal through Forsythe.

THIRD ROUND   22 February 1992

(replays in italics)

Att				Result
1537	Northwich Victoria	v	Macclesfield Town	0–1
1353	Redbridge Forest	v	Farnborough Town	3–2
3206	Colchester United	v	Morecambe	3–1
1755	Witton Albion	v	Stalybridge Celtic	1–0
1027	Telford United	v	Gateshead	0–0
533	*Gateshead*	v	*Telford United* (26.2.92)	*0–1*
1111	Marine	v	Kettering Town	2–1
2899	Bath City	v	Wycombe Wanderers	1–1
3542	*Wycombe Wanderers*	v	*Bath City* (25.2.92)	*2–0*
2679	Yeovil Town	v	Kidderminster Harriers	3–1

FOURTH ROUND

Wycombe Wanderers 1 Witton Albion 2

Wycombe Wanderers' 1991 FA Trophy victory over Kidderminster Harriers in front of a record crowd of 34,842, marked the arrival of manager Martin O'Neill. The former Northern Ireland international, with over 60 caps for his country, is probably best remembered for his League efforts with the mighty Nottingham Forest side of the late '70s with whom he collected League Championship, European Cup and League Cup winners' medals. But in managerial terms his previous experience is more modest, including a brief but successful spell with Grantham Town before joining Wanderers in early 1990.

O'Neill has brought Wycombe to the very fringes of the Football League and yielded them the FA Trophy. Their defence of the competition began in the first round against Salisbury, where they eased their way through to round two with a 2–0 win.

There, the Wanderers found themselves up against the runaway Diadora Premier Division leaders Woking, one-time FA Cup giant-killers over then Second Division West Brom. An enormous crowd of 5801 was drawn to Adams Park, where a Kim Casey goal was enough to put Wycombe into round three.

It required a replay to dispose of Bath to take the Wanderers into the last eight; thoughts of another Wembley appearance loomed large.

Their fourth round opponents, Witton Albion, had other ideas. Having beaten Colchester at the same stage of the competition the year before, Peter O'Brien's side were clearly no strangers to the big occasion. The visitors snatched an early lead through Mike Lutkevitch with Karl Thomas grabbing a second in the 89th minute. Despite a Mark West penalty deep into injury time, there was not enough time for the home side to force a replay. Witton Albion were on the march.

FOURTH ROUND   14 March 1992

(replays in italics)

Att				Result
1106	Marine	v	Redbridge Forest	1–1
1239	*Redbridge Forest*	v	*Marine* (17.3.92)	*0–1*
4269	Yeovil Town	v	Macclesfield Town	1–2
3894	Colchester United	v	Telford United	4–0
4636	Wycombe Wanderers	v	Witton Albion	1–2

SEMI-FINAL

Witton Albion 6 Marine 3 (aggregate)

When HFS Loans side Marine continued their breathtaking form of previous rounds to hold Vauxhall Conference Witton Albion 2–2 away from home in the first leg of the FA Trophy, the odds seemed to lean towards the Merseyside team who are forced to play their football in the shadow of more illustrious League neighbours.

However the dream was not to become a reality when a week later, in front of 2030 fans packed into the Mariners' Rossett Park ground in Crosby, Witton overwhelmed their hosts 4–1 to secure a Wembley ticket. Goals from Karl Thomas, Jim McCluskie, Mike Halliday and Mike Lutkevitch were enough to silence the home fans, who only had a Jon Gautrey effort to cheer.

It was a harsh result for the Mariners and their manager of over 20 years Roly Howard, who had to suffer the same agony at the semi-final stage of the Trophy in 1984 when Northwich were the victorious party.

But Mr Howard, whose window cleaning business includes cleaning and polishing the windows of one of Liverpool's most famous sons, Kenny Dalglish, can return to his work with great pride, with the comfort of an impressive Trophy campaign to look back on. It all started back in the first qualifying round in September, where Marine found themselves for the first time in 15 years. It required three matches to overcome Nuneaton Borough and other notable scalps included two Vauxhall Conference sides, Stafford Rangers and Redbridge Forest.

As for Witton, who had never been in the Trophy final before, and who knocked out highflying Wycombe Wanderers along the way to this year's May showdown, their opponents were Colchester United.

SEMI–FINAL First leg   4 April 1992

Att				Result
2030	Witton Albion	v	Marine	2–2
5443	Colchester	v	Macclesfield	3–0

Second leg   11 April 1992

2212	Marine	v	Witton Albion	1–4
1650	Macclesfield	v	Colchester	1–1

(Witton Albion won 6–3, Colchester United 4–1 on aggregate)

FINAL   Sunday 10 May 1992

Wembley Stadium

Att				Result
27806	Colchester United	v	Witton Albion	3–1

History of the FA Trophy

With the effective decline of the amateur game by the end of the 1960s, the FA Trophy was introduced in the 1969–70 season as a national knockout competition for the emerging senior semi-professional sides.

Running alongside the FA Amateur Cup, which was eventually to disappear altogether in 1974, the first winners of the Trophy were Macclesfield Town, who beat off the challenge of Telford United in a 2–0 win in front of 28,000 at Wembley. But Telford's albeit unsuccessful debut in the Trophy was to be a prelude to a further four final appearances, three of which were successful in 1971, 1983 and 1989, as well as six semi-final performances.

Scarborough, now a Football League side, have also won the Trophy a record three times, with their first taste of victory coming in 1973, followed by an astonishing three-year spell in the mid-70s when they reached the final three years running, from 1975 to 1977, with victories in 1976 and 1977.

At first the Trophy was contested largely by teams from the Northern Premier League and the Southern League, but the subsequent entry of sides from the Isthmian League in 1975 and the Alliance Premier League in 1980 added real spice to the competition.

These days the Trophy is a major target for teams from the GM Vauxhall Conference, as well as the Premier Divisions of the HFS Loans, Beazer Homes and Diadora Leagues, together with the HFS and Diadora First Divisions and the Northern League First Division. More illustrious recent wins have included Altrincham in 1986, with a 1–0 defeat

155

of Runcorn; Enfield's 3–2 victory over Telford in 1988, with two of the north Londoners' goals coming from Paul Furlong, now of Coventry City; and last year's winners Wycombe Wanderers, who beat Kidderminster Harriers 2–1 in front of a record attendance of 34,842.

In the 1991–92 season The Football Association agreed terms for the first-ever sponsorship of a senior FA competition, the FA Challenge Trophy. Vauxhall Motors Limited became the inaugural sponsors of the tournament, extending their support for one season, the deal coming into effect after the qualifying rounds had been completed. Prize money totalling £30,000 has been made available to this year's entrants, with the competition now becoming known as the 'Vauxhall FA Challenge Trophy'.

FA TROPHY FINAL 1970

Macclesfield Town 2 Telford United 0

In front of an encouraging crowd of 28,000 spectators, the inaugural FA Trophy Final proved to be a hard-fought contest between North and South, Macclesfield Town of the Northern Premier League versus Telford United of the Southern (now Beazer Homes) League.

Telford were led into the fray by their player/coach Ron Flowers, capped 49 times for England and boasting some 17 years' loyal service to Wolverhampton Wanderers. Joining Flowers in the Telford line-up were goalkeeper Bobby Irvine, capped nine times for Northern Ireland and with previous League experience at Stoke, Alan Harris, formerly of Aston Villa and Wolves, and Jimmy Murray, formerly of Manchester City and Walsall and a member of Wolves' 1960 FA Cup-winning team.

Macclesfield could not boast quite the same pedigree. Brandishing an assortment of players who were nearing the end of their modest careers, spent largely with teams from the lower divisions, player/manager Frank Beaumont was relying on the exuberance of the Fidler brothers, Dennis and Brian, and younger players such as David Lyon. He was not to be disappointed. Lyon responded to the challenge by putting the side 1–0 up after the Northerners had virtually laid siege to Irvine's goal.

And when, as promised, Brian Fidler also scored for Macclesfield, there followed celebrations the like of which the grand old stadium has rarely seen since. Fidler, now managing non-League Burton Albion, wheeled away in delight and ran fully 70 yards, vaulted a fence and pranced ecstatically in front of his delirious supporters.

It was an extravagant yet suitable demonstration of the pride and passion clearly evident in semi-professional football and provided the FA Trophy with the baptism it so richly deserved.

FA TROPHY FINAL 1972
Stafford Rangers 3 Barnet 0

The 1972 FA Trophy Final provided the young Stafford Rangers goal-keeper with a first taste of the Wembley experience he was to enjoy again nine years later. Milija Aleksic was between the posts that day for the Northern Premier League side, little knowing that he would be striding out on to the hallowed Wembley turf in 1981 as a member of Tottenham's FA Cup-winning side when the north Londoners defeated Manchester City in a replay.

But on that particular spring day in 1972, Aleksic and his Stafford team-mates were preoccupied with the challenge of a Barnet side whose own aspirations of playing League football were still a very dim and distant dream.

The Stafford manager of the day was none other than Roy Chapman, the late father of current Leeds United's much-travelled striker Lee Chapman, and his side, brimming with confidence and experience, did not disappoint him. In front of 24,000 fans, Stafford dominated for pro-longed spells, with Ray Williams scoring twice and Nick Cullerton adding the third.

Cullerton was to go on and join Port Vale, while Williams finished the season clutching a club goal-scoring record. Rangers confirmed their burgeoning reputation as the best non-League club in the country at the time by winning the Northern Premier League title and the County Cup. They were to return to Wembley again in 1976, only to face defeat by three goals to two at the hands of an impressive Scarborough. But the Midlands club did lift the Trophy once again in 1979 when they beat Kettering Town 2–0.

FA TROPHY FINAL 1982
Enfield 1 Altrincham 0*

The 1982 FA Trophy final brought together the two strongest teams of the year, Enfield and Altrincham, both of the Alliance Premier League.

Both sides could boast an impressive cluster of semi-professional England caps in their ranks, while Eddie McCluskey's Enfield side in-cluded central defender Tony Jennings, now England's semi-profes-sional manager.

For the north London club and their supporters it was a first Trophy final appearance, although Altrincham, under manager Tony Sanders, had been to Wembley once before, defeating Leatherhead 3–1 in 1978.

* *after extra time*

With the sides so evenly matched, the first 90 minutes were a mainly dour affair for the crowd of 18,678, with very little in the way of chances. It was left to Enfield midfielder Paul Taylor finally to decide the destination of the silverware when he popped up to score the winner in extra time, with the game's only moment of inspiration.

The Northerners made amends for the disappointment of defeat when they returned to Wembley in 1986 to beat Runcorn 1–0, while Enfield boss Eddie McCluskey coaxed another Trophy victory out of his side in 1988 when they beat Telford United in a replay at The Hawthorns following a goalless draw at Wembley.

McCluskey finally left the club in 1989 but returned in January 1992, to try to lift them back into the GM Vauxhall Conference from the Diadora Premier Division.

FA TROPHY WINNERS

Year/venue	Winner		Runner-up	Result
1970 Wembley	Macclesfield Town	v	Telford United	2–0
1971 Wembley	Telford United	v	Hillingdon Borough	3–2
1972 Wembley	Stafford Rangers	v	Barnet	3–0
1973 Wembley	Scarborough	v	Wigan Athletic	2–1*
1974 Wembley	Morecambe	v	Dartford	2–1
1975 Wembley	Matlock Town	v	Scarborough	4–0
1976 Wembley	Scarborough	v	Stafford Rangers	3–2*
1977 Wembley	Scarborough	v	Dagenham	2–1
1978 Wembley	Altrincham	v	Leatherhead	3–1
1979 Wembley	Stafford Rangers	v	Kettering Town	2–0
1980 Wembley	Dagenham	v	Mossley	2–1
1981 Wembley	Bishop's Stortford	v	Sutton United	1–0
1982 Wembley	Enfield	v	Altrincham	1–0*
1983 Wembley	Telford United	v	Northwich Victoria	2–1
1984 Wembley	Northwich Victoria	v	Bangor City	1–1
Stoke	Northwich Victoria	v	Bangor City	2–1
1985 Wembley	Wealdstone	v	Boston United	2–1
1986 Wembley	Altrincham	v	Runcorn	1–0
1987 Wembley	Kidderminster Harriers	v	Burton Albion	0–0
West Bromwich	Kidderminster Harriers	v	Burton Albion	2–1
1988 Wembley	Enfield	v	Telford United	0–0
West Bromwich	Enfield	v	Telford United	3–2
1989 Wembley	Telford United	v	Macclesfield Town	1–0*
1990 Wembley	Barrow	v	Leek Town	3–0
1991 Wembley	Wycombe Wanderers	v	Kidderminster Harriers	2–1
1992 Wembley	Colchester United	v	Witton Albion	3–1

after extra time

The Official FA Young England Soccer Club

The Young England Club is an exciting new idea for boys and girls who are loyal supporters of the England team.

The Club is aimed at developing involvement with young people between six to sixteen years old, and will offer members an opportunity to become more closely involved with the England team.

All members will receive a letter from Graham Taylor in their Welcome Pack. The pack will also contain exciting football items including an action team poster, membership card, club badge, club stickers, discount vouchers etc.

The first action-packed issue of the quarterly Club magazine will follow the Welcome Pack. The magazine will contain football action, coaching and soccer skills sections, quizzes, competitions and a brand new comic strip adventure series about a boy soccer hero.

At last young England supporters will have the chance to get behind their team whilst enjoying the many benefits the Club will provide.

The yearly Club subscription is £9.95, including P&P.

Application forms available from YOUNG ENGLAND CLUB, 3 Albion Buildings, 1 Back Hill, London EC1R 5EN

CHAPTER FIVE

The FA Vase

FA Vase Final 1992

Wimborne Town 5   Guiseley 3

Wembley Stadium, home to so many great matches over the years, has a seemingly unending capacity to inspire the best from its visitors. The stadium and its enormous pitch, which can be an engaging yet punishing host, staged yet another thrilling contest at the end of April when Guiseley from the HFS Loans League arrived to defend the FA Vase they had won the year before in such style. Having triumphed over Gresley Rovers 3–1 in a replay at Bramall Lane, following a 4–4 draw at Wembley, Guiseley returned to this most romantic of non-League football occasions, to face Wimborne from Dorset, soon to be crowned champions of the Jewson Wessex League.

It was an intriguing collision. Guiseley, the champions, boasting a team comprising several experienced former League players versus Wimborne, the surprise package of the competition who had exceeded all expectations in reaching Wembley, having previously never progressed further than the third round. It was Guiseley who began the match as the stronger team. Seemingly accustomed to the expansive size of the playing surface, they took the lead in the 14th minute when Ian Noteman, brother of Doncaster Rovers striker Kevin, pounced on an horrendous defensive mix-up when Wimborne keeper Kevin Leonard fluffed a punch, to steer the ball into the empty net.

The goal was just reward for a stylish Guiseley opening that had seen the Wimborne defence rigorously tested on a number of occasions. But the Dorset side gradually began to gain confidence and equalised in the 27th minute when skipper Steve Richardson surprised Guiseley keeper Paul Maxted with a viciously struck shot which rebounded off the Yorkshireman's chest and flew into the net. Three minutes later it was 2–1 to Wimborne when Tommy Killick streaked away down the left before sending in a perfect centre for Jamie Sturgess to power home with a thumping header.

As Guiseley struggled to find their early form, Wimborne swept forward in droves, keen to exploit the sudden indecision that had crept into their opponents' play. Wimborne got their just desserts three minutes before the break when the inspirational Richardson prodded forward a tantalising through ball which split the Guiseley defence. Strikers Sturgess and Killick immediately converged on the ball, but it was Killick, who just seven weeks earlier had torn cruciate ligaments in his knee and seemed certain to miss the big Wembley occasion, who got there first to sweep the ball home.

Guiseley gave their enthusiastic support amongst a crowd of 10,772, some renewed hope in the 51st minute when Noteman seized upon a rare mistake by Andy Taplin, to collect the defender's half-hearted back pass and beat Leonard from close range.

But Guiseley's joy was short-lived. Wimborne restored their two-goal advantage six minutes later when Killick skilfully managed to rob both Maxted and his defence before forcing the ball home with his left foot through a crowd of players.

The Dorset fans had by now begun to celebrate, sensing the FA Vase would be theirs. Wimborne, however, were not content just to sit on their lead, and they stretched their advantage to 5–2 in the 78th minute when Sturgess collected an optimistic through ball in space on the left, before cutting inside his man and unleashing an unstoppable shot from the edge of the area.

Guiseley for their part never stopped trying to score and they were rewarded with a late consolation effort in the dying seconds of normal time when substitute Bob Colville, a 28-year-old veteran of Stockport County and Bangor City, breached the Wimborne defence's obstinate resistance when he collected his own lobbed ball to plant a firm shot past the advancing Leonard.

But it was a case of too little too late and at the final whistle the Wimborne players were left to celebrate what had seemed an unlikely victory whilst Guiseley were left to ponder their performance on the long journey back to Yorkshire.More silverware was to follow for Wimborne a few weeks later, when the little Dorset club clinched the Dorset Senior Challenge Cup, admittedly in less grandiose surroundings.

Wimborne Town   Leonard, Langdown (Wilkins 55), Beacham, Allan, Taplin, Ames, Richardson, Bridle, Killick, Sturgess (Lovell 86), Lynn.

Guiseley   Maxted, Atkinson, Hogarth, Tetley (Wilson 66), Morgan, Brockie, Annan (Colville 75), Tennison, Noteman, A Roberts, B Roberts.

EXTRA PRELIMINARY ROUND

Prudhoe East End 2 Dunston FB 7

The streets of Dunston have frequently been full of football-crazy youngsters playing impromptu five-a-side games. These days the craze is as popular as ever, most likely due to the emergence of Paul Gascoigne, a native of Dunston, whose talent emerged from the cocoon of terraced streets to captivate a nation during the 1990 World Cup Finals in Italy.

Dunston Federation Breweries of the Northern League Second Division have acknowledged the contributions of Dunston's most famous son by naming a stand after him at their modest Federation Park home. During the 1991–92 season, the Paul Gascoigne Stand was regularly filled with a growing number of Dunston FB followers who had been enticed to the ground to witness the unlikely progress of their side through to the latter stages of the FA Vase.

To reach even the first round of the competition, Dunston had first to negotiate the extra preliminary round and preliminary round. Their first opponents were fellow Northern Leaguers Prudhoe East End and Dunston wasted no time and little ceremony in inflicting an overwhelming 7–2 defeat on their hosts, with David Wright (2), Ian Bensley (2), Mick Richmond, Steve Kendal and Tony Coyles all finding the back of the net.

In the preliminary round Coyles and Richmond struck again to oust Stockton 2–1 and in the first round proper a Matty Hillary last-minute winner in extra time, following Steve Cockburn's earlier effort, was enough to unseat Northern Alliance Seaton Delaval Amateurs.

Extra time was again required in round two as Kenny Cramman, Ian Bensley and Mick Richmond scored to beat Thackley 3–2. Belper Town, another North-East Counties League side, were Dunston's next victims in round three when, following the abandonment of their first match at 90 minutes due to a waterlogged pitch, Dunston triumphed 2–0 thanks to Cockburn and Tony Halliday.

This set up a fourth-round tie against the 1991 winners of the Vase, Guiseley of the HFS Loans League. Ian Mulholland scored for Dunston, but it was not enough to prevent experienced Guiseley winning 3–1, leaving the Newcastle side to reflect on their best-ever run in the competition.

Top: Wimborne Town victorious in the FA Vase

Bottom: Dave Morgan of Guiseley tackles Simon Lynn of Wimborne

EXTRA PRELIMINARY ROUND   7 September 1991

(replays in italics)

Result

28	Heaton Stannington	v	Marske United	0–1
30	Ponteland United	v	Sunderland IFG Roker	1–3
91	Prudhoe East End	v	Dunston FB	2–7
38	Whitehaven Miners	v	Newton Aycliffe	0–4
108	Pickering Town	v	Seaton Delaval ST	4–0
31	Seaton Delaval Amateurs	v	Sunderland Vaux Ryhope	2–0
60	Heswall	v	Poulton Victoria	4–0
52	General Chemicals	v	Christleton	3–1
50	Merseyside Police	v	Westhoughton Town	4–0
80	Ashville	v	Bamber Bridge	0–3
45	Atherton Collieries	v	Knypersley Victoria	4–3
46	Waterloo Dock	v	Cheadle Town	3–1
70	Redgate Clayton	v	St Dominics	4–4
45	*St Dominics*	v	*Redgate Clayton*	*7–1*
20	Newton (WC)	v	Vauxhall Motors (WC)	1–4
40	Maghull	v	Ayone	2–3
	Kidsgrove Athletic	v	Leyland DAF	†
22	Blidworth MW	v	Brodworth MW	1–0
35	Hatfield Main	v	Immingham Town	2–3
60	Dunkirk	v	Lincoln United	1–5
26	Radford	v	Louth United	3–2
25	Priory (Eastwood)	v	Rossington Main	5–1
113	Winterton Rangers	v	Bradford PA	4–1
46	Nettleham	v	Tadcaster Albion	0–0
55	*Tadcaster Albion*	v	*Nettleham*	*0–2*
61	Clipstone Welfare	v	RES Parkgate	1–1
30	*RES Parkgate*	v	*Clipstone Welfare*	*0–1*
45	Yorkshire Amateur	v	Worsboro Bridge MW	3–1
103	Mickleover RBL	v	Maltby MW	2–1
87	Liversedge	v	Kimberley Town	2–1*
31	Stocksbridge Park Steels	v	Bradley Rangers	2–1*
107	Selby Town	v	Glasshoughton Welfare	1–4
150	Shirebrook Colliery	v	Pontefract Collieries	2–1*
42	Hall Road Rangers	v	Hallam	2–2
45	*Hall Road Rangers*	v	*Hallam*	*1–2***
25	Bloxwich Town	v	Brackley Town	4–0
57	Harrowby United	v	Heath Hayes	5–2
56	Coleshill Town	v	Holwell Sports	1–1
204	*Holwell Sports*	v	*Coleshill Town*	*3–2*
30	Oldswinford	v	Knowle	0–0
34	*Knowle*	v	*Oldswinford*	*1–0*
60	Oadby Town	v	Pelsall Villa	1–0
33	West Bromwich Town	v	Anstey Nomads	2–2
103	*Anstey Nomads*	v	*West Bromwich Town*	*3–0*
68	Northfield Town	v	Tividale	4–0
15	Burton Park Wanderers	v	Pegasus Juniors	0–2
10	Wolverhampton Casuals	v	Westfields	1–0
55	Meir KA	v	Lutterworth Town	2–1
42	Kings Heath	v	Highfield Rangers	3–2
52	Stourport Swifts	v	Bolehall Swifts	2–0
82	St Andrews	v	Daventry Town	1–2
100	Stapenhill	v	Norton United	6–4

(replays in italics)

Att				Result
69	Eccleshall	v	Hamlet S & L	3–1
69	St Ives Town	v	Ramsey Town	1–2
112	Diss Town	v	Clarksteel Yaxley	2–0
92	Downham Town	v	Brightlingsea United	1–0
148	Stansted	v	Sawbridgeworth Town	2–1*
99	Norwich United	v	Somersham Town	0–2
52	Wroxham	v	Ipswich Wanderers	3–1
63	Brantham Athletic	v	Ely City	0–2
89	Chatteris Town	v	Woodbridge Town	1–2
51	Long Sutton Athletic	v	LBC Ortonians	1–2
25	Long Buckby	v	London Colney	2–2
30	*London Colney*	v	*Long Buckby*	*1–4*
30	Beaconsfield United	v	Milton Keynes Borough	3–1
68	Kempston Rovers	v	Langford	3–0
62	Wolverton	v	Brook House	0–3
59	Biggleswade Town	v	Wingate & Finchley	0–1
65	Viking Sports	v	Amersham Town	3–2
41	Waltham Abbey	v	Totternhoe	3–2
10	The 61	v	Cockfosters	1–4
72	Potters Bar Town	v	Pirton	1–0*
51	Stotfold	v	Bowers United	2–1
25	Winslow United	v	Rayners Lane	1–3
58	Brimsdown Rovers	v	Shillington	2–0
75	Petersfield United	v	Bedfont	1–0
190	Deal Town	v	Eastbourne Town	1–0
40	Horley Town	v	Slade Green	0–3
50	Ashford Town (Middx)	v	Hartley Wintney	3–0
65	Old Salesians	v	Farleigh Rovers	3–2
36	Godalming Town	v	Broadbridge Heath	0–1*
22	Cobham	v	Ash United	5–1
45	Sherborne Town	v	Bicester Town	3–2
42	Christchurch	v	Fleet Town	1–3
110	Oxford City	v	Wantage Town	3–1
44	Aerostructures	v	Milton United	0–1
65	Ryde Sports	v	Kintbury Rangers	3–2
66	AFC Lymington	v	Bishop's Cleeve	5–0
70	Brockenhurst	v	BAT	4–0
23	Flight Refuelling	v	Harrow Hill	5–1
169	Bridgwater Town	v	Brislington	2–0
103	Cinderford Town	v	Backwell United	1–1
72	*Backwell United*	v	*Cinderford Town*	*2–2*
130	*Cinderford Town*	v	*Backwell United*	*4–2*
40	Old Georgians	v	Keynsham Town	0–2
50	Fairford Town	v	Larkhall Athletic	2–3*
27	Clandown	v	Wotton Rovers	1–1
45	*Wotton Rovers*	v	*Clandown*	*2–1*
52	Almondsbury Picksons	v	Cirencester Town	4–4
100	*Cirencester Town*	v	*Almondsbury Picksons*	*0–1*
45	Bemerton Heath Harlequins	v	Swindon Athletic	2–3*
25	DRG (FP)	v	Clanfield	3–4
180	Truro City	v	St Austell	0–2

* *after extra time*
† *walkover for Kidsgrove Athletic, Leyland DAF removed from competition*

PRELIMINARY ROUND

Oldham Town 1 Newcastle Town 2

Newcastle-under-Lyme, Staffordshire, unlike its more illustrious Tyneside namesake, is not a town renowned for its footballing passion, fervour and commitment.

Indeed Newcastle Town, of the North-West Counties League Division Two, can boast only five years' Saturday footballing experience, having spent much of their previous life as a Sunday League team. But while Newcastle United of the Second Division grabbed many of football's more dramatic headlines towards the end of the season, Newcastle Town delighted their own more modest following with a rollercoaster ride through the 1991–92 FA Vase, from the preliminary round through to their eventual exit in the fifth round.

The long road began for Newcastle at Oldham Town, another North-West Counties League Division Two side. The visitors surged powerfully into a two-goal lead thanks to efforts from Paul Groves and Neil Prestige and despite a late rally from their Lancashire hosts, which was rewarded with a consolation goal, Newcastle matched their previous best Vase performance by reaching the first round proper.

There they encountered Glossop, and a single strike from Griffiths was enough to secure a second-round berth. A home tie against Sheffield produced goals from Trevor Brissett, once of Port Vale, Dave Ritchie, formerly of Stoke City and Stockport County, and Shaun Wade, as the Staffordshire outfit triumphed 3–2.

Having exceeded all but the most optimistic of expectations, by marching proudly into the last 64, Newcastle continued to delight their growing number of fans with an extra-time 3–2 victory over Penrith. Stevenson, Wade and Bright scored the all-important goals to set up the mouthwatering prospect of a home tie with the previous year's beaten finalists, Gresley Rovers. A crowd of 577, Newcastle's biggest of the season in the League or Cup, saw their heroes exact another pulsating 3–2 extra-time win, with Wade poaching his third and fourth goals of the competition and Neil Prestige hitting the winner with a penalty.

But Town's hopes of a Wembley appearance finally evaporated in the last 16 when, following a 1–1 draw with Wessex League Wimborne, the Dorset side won the return 1–0.

PRELIMINARY ROUND   5 October 1991

(replays in italics)

Att				Result
15	Evenwood Town	v	Seaton Delaval Amateurs	1–2
46	Ashington	v	Penrith	1–2
81	Cleator Moor Celtic	v	Langley Park	2–6
43	Marske United	v	West Allotment Celtic	2–1
250	Hebburn	v	Norton & Stockton Ancients	2–0*
30	West Auckland Town	v	Washington	2–0
22	Willington	v	Newton Aycliffe	0–4
57	Annfield Plain	v	Crook Town	3–1
50	Shotton Comrades	v	Durham City	0–6
105	Chester–le–Street Town	v	Pickering Town	2–1
	Stockton	v	Dunston FB	1–2
27	Horden CW	v	Darlington CB	6–1
97	Netherfield	v	Sunderland IFG Roker	1–2*
45	Esh Winning	v	Bedlington Terriers	1–4
30	Oldham Town	v	Newcastle Town	1–2
21	Vauxhall GM	v	Rocester	0–0
131	*Rocester*	v	*Vauxhall GM*	*1–2*
49	Irlam Town	v	Heswall	3–2*
80	St Helens Town	v	Burscough	2–3
32	Vauxhall Motors (WC)	v	Atherton LR	1–2
63	Curzon Ashton	v	Blackpool (Wren) Rovers	0–1
148	Nantwich Town	v	Wythenshawe Amateurs	1–1
115	*Wythenshawe Amateurs*	v	*Nantwich Town*	*2–1*
212	Ashton United	v	Lancaster City	4–0
27	Ayone	v	Bootle	1–1
138	*Bootle*	v	*Ayone*	*2–3*￼*
102	Chadderton	v	Flixton	4–6*
19	Formby	v	General Chemicals	1–1
58	*General Chemicals*	v	*Formby*	*0–0*
42	*Formby*	v	*General Chemicals*	*0–1*
135	Clitheroe	v	Skelmersdale United	2–1
132	Prescot AFC	v	Bamber Bridge	1–3*
144	Darwen	v	St Dominics	1–2
48	Atherton Collieries	v	Maine Road	1–1
61	*Maine Road*	v	*Atherton Collieries*	*3–1*
82	Salford City	v	Merseyside Police	2–0
80	Kidsgrove Athletic	v	Waterloo Dock	1–1
51	*Waterloo Dock*	v	*Kidsgrove Athletic*	*1–1*
63	*Waterloo Dock*	v	*Kidsgrove Athletic*	*1–1*
80	*Kidsgrove Athletic*	v	*Waterloo Dock*	*3–1*
73	Oakham United	v	Hallam	1–5*
190	Arnold Town	v	Lincoln United	0–0
334	*Lincoln United*	v	*Arnold Town*	*5–0*
114	Denaby United	v	Thackley	3–4
106	Mickleover RBL	v	Nettleham	3–2*
48	Ossett Albion	v	Immingham Town	2–5
100	Clipstone Welfare	v	Winterton Rangers	0–1
47	Yorkshire Amateurs	v	Glasshoughton Welfare	2–3

* *after extra time*

(replays in italics)

Att				Result
46	Armthorpe Welfare	v	Eccleshill United	4–1
25	Radford	v	Harworth CI	1–2
67	Brigg Town	v	Shirebrook Colliery	6–1
47	Priory (Eastwood)	v	Stocksbridge Park Steels	1–3
38	Sheffield	v	Friar Lane OB	2–1
23	Blidworth MW	v	Liversedge	1–3
174	Ilkeston Town	v	Belper Town	0–3
80	Stapenhill	v	Oldbury United	0–2
50	Wellingborough Town	v	Northfield Town	1–3
82	Pegasus Juniors	v	Northampton Spencer	0–1
35	Meir KA	v	Racing Club Warwick	0–1
46	Eccleshall	v	Wolverhampton Casuals	2–1
87	Halesowen Harriers	v	Holwell Sports	4–2
110	Daventry Town	v	West Midlands Police	0–0
30	*West Midlands Police*	v	*Daventry Town*	*0–0*
60	*West Midlands Police*	v	*Daventry Town*	*2–1**
48	Hinckley	v	Sandwell Borough	0–1
80	Bridgnorth Town	v	Irthlingborough Diamonds	4–1
52	Malvern Town	v	Oadby Town	1–0
33	APV Peterborough City	v	Stratford Town	1–0
45	Highgate United	v	Desborough Town	2–0
89	Blakenall	v	Mile Oak Rovers	8–0
85	Anstey Nomads	v	Kings Heath	2–1
77	Harrowby United	v	Boldmere St Michaels	1–5
74	Hinckley Town	v	Walsall Wood	1–0
102	Solihull Borough	v	Knowle	6–2
72	Rushall Olympic	v	Stourport Swifts	5–1*
105	Lye Town	v	Bilston Town	1–1
122	*Bilston Town*	v	*Lye Town*	*5–2*
37	Wednesfield	v	Evesham United	1–3
33	Bloxwich Town	v	Chasetown	0–0
79	*Chasetown*	v	*Bloxwich Town*	*2–0*
79	Clacton Town	v	Ely City	4–3
73	Canvey Island	v	Witham Town	0–1
68	Boston	v	Diss Town	0–1*
120	Eynesbury Rovers	v	Newmarket Town	0–0
110	*Newmarket Town*	v	*Eynesbury Rovers*	*0–0*
140	*Eynesbury Rovers*	v	*Newmarket Town*	*0–2**
167	Woodbridge Town	v	Royston Town	0–1
120	Halstead Town	v	Basildon Town	1–3
	Ramsey Town	v	March Town United	1–2
104	Mirrlees Blackstone	v	Lowestoft Town	1–4
26	Tiptree United	v	Downham Town	3–5
79	Berkhamsted Town	v	Soham Town Rangers	1–0
214	Stamford Town	v	Bourne Town	1–0
134	Gorleston	v	Stowmarket Town	4–2*
105	Stansted	v	Barton Rovers	3–0
171	Bury Town	v	LBC Ortonians	1–0
114	Wroxham	v	Somersham Town	3–0

* after extra time

Att				Result
45	Watton United	v	Felixstowe Town	1–2
45	Rayners Lane	v	Kingsbury Town	0–1*
54	Tilbury	v	Brook House	5–2
106	Wingate & Finchley	v	Hornchurch	5–0
51	Waltham Abbey	v	Leighton Town	1–0
66	Brimsdown Rovers	v	Viking Sports	0–1
30	Feltham & Hounslow Borough	v	Wootton Blue Cross	5–0
61	Stotfold	v	Tring Town	2–0
65	Ford United	v	Metropolitan Police	2–3*
61	Clapton	v	Haringey Borough	1–3
103	Hertford Town	v	Beaconsfield United	4–1*
150	Arlesey Town	v	Rainham Town	4–1
52	Flackwell Heath	v	Edgware Town	1–4
48	Bracknell Town	v	Hoddesdon Town	0–1
79	Kempston Rovers	v	Cockfosters	1–3*
40	Welwyn Garden City	v	Cheshunt	1–2
145	Hampton	v	Ruislip Manor	1–1
199	*Ruislip Manor*	v	*Hampton*	*2–3*
81	Northwood	v	Long Buckby	4–1
44	Letchworth Garden City	v	Potters Bar Town	1–1
84	*Potters Bar Town*	v	*Letchworth Garden City*	*2–1*
65	Hemel Hempstead	v	Barkingside	4–1
26	Eton Manor	v	Southall	2–3
105	Ware	v	Collier Row	0–2
95	Leatherhead	v	Burnham	0–1
130	Worthing	v	Slade Green	1–3
94	Shoreham	v	Peacehaven & Telscombe	1–3
31	Corinthian	v	Deal Town	1–0
55	Wick	v	Haywards Heath Town	4–0
28	Croydon Athletic	v	Banstead Athletic	2–4
147	Horsham	v	Cove	5–1
105	Tunbridge Wells	v	Cobham	7–6*
51	Old Salesians	v	Hailsham Town	2–7
84	Chipstead	v	Burgess Hill Town	0–4
69	Herne Bay	v	Arundel	8–1
271	Sittingbourne	v	Beckenham Town	3–1
52	Camberley Town	v	Southwick	1–2
72	Redhill	v	Alma Swanley	4–0
66	Pagham	v	Horsham YMCA	3–1
45	Broadbridge Heath	v	Oakwood	0–2
34	Worthing United	v	Ringmer	2–1
180	Petersfield United	v	Tonbridge	1–7
68	Whitehawk	v	Ashford Town (Middx)	2–1*
28	Three Bridges	v	Darenth Heathside	2–1*
103	Whitstable Town	v	Lancing	4–0
62	Lewes	v	Selsey	0–2
50	Steyning Town	v	Epsom & Ewell	0–3
89	Egham Town	v	Malden Vale	0–1
40	Portfield	v	Corinthian Casuals	0–1*

* after extra time

(replays in italics)

Att			Result
270	Langney Sports	v Eastbourne United	5–2
135	Sheppey United	v Faversham Town	1–4
27	Chichester City	v Chatham Town	3–0
60	Milton United	v Abingdon United	3–0
76	Newbury Town	v AFC Totton	3–0
58	AFC Lymington	v Ryde Sports	1–0
286	Newport (IOW)	v Oxford City	2–0
62	Sholing Sports	v Swanage Town & Herston	1–2
111	Thame United	v Horndean	6–0
90	Brockenhurst	v Romsey Town	1–2
40	East Cowes Victoria Athletic	v Witney Town	1–2
69	Fleet Town	v Banbury United	2–2
182	*Banbury United*	v *Fleet Town*	*1–3*
87	Sherborne Town	v First Tower United	2–2
75	*First Tower United*	v *Sherborne Town*	*1–2*
98	Westbury United	v Bournemouth	0–1
102	Minehead	v Melksham Town	4–1
43	Calne Town	v Odd Down	0–1
75	Glastonbury	v Mangotsfield United	2–4
52	Clanfield	v Devizes Town	1–3
71	Chard Town	v Swindon Athletic	2–0
49	Larkhall Athletic	v Bristol Manor Farm	1–2
58	Wotton Rovers	v Keynsham Town	2–3
150	Cinderford Town	v Frome Town	3–0
146	Shortwood United	v Radstock Town	5–2
170	Bridgwater Town	v Chippenham Town	0–2
62	Almondsbury Picksons	v Welton Rovers	0–1
110	Clevedon Town	v Flight Refuelling	7–1
119	Exmouth Town	v Liskeard Athletic	1–0
396	Tiverton Town	v Elmore	3–0
140	Torrington	v Barnstaple Town	1–1†
217	*Barnstaple Town*	v *Torrington*	*1–2*
88	Torpoint Athletic	v Ilfracombe Town	1–0
75	St Blazey	v Crediton United	1–2*
82	St Austell	v Ottery St Mary	2–0

* *after extra time*
† *extra time not played*

FIRST ROUND
AFC Lymington 0 Newport (IOW) 1

One team in this year's FA Vase competition had to negotiate a major stretch of water before embarking upon the first of many lengthy Cup journeys. Newport, Isle of Wight, the only non-mainland side in the competition, became even more familiar than usual with their route across the Solent from Newport to Southampton as they charted a course through the early rounds.

Following a comfortable 2–0 home win over Oxford City in the preliminary round, the Beazer Homes Southern Division side were confronted by a potentially hazardous trip to AFC Lymington in round one.

As expected the match was a close-fought affair, with both sides creating and then squandering several goalscoring opportunities. But Newport kept their Vase hopes very much alive when Mark 'Sparky' Hutton produced a moment of magic late in the game to send his side into round two.

The reward for a tenacious performance was the relatively short trip to nearby Havant, where they encountered surprisingly few difficulties, with Deacon and Greening bagging the Islanders' goals in a 2–1 victory.

Steve Greening was again on the mark in round three when he scored the only goal of the tie against Diadora League Division Three outfit Hampton, and Greening, in his by now customary role as the Islanders' goalscoring hero, pounced for his third and fourth goals of the campaign as Newport put out Burnham Ramblers in round four.

This victory secured a place in the last 16 for the first time in their history, and Newport's sight of Wembley's twin towers was brought abruptly into focus when former Aston Villa player Stuart Ritchie scored a penalty for the Islanders in their fifth-round tie against Bamber Bridge.

But it was not enough as the North-West Counties League Division Two side triumphed 2–1 to go through to the quarter-finals.

FIRST ROUND   2 November 1991

(replays in italics)

Att				Result
84	West Auckland Town	v	Horden CW	1–0
80	Durham City	v	Eppleton CW	2–2
161	*Eppleton CW*	v	*Durham City*	*2–2*
198	*Durham City*	v	*Eppleton CW*	*2–0*
65	Seaton Delaval Amateurs	v	Dunston FB	1–2*
30	Bedlington Terriers	v	Newton Aycliffe	0–1

* after extra time

171

Att				Result
41	Penrith	v	Sunderland IFG Roker	2–1
54	Chester–le–Street Town	v	Langley Park	3–3
97	*Langley Park*	v	*Chester–le–Street Town*	*1–3*
8	Billingham Town	v	Annfield Plain	4–3*
110	Hebburn	v	Marske United	3–2
70	Atherton LR	v	Clitheroe	2–1
71	Burscough	v	Irlam Town	5–1
35	Flixton	v	Kidsgrove Athletic	1–0
120	Glossop	v	Newcastle Town	0–1
30	Wythenshawe Amateurs	v	Eastwood Hanley	0–2
55	Salford City	v	Vauxhall GM	2–0
156	Bamber Bridge	v	St Dominics	6–1
32	General Chemicals	v	Maine Road	0–1
175	Rossendale United	v	Ayone	5–2*
55	Blackpool (Wren) Rovers	v	Ashton United	1–2
180	Lincoln United	v	Harworth CI	2–3
93	Hallam	v	Ossett Town	0–1*
50	Glasshoughton Welfare	v	Belper Town	0–3
46	Garforth Town	v	Heanor Town	4–1
80	Mickleover RBL	v	Borrowash Victoria	3–4
44	Liversedge	v	Rainworth MW	3–1
52	Brigg Town	v	Stocksbridge Park Steels	5–0
43	Armthorpe Welfare	v	Sheffield	2–4*
163	Harrogate Town	v	Winterton Rangers	4–1
100	Thackley	v	Immingham Town	3–1
42	Sandwell Borough	v	West Midlands Police	1–2*
69	Raunds Town	v	Bridgnorth Town	1–1
90	*Bridgnorth Town*	v	*Raunds Town*	*0–2*
51	Eccleshall	v	Halesowen Harriers	4–2
57	Chasetown	v	Northampton Spencer	2–1*
44	Rothwell Town	v	Evesham United	1–3
123	Solihull Borough	v	Paget Rangers	4–1
67	Rushall Olympic	v	Hinckley Town	2–1
39	Boldmere St Michaels	v	Racing Club Warwick	0–3
30	APV Peterborough City	v	Malvern Town	3–0
58	Anstey Nomads	v	Oldbury United	4–0
64	Bilston Town	v	Highgate United	1–0
49	Northfield Town	v	Blakenall	1–3
110	Newmarket Town	v	Stamford Town	5–0
169	Diss Town	v	Witham Town	3–1
70	Downham Town	v	Felixstowe Town	3–3
65	*Felixstowe Town*	v	*Downham Town*	*2–0*
70	Holbeach United	v	Thetford Town	2–1
42	Basildon United	v	Histon	5–3
66	Wroxham	v	Clacton Town	3–0
130	Gorleston	v	Stansted	2–1
63	Berkhamsted Town	v	Bury Town	2–0
344	King's Lynn	v	Lowestoft Town	2–1*
54	Royston Town	v	March Town United	2–1
35	Metropolitan Police	v	Stotfold	1–1

* after extra time

Att				Result
98	*Stotfold*	v	*Metropolitan Police*	*0–2**
63	Burnham Ramblers	v	Haringey Borough	2–2
38	*Haringey Borough*	v	*Burnham Ramblers*	*1–2*
45	Viking Sports	v	Feltham & Hounslow Borough	3–1
76	Collier Row	v	Wingate & Finchley	1–0
45	Purfleet	v	Southall	6–0
79	Northwood	v	Braintree Town	7–6*
64	Potters Bar Town	v	Hampton	0–0
187	*Hampton*	v	*Potters Bar Town*	*4–1*
65	Cheshunt	v	Waltham Abbey	2–1
150	Arlesey Town	v	Hertford Town	1–0
65	Cockfosters	v	Kingsbury Town	1–1
63	*Kingsbury Town*	v	*Cockfosters*	*1–4*
52	Hemel Hempstead	v	Edgware Town	0–2
31	Tilbury	v	Hoddesdon Town	1–0
18	Corinthian	v	Langney Sports	1–3
126	Peacehaven & Telscombe	v	Whitehawk	5–0
48	Merstham	v	Whitstable Town	0–6
74	Wick	v	Sittingbourne	0–2
78	Faversham Town	v	Southwick	6–0
148	Tunbridge Wells	v	Greenwich Borough	1–2*
63	Three Bridges	v	Burgess Hill Town	3–3
109	*Burgess Hill Town*	v	*Three Bridges*	*0–1*
91	Herne Bay	v	Hailsham Town	3–1
40	Worthing United	v	Selsey	2–1
88	Havant Town	v	Redhill	3–2
65	Pagham	v	Burnham	1–0
155	Horsham	v	Oakwood	1–0
51	Epsom & Ewell	v	Chertsey Town	0–2
33	Slade Green	v	Chichester City	4–0
45	Corinthian Casuals	v	Malden Vale	2–3*
348	Tonbridge	v	Banstead Athletic	2–1
72	Sherborne Town	v	Thatcham Town	0–2
100	AFC Lymington	v	Newport (IOW)	0–1
74	Witney Town	v	Bournemouth	4–3
37	Didcot Town	v	Romsey Town	2–1*
49	Fleet Town	v	Swanage Town & Herston	4–6*
90	Thame United	v	Milton United	3–0
65	Newbury Town	v	Eastleigh	3–0
52	Welton Rovers	v	Minehead	1–0
38	Devizes Town	v	Chard Town	0–3
100	Shortwood United	v	Clevedon Town	3–1
50	Wellington	v	Cinderford Town	1–3
35	Chippenham Town	v	Bristol Manor Farm	2–0*
46	Keynsham Town	v	Odd Down	1–0
127	Mangotsfield United	v	Wimborne Town	1–2
58	Torpoint Athletic	v	St Austell	2–0
103	Crediton United	v	Torrington	1–2*
245	Falmouth Town	v	Tiverton Town	1–3*
84	Exmouth Town	v	Newquay	0–6

* after extra time

173

SECOND ROUND

Burnham Ramblers 5 East Thurrock United 3

Having skilfully disposed of Haringey Borough in the first round of the competition, at Borough's modest White Hart Lane headquarters situated just one mile away from the towering floodlights of their more illustrious north London neighbours Tottenham Hotspur, Essex Senior League Burnham Ramblers returned home to prepare for a second-round clash with Essex rivals East Thurrock.

The Ramblers, whose previous Vase best had been reaching the last 16 of the competition in 1988, started the tie in lacklustre mood, and were quickly punished by the visitors as East Thurrock galloped into a 3–2 lead. The omens did not look good for the home side, but in true Cup tradition they found a saviour in striker Steven Harding, whose three goals in the two games against Haringey Borough had given his team the right to entertain East Thurrock.

Harding struck twice and, together with goals from Shaun Tracey, Gary Eves and Simon Connolly, the Ramblers snuffed out the threat from East Thurrock and progressed to round three.

Chasetown, from the Midlands League, were their next opponents, and the Ramblers were again grateful for the accurate firepower of Harding who, linking up with Gary Eves, instigated a 2–1 victory.

However, Burnham stumbled at the next hurdle as they neared the last 16. They were ousted from the competition in round five by Newport (IOW). Steve Howard had given the Ramblers hope when he took the tie into extra time with a late equaliser. But the Beazer Homes Southern Division side proved too strong for Burnham and eventually won 3–1.

SECOND ROUND   23 November 1991

(replays in italics)

Att				Result
102	Harrogate RA	v	Penrith	0–1
271	Great Harwood Town	v	Farsley Celtic	1–1
260	*Farsley Celtic*	v	*Great Harwood Town*	*4–0*
100	Dunston FB	v	Thackley	3–2*
113	Liversedge	v	Bamber Bridge	3–8
108	Newton Aycliffe	v	Hebburn	2–2
	Hebburn	v	*Newton Aycliffe*	*2–4**
253	Chester–le–Street Town	v	Durham City	2–0
214	Bridlington Town	v	Billingham Town	5–0
112	North Ferriby United	v	West Auckland Town	1–0
80	Newcastle Town	v	Sheffield	3–2
601	Guiseley	v	Garforth Town	2–0
61	Eastwood Hanley	v	Harrogate Town	4–1

* *after extra time*

174

Att				Result
160	Belper Town	v	Harworth CI	2–1
95	Ossett Town	v	Atherton LR	3–3
200	*Atherton LR*	v	*Ossett Town*	*3–1*
92	Flixton	v	Borrowash Victoria	8–3
282	Knowsley United	v	Cammell Laird	1–0
183	Burscough	v	Rossendale United	2–0
323	Ashton United	v	Maine Road	2–1
80	Salford City	v	Brigg Town	0–1
268	Eccleshall	v	Wisbech Town	0–2
589	Gresley Rovers	v	Blakenall	1–0
105	Chasetown	v	Witney Town	3–2*
105	Bilston Town	v	APV Peterborough City	3–1
109	Anstey Nomads	v	Spalding United	3–2
97	Raunds Town	v	Holbeach United	3–0
287	Hinckley Athletic	v	Hucknall Town	3–2
52	West Midlands Police	v	Rushall Olympic	3–1*
141	Racing Club Warwick	v	Solihull Borough	1–3
233	Evesham United	v	Buckingham Town	3–1
108	Potton United	v	Walthamstow Pennant	0–4
240	Diss Town	v	Viking Sports	4–0
125	Felixstowe Town	v	Cheshunt	2–0
110	Arlesey Town	v	Newmarket Town	0–2
90	Great Yarmouth Town	v	Cockfosters	2–1
211	Edgware Town	v	Basildon United	4–3
119	Burnham Ramblers	v	East Thurrock United	5–3
98	Collier Row	v	Harefield United	4–0
150	Saffron Walden Town	v	Wroxham	3–1
120	Berkhamsted Town	v	Harwich & Parkeston	2–1
45	Metropolitan Police	v	Royston Town	1–0
157	Gorleston	v	Hampton	0–2
539	Haverhill Rovers	v	Sudbury Town	1–1
577	*Sudbury Town*	v	*Haverhill Rovers*	*2–1*
404	Billericay Town	v	King's Lynn	4–2
405	Horsham	v	Littlehampton Town	2–2
490	*Littlehampton Town*	v	*Horsham*	*0–1*
314	Sittingbourne	v	Tilbury	4–2*
91	Malden Vale	v	Thatcham Town	2–2
158	*Thatcham Town*	v	*Malden Vale*	*2–3*
334	Hythe Town	v	Herne Bay	1–1
216	*Herne Bay*	v	*Hythe Town*	*1–2*
161	Chertsey Town	v	Peacehaven & Telscombe	3–2
271	Faversham Town	v	Whitstable Town	1–0
78	Three Bridges	v	Greenwich Borough	2–0
498	Langney Sports	v	Hastings Town	3–3
637	*Hastings Town*	v	*Langney Sports*	*2–1*
304	Havant Town	v	Newport (IOW)	1–2
102	Didcot Town	v	Worthing United	1–2*
469	Tonbridge	v	Thame United	1–6
90	Pagham	v	Slade Green	3–0
109	Northwood	v	Purfleet	3–2
82	Chippenham Town	v	Paulton Rovers	1–3

* after extra time

175

Att				Result
160	Shortwood United	v	Bridport	3–1
122	Torrington	v	Keynsham Town	1–0
215	Yate Town	v	Newbury Town	3–0
250	Cinderford Town	v	Newquay	3–1
210	Wimborne Town	v	Chard Town	5–2
171	Hungerford Town	v	Torpoint Athletic	2–1
64	Dawlish Town	v	Welton Rovers	1–2
241	Tiverton Town	v	Swanage Town & Herston	2–0

* after extra time

THIRD ROUND

Wimborne Town 1 Horsham 0*

Wessex League Wimborne Town had a modest footballing record before the 1991–92 season. Having reached the first round proper of the FA Cup only once, at the beginning of the 1980s, the club's record of three appearances in the third round of the FA Vase was arguably their best achievement.

But under the aegis of policeman and manager Alex Pike, Wimborne embarked upon a spectacular FA Vase journey which took them all the way from the first round to a Wembley final.

Having disposed of Mangotsfield 2–1 in round one thanks to goals from Richardson and Allan, and enjoyed the pleasure of beating a side that featured none other than Mickey Tanner, brother of Liverpool defender Nicky, the Dorset side then faced Chard in round two.

A thumping 5–2 win was the result, with Sturgess, Allan, Richardson, Lynn and Killick all finding the net to set up a third-round tie with Horsham, the Diadora League Division Three leaders.

The visitors made the better start but spurned a glorious opportunity to go in front when they missed a penalty after only 10 minutes. This let off inspired Wimborne, who came back into the match strongly. But they made the home crowd of 243 wait until the 95th minute, deep into injury time, for the winner, which eventually came from the boot of Jamie Sturgess. His goal could not have been more timely. There was no time to restart and the Dorset side had booked a place in round four against Hastings Town.

The first match between the two sides attracted some 626 spectators and produced six goals. Wimborne hit three through Killick, Richardson and Allan, but they were forced to wait until the replay in Sussex before they could guarantee a fifth-round berth, eventually winning 2–1 with goals from Lynn and Turner. Their opponents in the last 16,

* after extra time

Newcastle Town, again forced a replay after Allan's goal, his fourth of the competition, had given Wimborne the advantage. However, the North-West Counties side were outgunned in their next meeting, and Sturgess again popped up with the winner to send his side into the quarter-finals.

THIRD ROUND   14 December 1991

(replays in italics)

Att			Result
150	Atherton LR	v Brigg Town	3–3
94	*Brigg Town*	v *Atherton LR*	*3–2*
607	Farsley Celtic	v Guiseley	2–5
212	Belper Town	v Dunston FB	1–1†
193	*Dunston FB*	v *Belper Town*	*2–0*
153	Bridlington Town	v Eastwood Hanley	2–3*
175	Chester–le–Street Town	v Ashton United	2–1
120	Newton Aycliffe	v Burscough	2–4*
283	Bamber Bridge	v Flixton	2–1
112	North Ferriby United	v Knowsley United	1–2
121	Newcastle Town	v Penrith	3–2*
329	Anstey Nomads	v Felixstowe Town	2–1
190	Newmarket Town	v Solihull Borough	2–1
120	Collier Row	v West Midlands Police	2–3
121	Raunds Town	v Diss Town	0–2
42	Walthamstow Pennant	v Evesham United	2–3*
226	Edgware Town	v Hinckley Athletic	2–1
545	Wisbech Town	v Great Yarmouth Town	2–2
330	*Great Yarmouth Town*	v *Wisbech Town*	*2–4*
337	Berkhamsted Town	v Gresley Rovers	1–2*
132	Burnham Ramblers	v Chasetown	2–1
411	Billericay Town	v Bilston Town	2–0
325	Saffron Walden Town	v Sudbury Town	1–2*
476	Hastings Town	v Torrington	3–0
320	Tiverton Town	v Sittingbourne	2–3
171	Pagham	v Hythe Town	1–2
147	Chertsey Town	v Cinderford Town	1–1
285	*Cinderford Town*	v *Chertsey Town*	*0–0*
450	*Cinderford Town*	v *Chertsey Town*	*1–2*
51	Metropolitan Police	v Three Bridges	2–0
90	Welton Rovers	v Malden Vale	2–1
150	Shortwood United	v Yate Town	2–3
110	Hungerford Town	v Faversham Town	4–1
155	Worthing United	v Northwood	1–2
243	Wimborne Town	v Horsham	1–0*
226	Hampton	v Newport (IOW)	0–1
185	Paulton Rovers	v Thame United	4–2

* *after extra time*
† *abandoned after 90 mins, waterlogged*

177

FOURTH ROUND

Billericay Town 3 Yate Town 4*

Billericay Town are one of the great FA Vase sides. The Essex team dominated the competition in the late 1970s when they lifted the Vase three times in the space of four years from 1976 to 1979.

But in recent years there has been little apparent sign of a revival of Vase-winning form, with a series of disappointing exits at early stages of the competition. However, memories of Wembley were evoked as Billericay, automatically exempt from round one, negotiated round two with ease when a Steve Jones hat-trick and a solo effort from Lee Fulling swept aside King's Lynn 4–2.

An invaluable Steve Munday brace against Bilston in round three set up a fourth-round clash with their third successive Beazer Homes Midlands Division opponents, Yate Town.

It was a tumultuous Cup-tie. With the scores at 2–2 after normal time the match went into extra time, with Billericay immediately taking the lead. But just when it seemed as if the goals of Mark Jenkins, Andy Jones and Steve Jones were going to be enough to send the home side safely through to the next round, Yate produced an amazing come-back and scored two goals in the dying moments of the match to kill off Billericay.

So the Essex side's dream of a long-overdue return to Wembley was to be denied for at least another year. As for Yate, their progress in the Vase came to an abrupt halt in the next round when they were defeated 3–1 by Chertsey Town.

* after extra time

FOURTH ROUND   18 January 1992

(replays in italics)

Att				Result
423	Dunston FB	v	Guiseley	1–3
410	Brigg Town	v	Bamber Bridge	4–4
1045	Bamber Bridge	v	Brigg Town	1–0*
577	Newcastle Town	v	Gresley Rovers	3–2*
314	Burscough	v	Eastwood Hanley	0–1
305	Chester–le–Street Town	v	Knowsley United	1–5*
388	Edgware Town	v	Welton Rovers	3–1
400	Sittingbourne	v	Metropolitan Police	1–2
450	Anstey Nomads	v	Diss Town	0–1
213	Northwood	v	Chertsey Town	1–4
626	Wimborne Town	v	Hastings Town	3–3
677	Hastings Town	v	Wimborne Town	1–2*
758	Sudbury Town	v	Newmarket Town	3–2

* after extra time

Att				Result
320	West Midlands Police	v	Wisbech Town	4–3
205	Paulton Rovers	v	Hungerford Town	1–3*
438	Billericay Town	v	Yate Town	3–4*
581	Newport (IOW)	v	Burnham Ramblers	3–1*
279	Hythe Town	v	Evesham United	3–3*
636	*Evesham United*	v	*Hythe Town*	2–0†

* *after extra time*
† *after abandoned match, 0–0 half-time*

FIFTH ROUND

Knowsley United 2 Sudbury Town 4

With a man like Brian Talbot in your side, you could ask for little more Cup and League experience. The former Arsenal, Ipswich, Watford, Stoke and West Bromwich midfielder, who clinched FA Cup winners' medals with Ipswich in 1978 and Arsenal a year later when he scored one of the goals, was capped six times by England.

In the twilight of his playing career Talbot joined West Brom and promptly took over as manager. He then discovered the perils of looking after a football team when he lost his job following a disastrous FA Cup defeat at the hands of Woking.

But with a spell as boss of Aldershot completed with little success, Talbot needed a new challenge and he found it in the unlikely form of East Anglian side Sudbury Town. The Suffolk team had successfully negotiated two rounds of the Vase against Haverhill Rovers and Saffron Walden Town before Talbot arrived to help them through round four with a 3–2 defeat of local rivals Newmarket Town.

This set up a fifth-round clash with HFS Loans Division One Knowsley United, and Talbot's contribution was again to prove invaluable. He scored a 52nd-minute penalty to add to earlier goals from Andy Crane and Dean Barker, and when Keith Bain notched his second goal of the competition, the Beazer Homes side were in an unassailable position.

They eventually ran out 4–2 winners as Knowsley added two consolation goals in the closing four minutes and suddenly the 1989 FA Vase runners-up, having lost to Tamworth in a replay, found themselves in the last eight.

Manager Richie Powling, himself a veteran of 50 League appearances for Arsenal, took his team to face a West Midlands Police side which had enjoyed one of their best-ever runs in the Vase.

It was a close match, but Sudbury eventually triumphed 2–1 thanks to another Keith Bain strike and an own goal, and Sudbury were in the semi-finals against last year's winners Guiseley.

179

FIFTH ROUND   8 February 1992

(replays in italics)

Att				Result
421	Chertsey Town	v	Yate Town	3–1
975	Guiseley	v	Edgware Town	4–0
950	Bamber Bridge	v	Newport (IOW)	2–1
425	Newcastle Town	v	Wimborne Town	1–1
912	*Wimborne Town*	v	*Newcastle Town*	*1–0*
320	Hungerford Town	v	West Midlands Police	0–3
235	Metropolitan Police	v	Diss Town	0–2
652	Knowsley United	v	Sudbury Town	2–4
1202	Evesham United	v	Eastwood Hanley	2–1

SIXTH ROUND

Chertsey Town 0 Bamber Bridge 1

Prior to the 1991–92 FA Vase, Diadora League Division Three Chertsey Town's best performance in that competition was in reaching the last eight in 1987–88.

But Chertsey's 1991–92 campaign was destined to match their best-ever showing, with a string of competent displays that thrust manager Jim Kelman's side into the last eight once more. Their progress to the latter stages of the competition began with a sweet 2–0 victory against local rivals Epsom & Ewell. Peacehaven & Telscombe were their next victims, succumbing 3–2 in a thrilling second-round tie in which Chertsey twice had to come from behind.

Cinderford Town were dispatched from the competition in round three, after three matches, and Northwood were the next club to be ousted by Chertsey, by a comprehensive 4–1 scoreline. Following a 3–1 defeat of Yate Town in round five, the Curlews prepared for the quarter-final challenge of Bamber Bridge, a surprise package from the Bass North West Counties League, who had negotiated a stealthy passage through the competition to the last eight.

Chertsey, who rely largely on a turnover of mainly non-League players rather than former League men, could boast some important FA Vase experience in Kevin Hall and Paul Sweales, who had both played in the 1990 Vase final with winners Yeading.

Ironically, Bamber fielded a couple of players who had played for 1990 beaten finalists Bridlington Town. However it was Sweales, Chertsey's influential midfielder, who played the most significant role in the match, being dismissed in the opening 20 minutes for allegedly striking an opponent.

Chertsey's remaining men battled on valiantly, but when Bamber scored a vital penalty in the second half, there was no way back for the home side, who were left to reflect on the fact that their semi-final aspirations had again been foiled at home by a 1–0 scoreline.

SIXTH ROUND   29 February 1992
(replays in italics)

Att				Result
1668	Guiseley	v	Evesham United	4–0
1528	Diss Town	v	Wimborne Town	0–0
1172	*Wimborne Town*	v	*Diss Town* (7.3.92)	*1–0*
1072	West Midlands Police	v	Sudbury Town	1–2
1121	Chertsey Town	v	Bamber Bridge	0–1

SEMI-FINAL

Wimborne Town 2 Bamber Bridge 0 (aggregate)

In August few but the most ardent of Bamber Bridge supporters would have been brave enough to predict that by March a Wembley appearance in the FA Vase final would be only 180 minutes away. Equally few would have predicted that the Lancashire club, newly promoted to the Bass North West Counties Division Two, would also be leading the division in the same month and pressing emphatically for promotion.

But then football can be a funny old game; it requires the bravest of men to predict anything with a degree of certainty. Bamber Bridge's passage to the last four of the FA Vase in their first year in the competition began back in September with an extra-preliminary-round 3–0 victory over Ashville. Eight matches and 27 goals later Barry Massie's side stood on the threshold of a dream appearance at Wembley, with only Dorset side Wimborne between them and a place in history.

Bamber's progress towards the latter stages of the competition was indeed relentless. In a cup run that took them past Brigg Town, Newport (IoW) and Flixton, they also recorded astonishing wins over Liversedge (8–3) and St Dominics (6–1), although the Lancashire side had to rely on a Stewart Procter penalty over Diadora Division Three outfit Chertsey Town, before their place in the last four was secure.

In the first leg against Wimborne at Bamber's Irongate ground, the two sides battled courageously for 90 minutes, but were unable to break the deadlock. Another goalless stalemate seemed possible in the return at Wimborne, until the 37th minute when home striker and former Aston Villa and Hereford player Trevor Ames popped up to give his side a 1–0 lead. Despite a fightback of titanic proportions, in which Bamber came desperately close to clinching the equaliser they craved, it was Wimborne who again found the target, with Ames securing their first-ever Wembley appearance with a second goal ten minutes from time.

SEMI–FINAL First leg   21 March 1992

Att				Result
2020	Bamber Bridge	v	Wimborne Town	0–0
2142	Guiseley	v	Sudbury Town	2–2

Second leg   28 March 1992

2819	Wimborne Town	v	Bamber Bridge	2–0
2987	Sudbury Town	v	Guiseley	1–3

(Wimborne Town won 2–0, Guiseley 5–3 on aggregate)

FINAL   25 April 1992

Wembley Stadium

10772	Wimborne Town	v	Guiseley	5–3

History of the FA Vase

After the demise of the FA Amateur Cup in 1974 and the disappearance of amateur and professional guidelines, the smaller amateur clubs found they had no trophy to compete for.

With the top amateur sides entering the FA Trophy, the FA Vase was formed. Organised as a straight knock-out competition on a national basis, culminating in a Wembley final, the Vase accommodated clubs in the feeder leagues to what are now the Beazer Homes, HFS Loans and Diadora Leagues.

Subsequently clubs from even lower leagues have gained admittance to the FA Vase, although they are usually teams who can provide satisfactory ground facilities and are regularly at, or near, the top of their leagues.

Hoddesdon Town were the first winners of the Vase when they overcame Epsom & Ewell 2–1 in front of 10,000 enthusiastic supporters in 1975. The following season Billericay Town clinched the first of what was to become three FA Vase triumphs in four years, when they disposed of Stamford 1–0. Only Newcastle Blue Star were able to break the Essex stranglehold on the competition when they beat Barton Rovers in 1978, but the balance of power did eventually shift northwards during the mid 1980s when Halesowen Town reached Wembley three times in four years, winning the competition in 1985 and 1986.

More recently only Yeading have been able to interrupt a succession of northern winners, with their 1–0 defeat of Bridlington Town in a replay in 1990. And in 1989 Tamworth and Sudbury Town set an attendance record of 26,487, before the Midlands side won 3–0 in a replay.

FA Vase Final 1975

Hoddesdon Town 2 Epsom & Ewell 1

The Hertfordshire town of Hoddesdon was virtually deserted on Saturday 19 April 1975 as most of its inhabitants made the modest pilgrimage to Wembley for the inaugural final of the first FA Vase.

For the Lilywhites and their manager Billy Moye, that day was the culmination of a sequence of tenacious Cup performances and victories at the expense of some unlikely casualties.

Farnborough Town, Basildon United, Baldock Town and Billericay Town, whose FA Vase ambitions would be realised the following year, all lay littered in Hoddesdon's wake as the Lilywhites prepared to meet Epsom & Ewell from the Surrey Senior League.

Epsom's player/manager Pat O'Connell had played on over 200 occasions for Fulham and, against a Hoddesdon side whose main source of supply was local football, he could boast a side that included an assortment of former League players and Surrey Juniors.

But in keeping with the true romance of any cup competition, it was the underdogs, Hoddesdon, who rose to the occasion. Striker Dickie Sedgewick scored twice to put Hoddesdon 2–0 in front, and despite a late flurry from Epsom which produced a consolation goal from Wales, there was little doubt about the eventual outcome of the match.

FA VASE WINNERS

Year/venue	Winner		Runner-up	Result
1975 Wembley	Hoddesdon Town	v	Epsom & Ewell	2–1
1976 Wembley	Billericay Town	v	Stamford	1–0*
1977 Wembley	Billericay Town	v	Sheffield	1–1*
Nottingham	Billericay Town	v	Sheffield	2–1
1978 Wembley	Blue Star	v	Barton Rovers	2–1
1979 Wembley	Billericay Town	v	Almondsbury Greenway	4–1
1980 Wembley	Stamford	v	Guisborough Town	2–0
1981 Wembley	Whickham	v	Willenhall Town	3–2*
1982 Wembley	Forest Green Rovers	v	Rainworth Miners' Welfare	3–0
1983 Wembley	VS Rugby	v	Halesowen Town	1–0
1984 Wembley	Stansted	v	Stamford	3–2
1985 Wembley	Halesowen Town	v	Fleetwood Town	3–1
1986 Wembley	Halesowen Town	v	Southall	3–0
1987 Wembley	St Helens Town	v	Warrington Town	3–2
1988 Wembley	Colne Dynamos	v	Emley	1–0*
1989 Wembley	Tamworth	v	Sudbury Town	1–1*
Peterborough	Tamworth	v	Sudbury Town	3–0
1990 Wembley	Yeading	v	Bridlington Town	0–0*
Leeds	Yeading	v	Bridlington Town	1–0
1991 Wembley	Guiseley	v	Gresley Rovers	4–4*
Sheffield	Guiseley	v	Gresley Rovers	3–1
1992 Wembley	Wimborne Town	v	Guiseley	5–3

* after extra time

183

CHAPTER SIX

The FA Charity Shield

The FA Charity Shield is now the traditional curtain-raiser to the season. It was introduced in 1908 and now pits the FA Cup winners against the League champions. That was not always the case. In the 1920s there was an equivalent of cricket's 'Gentlemen v Players' when the 'Professionals' met the 'Amateurs'. In 1950 the fixture was taken on by the England World Cup team, just returned from Brazil. They played and beat a Canadian touring team 4–2.

When teams have won the 'double' (Tottenham in 1961, Arsenal in 1971 and Liverpool in 1986) there have been variations on the League champions v Cup winners theme.

In 1961 Tottenham played and beat an FA XI; Arsenal did not compete in 1971 (there was a three-year period when neither the Cup winners not the League champions took part); and in 1986 Liverpool played Everton who had finished second in the League and were beaten FA Cup finalists.

In his first year as FA secretary Ted Croker moved the fixture to Wembley Stadium and in that first Wembley match in 1974 the game was decided on penalty-kicks – the first and only time that has happened. In every other drawn game the two clubs have shared the trophy, holding it for six months each. The only replay was in the first year, after Manchester United had drawn 1–1 with Queen's Park Rangers. United won the replay 4–0.

FA CHARITY SHIELD WINNERS

Year	Winner		Runner-up	Result
1908	Manchester United	v	Queen's Park Rangers	1–1
	Manchester United	v	*Queen's Park Rangers*	*4–0*
1909	Newcastle United	v	Northampton Town	2–0
1910	Brighton	v	Aston Villa	1–0
1911	Manchester United	v	Swindon	8–4
1912	Blackburn	v	Queen's Park Rangers	2–1
1913	Professionals	v	Amateurs	7–2
1914-19		not played		
1920	West Bromwich Albion	v	Tottenham Hotspur	2–0
1921	Tottenham Hotspur	v	Burnley	2–0
1922	Huddersfield	v	Liverpool	1–0
1923	Professionals	v	Amateurs	2–0
1924	Professionals	v	Amateurs	3–1
1925	Amateurs	v	Professionals	6–1
1926	Amateurs	v	Professionals	6–3
1927	Cardiff	v	Corinthians	2–1
1928	Everton	v	Blackburn	2–1
1929	Professionals	v	Amateurs	3–0
1930	Arsenal	v	Sheffield Wednesday	2–1
1931	Arsenal	v	West Bromwich Albion	1–0
1932	Everton	v	Newcastle United	5–3
1933	Arsenal	v	Everton	3–0
1934	Arsenal	v	Manchester City	4–0
1935	Sheffield Wednesday	v	Arsenal	1–0
1936	Sunderland	v	Arsenal	2–1
1937	Manchester City	v	Sunderland	2–0
1938	Arsenal	v	Preston North End	2–1
1939-47		not played		
1948	Arsenal	v	Manchester United	4–3
1949	Portsmouth	v	Wolverhampton Wanderers	1–1
1950	World Cup XI	v	Canadian Touring Team	4–2
1951	Tottenham Hotspur	v	Newcastle United	2–1
1952	Manchester United	v	Newcastle United	4–2
1953	Arsenal	v	Blackpool	3–1
1954	Wolverhampton Wanderers	v	West Bromwich Albion	4–4
1955	Chelsea	v	Newcastle United	3–0
1956	Manchester United	v	Manchester City	1–0
1957	Manchester United	v	Aston Villa	4–0
1958	Bolton	v	Wolverhampton Wanderers	4–1
1959	Wolverhampton Wanderers	v	Nottingham Forest	3–1
1960	Burnley	v	Wolverhampton Wanderers	2–2
1961	Tottenham Hotspur	v	FA XI	3–2
1962	Tottenham Hotspur	v	Ipswich Town	5–1
1963	Everton	v	Manchester United	4–0
1964	Liverpool	v	West Ham United	2–2
1965	Manchester United	v	Liverpool	2–2
1966	Liverpool	v	Everton	1–0
1967	Manchester United	v	Tottenham Hotspur	3–3
1968	Manchester City	v	West Bromwich Albion	6–1
1969	Leeds United	v	Manchester City	2–1

Year	Winner		Runner-up	Result
1970	Everton	v	Chelsea	2–1
1971	Leicester City	v	Liverpool	1–0
1972	Manchester City	v	Aston Villa	1–0
1973	Burnley	v	Manchester City	1–0
1974	Liverpool	v	Leeds United	2–1**
1975	Derby County	v	West Ham United	2–0
1976	Liverpool	v	Southampton	1–0
1977	Liverpool	v	Manchester United	0–0
1978	Nottingham Forest	v	Ipswich Town	5–0
1979	Liverpool	v	Arsenal	3–1
1980	Liverpool	v	West Ham United	1–0
1981	Aston Villa	v	Tottenham Hotspur	2–2
1982	Liverpool	v	Tottenham Hotspur	1–0
1983	Manchester United	v	Liverpool	2–0
1984	Everton	v	Liverpool	1–0
1985	Everton	v	Manchester United	2–0
1986	Everton	v	Liverpool	1–1
1987	Everton	v	Coventry City	1–0
1988	Liverpool	v	Wimbledon	2–1
1989	Liverpool	v	Arsenal	1–0
1990	Liverpool	v	Manchester United	1–1
1991	Arsenal	v	Tottenham Hotspur	0–0

** *match won on penalties*

FA Charity Shield 1991

Arsenal 0 Tottenham Hotspur 0

When Arsenal arrived at Wembley Stadium in August 1991 to contest the annual Tennents FA Charity Shield game, against Tottenham, they came with the determination to wipe out memories of the FA Cup semi-final defeat in April which effectively cost the Gunners the coveted League and Cup 'double'.

Both Arsenal and Tottenham have achieved the 'double'. Arsenal did it under Bertie Mee in 1971, while Spurs achieved the feat under Bill Nicholson ten years earlier.

Having won the League for the second time in three seasons Arsenal fancied their chances in the FA Cup semi-final, but a Paul Gascoigne-inspired performance meant that it was Tottenham and not Arsenal who would progress to a final meeting with Brian Clough's Nottingham Forest.

Spurs won the Cup, qualified for the European Cup Winners' Cup and won the right to contest the Charity Shield with their north London rivals.

Top: Arsenal and Spurs line-up with the Charity Shield

Nayim tackles Arsenal's Alan Smith

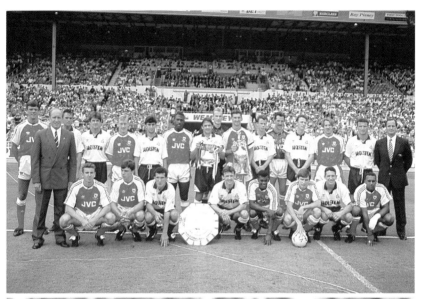

They came to Wembley without Gascoigne, whose early injury during the Cup Final victory over Forest had proved to be a serious one, delaying, for the time being, a multi-million-pound move to Lazio of Italy.

Spurs, involved in a massively busy pre-season programme, elected to use Vinny Samways in Gascoigne's midfield role, although Gascoigne gave a tantalising display when he took a tentative part in the pre-match warm-up.

Arsenal, too, were without one of their more colourful characters. Anders Limpar, the dashing winger, had been injured playing for Sweden in an international, so the Charity Shield game had been robbed of two of its potentially most exciting match-winners.

That, however, did not stop Arsenal from being determined to put behind them the semi-final defeat, and the game, while often dour, was always competitive.

Both sides had chances to sneak a win, with Arsenal coming closest when Paul Davis set up Kevin Campbell for a shot that he wasted. Alan Smith actually got the ball in the net but was judged offside.

Spurs – who left Wembley immediately after the game to play in a prestigious four-team tournament involving Juventus in Italy – decided to continue their experiment with a 4–5–1 formation in which Gary Lineker was used as a lone striker very much in the way Clive Allen had been deployed a few seasons earlier when he scored 49 goals.

Lineker's chances were limited on the day and the game, not surprisingly, ended in a goalless draw with the two teams left to argue as to who would hold the Shield for the first six months.

Peter Shreeves, newly installed as the Tottenham manager, declared himself satisfied with the performance and then left for Italy.

George Graham, the Arsenal manager, was also satisfied with the work-out considering the heat. 'I have been very happy with the build-up,' he said. 'Now we are ready.'

It was only the second time in history that the Charity Shield had ended in a goalless draw. The other occasion was the 1977 match between Manchester United and Liverpool.

Arsenal Seaman, Dixon, Winterburn, Hillier, O'Leary, Adams, Rocastle (Thomas), Davis, Smith, Merson, Campbell (Cole). Subs not used: Linighan, Jonsson, Miller.

Tottenham Hotspur Thorstvedt, Fenwick, Van den Hauwe, Sedgley, Howells, Mabbutt, Stewart, Nayim, Samways, Lineker, Allen. Subs not used: Walsh, Bergsson, Edinburgh, Hendon, Walker.

Att 65,483   *Referee* T Holbrook (Staffordshire).

CHAPTER SEVEN

Other FA Competitions

FA SUNDAY CUP FINAL 1992

Theale 3   Marston Sports 2

The twenty-eighth FA Sunday Cup Final was a contest between Theale, just outside Reading, the first-ever Berkshire finalists in the competition, and Marston Sports from the West Midlands, who had experienced the bitter-sweet taste of defeat in the 1990 final.

Theale, who had just won the Reading & District Sunday League Senior Division title for a third successive year, had previously never progressed further than the third round. But with a squad bulging with young talent, as well as a handful of semi-professional footballers from Diadora Premier Division champions Woking, they had suffered just one defeat all season, a 3–1 reverse at the hands of Dee Road Rangers in the Berks & Bucks Intermediate Cup.

Roared on by the largely partisan 2427 crowd assembled at Reading's Elm Park Stadium for the cup final clash, the prospect of a popular local victory seemed high. But their opponents from the Wolverhampton Sunday League had other ideas. Despite the disappointment of defeat against Sunderland side Humbledon Plains Farm two years before, Marston could rely on the playing experience of former Hereford striker Ian Wells, as well as a host of players drawn from West Midland teams such as Atherstone, Bromsgrove, Stourbridge and Alcester. Fresh from their Wolverhampton Charity Cup success of the week before, the Sunday Cup Final promised to provide an intriguing collision of interests.

Marston opened the contest with the better football, immediately carving through the tentative Theale defence to create early chances for Mick Osborne, Evron Wright and Neil Morgan. But thanks to the timely interventions of Theale keeper Andy Howell the scores remained goalless until the 31st minute, when a rare Theale raid into Marston territory wrought a surprise lead for the Berkshire side.

Andy Parr and Noel Newton were the instigators of the move which released Parr down the left flank. The Theale skipper (and Woking midfield dynamo) cut into the penalty area, only to be scythed unceremoniously to the ground by John Horne. Referee Gallagher from the Oxfordshire FA had no alternative but to point to the penalty spot.

Parr promptly picked himself gingerly off the turf and sent Marston keeper Kevin Williams the wrong way, to give Theale a 1–0 lead.

But the ecstatic celebrations of the local supporters were relatively short-lived, as Marston responded with a 10-minute spell of intense pressure which eventually produced an equaliser. A move down the left saw Wright skip away from the challenge of Steve Dale and race un-opposed into the area before tumbling headlong under the clumsy challenge of full-back Jamie Murray. Mr Gallagher again had little option but to award a penalty. David Wells stepped up to take the spot-kick which he drove with almighty power straight at Howell, and although the Theale keeper made a spectacular attempt to palm the shot away, the ball ricocheted onto the crossbar and drifted into the net to make it 1–1 with just a minute of the half to go.

After the break as the crowd lapped up the warm sunshine of a glorious early May afternoon, it was Marston who began to look more capable of lifting the trophy, as they swarmed through a congested mid-field and began to unsettle the Theale defence. Ian Wells and Jim Skid-more sent headers spinning just wide of both posts before the Midlands side took the lead with a goal of bizarre proportions.

There seemed little danger as Parr, Theale's man-of-the-match, col-lected a miscued cross in his own penalty area, and shaped to clear upfield. But as Parr delayed, Marston midfielder Clive Walker sprinted forward to try and block his clearance and succeeded in deflecting Parr's pass back past the surprised keeper and into the net.

As Marston rejoiced there seemed precious little time for the local side to recover from such a numbing blow. There were just 13 minutes left on the watch and the Theale attack had offered little evidence during the second half, to suggest that they would be capable of forcing the game even to extra-time. However three minutes later they were level. Newton embarked on a mazy burst down the left flank before con-juring an exquisite centre for substitute Dave Eales to dispatch past Williams at the far post with a glorious looping header.

As the Berkshire legions exploded into song, there was scarcely time to draw breath before Theale's delirious fans were celebrating yet another goal. Murray, the man whose earlier indiscretion had allowed Marston to equalise at the end of the first half, started the move on the right when he powered in a low, skidding centre for Dale. His flick deceived the Marston defence and Graham Hambridge timed his run to perfection, arriving just in time to rifle an unstoppable drive past Williams.

As Marston reeled, Theale could almost have made it 4–2 a minute later on 85 minutes when Paul Mulvaney, another player who had en-joyed part of Woking's remarkable season, saw his shot spectacularly blocked by Williams, as the Marston defence disintegrated.

Theale, winners of the 1992 FA Sunday Cup

Marston threw on substitutes Roy Green and Dave Trend, and but for a brilliant reflex save from Howell at the feet of Green, the outcome of the cup could have been very different, but as it was, Theale held on to lift the FA Sunday Cup for the first time in their history and emerge triumphant from the cluster of 106 expectant clubs who had first entered the competition back in the autumn of 1991.

Theale Howell, Murray, Cox, Ferguson, Webb, Hambridge, Dale, Parr, Cook (Eales 68), Newton, Mulvaney. Sub not used: Wylie.

Marston Sports Williams, Walton, D. Wells, Horne, Skidmore, Walker, Astley (Trend 87), Morgan (Green 81), Osborne, Wright, I. Wells.

Att 2427 *Referee* D J. Gallagher (Oxfordshire).

FA Sunday Cup 1991-92

FIRST ROUND   13 October 1991

(replays in italics)   Result

Queens Arms	v	Nenthead	0–4
Dudley & Weetslade	v	Blyth Waterloo SC	3–2
Mayfield United	v	Stanton Dale	1–4
Lobster	v	Whetley Lane	4–0
Carlisle United	v	Iron Bridge	2–4
Lynemouth	v	Croxteth & Gilmoss RBL	0–4

Framwellgate Moor & Pity Me	v	Woodlands 84	7–1
Seymour	v	Hartlepool Lion Hotel	3–5*
Western Approaches	v	Railway Hotel	2–1
Bolton Woods	v	Oakenshaw	2–2*
Bolton Woods	v	*Oakenshaw*	*0–2*
Littlewoods	v	B & A Scaffolding	2–3
Almithak	v	AC Sparks	3–2
Netherley RBL	v	East Bowling Unity	1–1
Netherley RBL	v	*East Bowling Unity*	*3–3*
Netherley RBL	v	*East Bowling Unity*	*2–3*
Hare	v	Clubmoor Nalgo	2–2
Hare	v	*Clubmoor Nalgo*	*2–3*
Carnforth	v	Britannia VNC	2–1
BRNECSC	v	Blue Union	1–3
Baildon Athletic	v	FC Coachman	1–3
Jolly Farmers	v	Dock	2–2
Jolly Farmers	v	*Dock*	*2–1*
Radford Park Rangers	v	Bricklayers Sports	4–5*
Altone Steel	v	Birmingham Celtic	4–0
Kenwick Dynamo	v	Brookvale Athletic	1–2
Ansells Stockland Star	v	AD Bulwell	0–2
Dereham Hobbies Sunday	v	Shouldham Sunday	0–1
Girton Eagles	v	Watford Labour Club	1–4
Sawston Keys	v	Gamlingay OBs	3–0
Inter Volante	v	Cork & Bottle	3–1†
Boreham Wood Royals	v	Chequers	1–2
Chapel United	v	Evergreen	2–4*
Old Paludians	v	Broad Plain House	0–5
Sandwell	v	Olympic Star	2–0
St Josephs (S Oxley)	v	BRSC Aidan	2–1*
Theale	v	Northfield Rangers	1–0
Hanham Sunday	v	Bedfont Sunday	2–1
Phoenix	v	Lebeq Tavern	1–2
Bishopstoke AFC	v	Santogee 66	2–3*
Sarton United	v	Somerset Ambury V & E	1–0
Inter Royalle	v	Rolls Royce (Sunday)	2–0
Continental	v	Concord Rangers	0–0
Continental	v	*Concord Rangers*	*1–2*
Priory Sports	v	Fryerns Community	2–1
Oxford Road Social	v	St Clements Hospital	0–3
Chesterfield Park	v	Rob Roy	††

* *after extra time*
† *Inter Volante expelled for fielding ineligible player*
†† *walkover for Chesterfield Park, Rob Roy withdrawn from competition*

SECOND ROUND   10 November 1991

B & A Scaffolding	v Green Man 88	3–0
Almithak	v Lobster	5–4*
Avenue Victoria Lodge	v A3	0–1
Eagle-Knowsley	v Clubmoor Nalgo	4–1
Nenthead	v Northwood	0–1
Hartlepool Lion Hotel	v Carnforth	1–0
Jolly Farmers	v FC Coachman	†
Blue Union	v East Levenshulme	2–2
East Levenshulme	v *Blue Union*	*2–3*
Framwellgate Moor & Pity Me	v Dudley & Weetslade	2–0
Western Approaches	v Oakenshaw	2–3
Toshiba Sharples	v Stanton Dale	1–1
Stanton Dale	v *Toshiba Sharples*	*5–4*
Humbledon Plains Farm	v Croxteth & Gilmoss RBL	2–0
Iron Bridge	v Chesterfield Park	3–0
Nicosia	v East Bowling Unity	1–1
East Bowling Unity	v *Nicosia*	*1–2*
Poringland Wanderers	v Marston Sports	2–4
A D Bulwell	v Brookvale Athletic	1–2*
Sawston Keys	v Bournville Wanderers	3–2
Cork & Bottle	v Lodge Cottrell	0–1
Slade Celtic	v Priory Sports	2–2
Priory Sports	v *Slade Celtic*	*2–1*
Ford Basildon	v Shouldham Sunday	2–1
St Clements Hospital	v Chequers	0–1
Watford Labour Club	v Sandwell	1–4
Bricklayers Sports	v Brerton Town	3–2
Altone Steels	v St Josephs (Luton)	0–1
Ranelagh Sports	v Evergreen	2–0
Sartan United	v St Josephs (S Oxley)	1–0
Ouzavich	v Leyton Argyle	3–2
Lee Chapel North	v Concord Rangers	2–1
Theale	v Lebeq Tavern	3–0
Broad Plain House	v Inter Royalle	2–0
Reading Borough	v Hanham Sunday	1–2
Colliers Row Supporters	v Santogee 66	2–1

* *after extra time*
† *walkover for FC Coachman, Jolly Farmers expelled for playing 2 contract players in previous round*

THIRD ROUND   8 December 1991

Stanton Dale	v A3	1–2
Iron Bridge	v Humbledon Plains Farm	2–0
FC Coachman	v Framwellgate Moor & Pity Me	4–3
Marston Sports	v B & A Scaffolding	1–0*
Hartlepool Lion Hotel	v Almithak	3–2
Northwood	v Oakenshaw	2–2

			Result
Oakenshaw	v	*Northwood*	*3–2*
Nicosia	v	Bricklayers Sports	0–1
Blue Union	v	Eagle-Knowsley	0–1
Ouzavich	v	Lodge Cottrell	0–2
Theale	v	Lee Chapel North	3–2
Sandwell	v	Ranelagh Sports	1–4
Colliers Row Supporters	v	Brookvale Ath	1–2*
Chequers	v	Sawston Keys	2–1*
Ford Basildon	v	Sartan United	1–0
Broad Plain House	v	Hanham Sunday	0–3
St Josephs (Luton)	v	Priory Sports	5–1

FOURTH ROUND   19 January 1992

			Result
Oakenshaw	v	FC Coachman	2–1
Marston Sports	v	Hartlepool Lion Hotel	5–3
Iron Bridge	v	Bricklayers Sports	0–2
A3	v	Eagle-Knowsley	2–1*
Chequers	v	Theale	2–3
St Josephs (Luton)	v	Brookvale Athletic	1–0*
Ranelagh Sports	v	Hanham Sunday	2–0
Lodge Cottrell	v	Ford Basildon	3–0

FIFTH ROUND   16 February 1992

(replays in italics)   Result

Marston Sports	v	Bricklayers Sports	2–1
A3	v	Oakenshaw	1–1
Oakenshaw	v	*A3*	*1–1*
A3	v	*Oakenshaw*	*0–2*
Lodge Cottrell	v	Ranelagh Sports	3–0
Theale	v	St Josephs (Luton)	2–0

SEMI-FINAL   22 March 1992

(replays in italics)   Result

Lodge Cottrell	v	Marston Sports	0–1
at Moor Green			
Theale	v	Oakenshaw	2–2*
at Wokingham Town			
Oakenshaw	v	*Theale*	*0–2*
at Thackley			

FINAL   3 May 1992 (at Reading)

			Result
Theale	v	Marston Sports	3–2

* *after extra time*

194

FA SUNDAY CUP WINNERS

Year/venue	Winner		Runner-up	Result
1965	London	v	Staffordshire	6–2†
1966 Dudley	Unique United	v	Aldridge Fabrications	1–0
1967 Hendon	Carlton United	v	Stoke Works	2–0
1968 Cambridge	Drovers	v	Brook United	2–0
1969 Romford	Leigh Park	v	Loke United	3–1
1970 Corby	Vention United	v	Unique United	1–0
1971 Leamington	Beacontree Rovers	v	Saltley United	2–0
1972 Dudley	Newton Unity	v	Springfield Colts	4–0
1973 Spennymoor	Carlton United	v	Wear Valley	2–1*
1974 Birmingham	Newton Unity	v	Brentford East	3–0
1975 High Wycombe	Fareham Town Centipedes	v	Players Athletic Engineers	1–0
1976 Spennymoor	Brandon United	v	Evergreen	2–1
1977 Spennymoor	Langley Park RH	v	Newton Unity	2–0
1978 Nuneaton	Arras	v	Lion Rangers	2–2
Bishop's Stortford	Arras	v	Lion Rangers	2–1
1979 Southport	Lobster	v	Carlton United	3–2
1980 Letchworth	Fantail	v	Twin Foxes	1–0
1981 Birkenhead	Fantail	v	Mackintosh	1–0
1982 Hitchin	Dingle Rail	v	Twin Foxes	2–1
1983 Walthamstow	Eagle	v	Lee Chapel North	2–1
1984 Runcorn	Lee Chapel North	v	Eagle	1–1
Dagenham	Lee Chapel North	v	Eagle	4–3*
1985 Norwich	Hobbies	v	Avenue	1–1
Birkenhead	Hobbies	v	Avenue	2–2
Nuneaton	Hobbies	v	Avenue	2–1
1986 Birkenhead	Avenue	v	Glenn Sports	1–0
1987 Birmingham	Lodge Cottrell	v	Avenue	1–0*
1988 Newcastle	Nexday	v	Sunderland Humb Plains	2–0
1989 Stockport	Almethak	v	East Levenshulme	3–1
1990 West Bromwich	Humbledon Plains Farm	v	Marston Sports	2–1
1991 Wigan	Nicosia	v	Ouzavich	3–2*
1992 Reading	Theale	v	Marston Sports	3–2

* after extra time
† two legs

History of the FA Sunday Cup

Back in the early days of the 1950s, when the nation thrilled to the talents of the likes of Matthews, Lofthouse and Wright, it still seemed inconceivable that The Football Association would ever sanction the introduction of Sunday football.

The Sabbath, they insisted, should be kept as a day of religious reflection and worship. As a result, Saturday afternoon football fans were forced to ponder in quiet solitude the feats of their heroes on the football pitches of England the previous day, rather than attempting to emulate them. But moods gradually changed and in 1955 the FA did relent and allow member clubs to take part in organised football on a Sunday. However there was still no indication that any sort of League football would be installed, but the FA was to alter course once more on this issue and allow the affiliation of Sunday Leagues in 1960.

The FA Sunday Cup finally arrived in 1964, the competition that Sunday football had been waiting for. The first final was contested between County Associations, London and Staffordshire, with London running out 6–2 winners over two legs in the spring of 1965. The competition was then thrown open to Sunday clubs and ever since the 1–0 victory for Unique United over Aldridge Fabrications at Dudley in 1966, the competition has grown steadily, with the FA constantly promoting the merits of the cup amongst its 40,000 member clubs.

Despite the problem of a lack in continuity of membership, with a great deal of clubs folding after a relatively short lifespan, the competition continues to serve its initial purpose – providing Sunday League football clubs with the chance to compete nationally against teams of similar stature and quality. In the competition's previous 27 finals, only three clubs have ever won the cup more than once, with Carlton United (1967, 1973), Newtown Unity (1972, 1974) and Fantail (1980, 1981) all winning twice.

The main requirements for entry to the Sunday Cup are that each club participate in the Premier Division of their Sunday League, and that they have the use of a ground that meets FA Vase requirements. In addition they must be able to prove that they can finance a lengthy run in the competition, which can be quite expensive.

FA County Youth Cup 1991-92

FIRST ROUND   5-19 October 1991

(replays in italics)   *Result*

Cheshire	v	Derbyshire	2–3
Devon	v	Somerset & Avon	1–0
Northumberland	v	Cumberland	3–1
Oxfordshire	v	Bedfordshire	4–1
Army	v	Sussex	1–7
Berks & Bucks	v	Kent	5–1
Birmingham	v	Northamptonshire	8–0
Cambridgeshire	v	Suffolk	4–5
East Riding	v	Durham	0–0
Durham	v	*East Riding*	*1–0*
Essex	v	Norfolk	3–2
Gloucestershire	v	Cornwall	0–2
Manchester	v	North Riding	2–3
Worcestershire	v	Staffordshire	1–3

SECOND ROUND   2-30 November 1991

Westmorland	v	Lancashire	2–3*
Hampshire	v	Devon	1–2
Nottinghamshire	v	Staffordshire	4–1
Royal Navy	v	Berks & Bucks	0–2
Shropshire	v	Derbyshire	1–2
Middlesex	v	Oxfordshire	0–3
Sheffield & Hallamshire	v	Durham	3–1
West Riding	v	Northumberland	4–3*
Dorset	v	Cornwall	1–0
Herefordshire	v	Birmingham	0–7
Hertfordshire	v	Essex	0–1
Lincolnshire	v	Leicestershire & Rutland	1–3
Liverpool	v	North Riding	1–1
North Riding	v	*Liverpool*	*1–2*
Surrey	v	Huntingdonshire	3–1
Wiltshire	v	Sussex	1–3
London	v	Suffolk	3–4*

THIRD ROUND   14 December 1991 - 18 January 1992

Result

Sussex	v	Devon	1–5
Nottinghamshire	v	Leicestershire & Rutland	4–3*
Berks & Bucks	v	Dorset	2–0
Derbyshire	v	Birmingham	3–3
Birmingham	v	*Derbyshire*	*1–3*
Essex	v	Oxfordshire	2–1
Lancashire	v	Liverpool	2–0
Suffolk	v	Surrey	3–3
Surrey	v	*Suffolk*	*2–1**
West Riding	v	Sheffield & Hallamshire	4–2

FOURTH ROUND   8-15 February 1992

Result

Devon	v	Surrey	0–3
Essex	v	Berks & Bucks	3–1
Lancashire	v	Derbyshire	1–0
Nottinghamshire	v	West Riding	3–2

SEMI–FINAL   7-14 March 1992

Result

Nottinghamshire	v	Essex	2–1
Lancashire	v	Surrey	3–4

FINAL   2 May 1992 (at Woking)

Surrey	v	Nottinghamshire	0–1

* after extra time

FA COUNTY YOUTH CUP WINNERS

From 1945 to 1969 the FA County Youth Cup final was played over two legs. Since 1970 it has been a straight final and only twice (in 1988 and 1990) has a replay been required.

Year				Result
1945	Staffordshire	v	Wiltshire	3–2
1946	Berks & Bucks	v	Durham	4–3
1947	Durham	v	Essex	4–2
1948	Essex	v	Liverpool	5–3
1949	Liverpool	v	Middlesex	4–3
1950	Essex	v	Middlesex	4–3
1951	Middlesex	v	Leicestershire & Rutland	3–1
1952	Sussex	v	Liverpool	3–1
1953	Sheffield & Hallam	v	Hampshire	5–3
1954	Liverpool	v	Gloucestershire	4–1
1955	Bedfordshire	v	Sheffield & Hallam	2–0
1956	Middlesex	v	Staffordshire	3–2
1957	Hampshire	v	Cheshire	4–3
1958	Staffordshire	v	London	8–0
1959	Birmingham	v	London	7–5
1960	London	v	Birmingham	6–4
1961	Lancashire	v	Nottinghamshire	6–3
1962	Middlesex	v	Nottinghamshire	6–3
1963	Durham	v	Essex	3–2
1964	Sheffield & Hallam	v	Birmingham	1–0
1965	Northumberland	v	Middlesex	7–4
1966	Leicestershire & Rutland	v	London	6–5
1967	Northamptonshire	v	Herts	5–4
1968	North Riding	v	Devon	7–4
1969	Northumberland	v	Sussex	1–0
1970	Herts	v	Cheshire	2–1
1971	Lancashire	v	Gloucestershire	2–0
1972	Middlesex	v	Liverpool	2–0
1973	Herts	v	Northumberland	3–0
1974	Nottinghamshire	v	London	2–0
1975	Durham	v	Bedfordshire	2–1
1976	Northamptonshire	v	Surrey	7–1
1977	Liverpool	v	Surrey	3–0
1978	Liverpool	v	Kent	3–1
1979	Herts	v	Liverpool	4–1
1980	Liverpool	v	Lancashire	2–0
1981	Lancashire	v	East Riding	3–1
1982	Devon	v	Kent	3–2*
1983	London	v	Gloucestershire	3–0
1984	Cheshire	v	Manchester	2–1
1985	East Riding	v	Middlesex	2–1
1986	Herts	v	Manchester	4–0
1987	North Riding	v	Gloucestershire	3–1
1988	East Riding	v	Middlesex	1–1
	East Riding	v	*Middlesex*	*5–3*
1989	Liverpool	v	Herts	2–1
1990	Staffordshire	v	Hampshire	1–1
	Staffordshire	v	*Hampshire*	*2–1*
1991	Lancashire	v	Surrey	6–0
1992	Nottinghamshire	v	Surrey	1–0

* *after extra time*

198

FA Representative and Semi-Professional Matches 1991-92

5 November 1991
FA XI beat British Students 2–1.
Paul Davies, from Kidderminster Harriers, scored both goals.
The match was played at Bromsgrove Rovers.
FA XI   Ron Green (*Kidderminster Harriers*), Kevin Willetts (*Cheltenham Town*), Stewart Brighton (*Bromsgrove Rovers*), David Barnett (*Kidderminster Harriers*), Chris Brindley (*Telford United*), Steve Stott (*Bromsgrove Rovers*), Ian Taylor (*Moor Green*), Peter Howell (*Kidderminster Harriers*), Mark Whitehouse (*Kidderminster Harriers*), Stephen Lilwall (*Kidderminster Harriers*), Delwyn Humphreys (*Kidderminster Harriers*). *Subs* Darren Acton (*Telford United*) for Green, Martin Weir (*Kidderminster Harriers*) for Barnett, Paul Davies (*Kidderminster Harriers*) for Whitehouse, Craig Gillett (*Kidderminster Harriers*) for Lilwall.

19 November 1991
FA XI lost to Northern Premier League 1–3.
Malcolm O'Connor, from Northwich Victoria, scored.
The match was played at Marine.
FA XI   Stephen Farrelly (*Macclesfield Town*), Andy Lee (*Altrincham*), Tony Chilton (*Barrow*), Stephen McNeilis (*Witton Albion*), Mark Hancock (*Northwich Victoria*), Stuart Anderson (*Witton Albion*), Malcolm O'Connor (*Northwich Victoria*), Gary Anderson (*Altrincham*), Karl Thomas (*Witton Albion*), Ken McKenna (*Altrincham*), Steve Hanlon (*Macclesfield Town*). *Sub:* Paul Rowlands (*Altrincham*) for Hancock. *Other Subs* Steve Berryman (*Altrincham*), Nicky Daws (*Altrincham*).

21 January 1992
FA XI drew with Combined Services 1–1 (match abandoned after 60 minutes due to bad weather).
Nick Tilly, from Matlock Town, scored.
The match was played at Ossett Albion.
FA XI   Ryan Price (*Stafford Rangers*), Paul Shirtliff (*Boston United*), Paul Watson (*Gainsborough Trinity*), Wayne Simpson (*Stafford Rangers*), Paul Nicol (*Kettering Town*), Martin Hardy (*Boston United*), Nick Tilly (*Matlock Town*), Paul Richardson (*Redbridge Forest*), Paul Cavell (*Redbridge Forest*), Phil Brown (*Kettering Town*), Paul Devlin (*Stafford Rangers*). *Subs* Mick Farrar (*Emley*) for Watson, Brown for Tilly, Gary Jones (*Boston United*) for Brown.

FA XI beat Isthmian League 7–1.

Gary Abbott from Welling United, scored five goals; Colin Fielder, from Slough Town, scored once; and Simon Reade, from Farnborough Town, also scored.

The match was played at Aylesbury.

FA XI   Paul Hyde (*Wycombe Wanderers*), Mark Hone (*Welling United*), Steve Connor (*Redbridge Forest*), Glyn Creaser (*Wycombe Wanderers*), Paul Watts (*Redbridge Forest*), Robert Mayes (*Redbridge Forest*), Colin Fielder (*Slough Town*), Mark Golley (*Welling United*), Steve Guppy (*Wycombe Wanderers*), Gary Abbott (*Welling United*), Simon Reade (*Farnborough Town*). *Subs* John Power (*Farnborough Town*) for Hyde, Terry Robbins (*Welling United*) for Hone, David Jacques (*Redbridge Forest*) for Golley, Reade for Abbott, Jason Cousins (*Wycombe Wanderers*) for Reade.

3 March 1992

England Semi-professional team beat Wales 1–0.

Bobby Mayes, from Redbridge Forest, scored the goal.

The match was played at Aberystwyth.

ENGLAND   John McKenna (*Boston United*), Paul Shirtliff (*Boston United*), Paul Watts (*Redbridge Forest*), Paul Nicol (*Kettering Town*), Steve Connor (*Redbridge Forest*), Delwyn Humphreys (*Kidderminster Harriers*), Paul Richardson (*Redbridge Forest*), Mark Golley (*Welling United*), Bobby Mayes (*Redbridge Forest*), Terry Robbins (*Welling United*), Paul Cavell (*Redbridge Forest*). *Subs* Ryan Price (*Stafford Rangers*) for Mckenna, Gary Abbott (*Welling United*) for Humphreys, Simon Reade (*Farnborough Town*) for Robbins. *Other Sub* James Wigmore (*Farnborough Town*).

History of the FA Amateur Cup

With the passion and excitement generated by the introduction of the FA Cup for the leading clubs in 1871, the FA decided that the amateur clubs would benefit from a similar national knock-out competition.

Therefore, in the 1893–94 season, the FA Amateur Cup was born, billed as a cup competition purely for the country's amateur sides and to be run along exactly the same lines as the FA Cup.

A modest 81 clubs entered the competition in the first season, Old Carthusians winning the final with a 2–1 defeat of Casuals in front of 3500 spectators at Richmond. The early years of the competition were dominated largely by public schools old boys' teams, but with the inauguration of the Arthur Dunn Cup the schools gave way to the new champions of the event, the North-East.

Bishop Auckland and the FA Amateur Cup are almost synonymous, with the northern side winning the competition a staggering 10 times. Their first taste of Amateur Cup success came in 1896, a year after Middlesbrough had notched the first of two wins in four years. Bishop Auckland followed this up with another victory in 1900.

With the departure of many sides to the Amateur Football Association (now the Alliance) the northern monopoly on the competition continued largely unchallenged, although Clapton managed the first of their five Cup wins in 1907.

Indeed, after the First World War the balance of power swung southwards with Leyton, Clapton and Ilford all capturing the Cup twice in successive years. As the battle between the teams from the Northern League and the Isthmian League gathered momentum, crowds for the competition began to rise. In 1949, a staggering 93,000 watched the first Wembley final between Bromley and Romford, with the attendance reaching 100,000 two years later as the combined Oxford and Cambridge Universities side Pegasus beat Bishop Auckland 2–1.

Bishop Auckland retaliated with three successive triumphs from 1955 to 1957, but from the start of the 1960s the competition was to become increasingly the domain of the London clubs. Hendon, Enfield and Wealdstone all won the Cup in the next 10 years, although it was perhaps fitting that another Bishop, Bishop's Stortford, should draw a veil across the event in 1974, when they won the last-ever FA Amateur Cup with a 4–1 defeat of Ilford in front of 30,500 fans at Wembley.

FA AMATEUR CUP WINNERS

Year/venue				Result
1894 Richmond	Old Carthusians	v	Casuals	2–1
1895 Leeds	Middlesbrough	v	Old Carthusians	2–1
1896 Leicester	Bishop Auckland	v	RA (Portsmouth)	1–0
1897 Tufnell Park	Old Carthusians	v	Stockton	1–1
Darlington	Old Carthusians	v	Stockton	4–1
1898 Crystal Palace	Middlesbrough	v	Uxbridge	2–1
1899 Middlesbrough	Stockton	v	Harwich & Parkeston	1–0
1900 Leicester	Bishop Auckland	v	Lowestoft	5–1
1901 Harwich	Crook Town	v	King's Lynn	1–1
Ipswich	Crook Town	v	King's Lynn	3–0
1902 Leeds	Old Malvernians	v	Bishop Auckland	5–1
1903 Reading	Stockton	v	Oxford City	0–0
Darlington	Stockton	v	Oxford City	1–0
1904 Bradford	Sheffield	v	Ealing	3–1
1905 Shepherds Bush	West Hartlepool	v	Clapton	3–2
1906 Stockton	Oxford City	v	Bishop Auckland	3–0

FA Amateur Cup Final 1963 – Wimbledon celebrate victory at Wembley

Year/venue				*Result*
1907 Chelsea	Clapton	v	Stockton	2–1
1908 Bishop Auckland	Depot BNRE	v	Stockton	2–1
1909 Ilford	Clapton	v	Eston United	6–0
1910 Bishop Auckland	RMLI (Gosport)	v	South Bank	2–1
1911 Herne Hill	Bromley	v	Bishop Auckland	1–0
1912 Middlesbrough	Stockton	v	Eston United	0–0
Middlesbrough	Stockton	v	Eston United	1–0
1913 Reading	South Bank	v	Oxford City	1–1
Bishop Auckland	South Bank	v	Oxford City	1–0
1914 Leeds	Bishop Auckland	v	Northern Nomads	1–0
1915 Millwall	Clapton	v	Bishop Auckland	1–0
1920 Millwall	Dulwich Hamlet	v	Tufnell Park	1–0*
1921 Middlesbrough	Bishop Auckland	v	Swindon Victoria	4–2
1922 Middlesbrough	Bishop Auckland	v	South Bank	5–2*
1923 Crystal Palace	London Caledonians	v	Evesham Town	2–1*
1924 Millwall	Clapton	v	Erith & Belvedere	3–0
1925 Millwall	Clapton	v	Southall	2–1
1926 Sunderland	Northern Nomads	v	Stockton	7–1

* *after extra time*

1927 Millwall	Leyton	v	Barking Town	3–1
1928 Middlesbrough	Leyton	v	Cockfield	3–2
1929 Arsenal	Ilford	v	Leyton	3–1
1930 West Ham	Ilford	v	Bournemouth Gas Ath	5–1
1931 Arsenal	Wycombe Wanderers	v	Hayes	1–0
1932 West Ham	Dulwich Hamlet	v	Marine	7–1
1933 Dulwich	Kingstonian	v	Stockton	1–1*
Darlington	Kingstonian	v	Stockton	4–1
1934 West Ham	Dulwich Hamlet	v	Leyton	2–1
1935 Middlesbrough	Bishop Auckland	v	Wimbledon	0–0*
Chelsea	Bishop Auckland	v	Wimbledon	2–1
1936 Selhurst Park	Casuals	v	Ilford	1–1*
West Ham	Casuals	v	Ilford	2–0
1937 West Ham	Dulwich Hamlet	v	Leyton	2–0
1938 Millwall	Bromley	v	Erith & Belvedere	1–0
1939 Sunderland	Bishop Auckland	v	Willington	3–0
1946 Chelsea	Barnet	v	Bishop Auckland	3–2
1947 Arsenal	Leytonstone	v	Wimbledon	2–1
1948 Chelsea	Leytonstone	v	Barnet	1–0
1949 Wembley	Bromley	v	Romford	1–0
1950 Wembley	Willington	v	Bishop Auckland	4–0
1951 Wembley	Pegasus	v	Bishop Auckland	2–1
1952 Wembley	Walthamstow Av	v	Leyton	2–1*
1953 Wembley	Pegasus	v	Harwich & Parkeston	6–0
1954 Wembley	Crook Town	v	Bishop Auckland	2–2*
Newcastle	Crook Town	v	Bishop Auckland	2–2*
Middlesbrough	Crook Town	v	Bishop Auckland	1–0
1955 Wembley	Bishop Auckland	v	Hendon	2–0
1956 Wembley	Bishop Auckland	v	Corinthian-Casuals	1–1
Middlesbrough	Bishop Auckland	v	Corinthian-Casuals	4–1
1957 Wembley	Bishop Auckland	v	Wycombe Wanderers	3–1
1958 Wembley	Woking	v	Ilford	3–0
1959 Wembley	Crook Town	v	Barnet	3–2
1960 Wembley	Hendon	v	Kingstonian	2–1
1961 Wembley	Walthamstow Av	v	West Auckland Town	2–1
1962 Wembley	Crook Town	v	Hounslow	1–1
Middlesbrough	Crook Town	v	Hounslow	4–0
1963 Wembley	Wimbledon	v	Sutton United	4–2
1964 Wembley	Crook Town	v	Enfield	2–1
1965 Wembley	Hendon	v	Whitby Town	3–1
1966 Wembley	Wealdstone	v	Hendon	3–1
1967 Wembley	Enfield	v	Skelmersdale United	0–0
Manchester	Enfield	v	Skelmersdale United	3–0
1968 Wembley	Leytonstone	v	Chesham United	1–0
1969 Wembley	North Shields	v	Sutton United	2–1
1970 Wembley	Enfield	v	Dagenham	5–1
1971 Wembley	Skelmersdale United	v	Dagenham	4–1
1972 Wembley	Hendon	v	Enfield	2–0
1973 Wembley	Walton & Hersham	v	Slough Town	1–0
1974 Wembley	Bishop's Stortford	v	Ilford	4–1

* *after extra time*

CHAPTER EIGHT

England Matches 1991-92

Wembley, 11 September 1991
England v Germany

Friendly, lost 0–1

Woods (Sheffield Wednesday), Dixon (Arsenal), Dorigo (Leeds United), Batty (Leeds United), Pallister (Manchester United), Parker (Manchester United), Platt (Bari), Steven (Marseille), Smith (Arsenal), Lineker (Tottenham Hotspur), Salako (Crystal Palace) *Subs* Stewart (Tottenham Hotspur) for Steven, Merson (Arsenal) for Salako

Wembley, 16 October 1991
England v Turkey

European Championship qualifying game, won 1–0 (Smith)

Woods (Sheffield Wednesday), Dixon (Arsenal), Pearce (Nottingham Forest), Batty (Leeds United), Walker (Nottingham Forest), Mabbutt (Tottenham Hotspur), Robson (Manchester United), Platt (Bari), Smith (Arsenal), Lineker (Tottenham Hotspur), Waddle (Marseille)

This was a critical European Championship qualifier for England and one where they might have hoped to improve their goal differential over the other three teams in the group. That was not to be the case as a swirling wind around Wembley made it difficult for England to assert their clear superiority.

Bryan Robson was back at the heart of England's midfield but it was to be a comfortable passage against a Turkey side that had not come to Wembley to have its neck wrung.

The Turks broke at England from midfield and caused Chris Woods just a few problems. Chris Waddle, on what was to be his final England appearance, had difficulty making any impression on the match.

And it was Stuart Pearce who set up the decisive goal, surging past defender Riza and placing his cross perfectly on to the target, which happened to be Alan Smith's forehead.

From three yards the Arsenal striker could hardly miss, underlining his ability in the air and for once showing his old Leicester team-mate Gary Lineker the route to goal.

Poznan, 11 November 1991
Poland v England

European Championship qualifying game, drew 1–1 (Lineker)

Woods (Sheffield Wednesday), Dixon (Arsenal), Pearce (Nottingham Forest), Gray (Crystal Palace), Walker (Nottingham Forest), Mabbutt (Tottenham Hotspur), Platt (Bari), Thomas (Crystal Palace), Rocastle (Arsenal), Lineker (Tottenham Hotspur), Sinton (Queen's Park Rangers)   *Subs*   Smith (Arsenal) for Gray, Daley (Aston Villa) for Sinton

This was the match where England needed a point to ensure a place in the final eight of the European Championship and they got there courtesy of a goal from, perhaps inevitably, Gary Lineker.

When the history of English soccer is written there can be no doubt Lineker will merit a chapter all on his own for his scoring exploits in the hour of need. European exit was staring England in the face for part of this night in Poznan.

The Poles, playing sweet, slick football, had taken the lead in the 40th minute when Gary Mabbutt deflected a long free-kick past the un-suspecting Chris Woods.

English fans were left in suspense until David Rocastle, one of the heroes of the night, swung over a 76th minute corner which Mabbutt got his head to and Lineker hooked into the net.

The strains of 'Swing Low, Sweet Chariot' drifted across the night air since a draw was enough to see Taylor over his first major hurdle as manager, qualification for the European finals, a feat which eluded Bobby Robson in his early career.

Wembley, 19 February 1992
England v France

Friendly, won 2–0 (Shearer, Lineker)

Woods (Sheffield Wednesday), Jones (Liverpool), Pearce (Nottingham Forest), Keown (Everton), Walker (Nottingham Forest), Wright (Liverpool), Webb (Manchester United), Thomas (Crystal Palace), Clough (Nottingham Forest), Shearer (Southampton), Hirst (Sheffield Wednesday)   *Sub* Lineker (Tottenham Hotspur) for Hirst

Prague, 25 March 1992
Czechoslovakia v England

Friendly, drew 2–2 (Merson, Keown)

Seaman (Arsenal), Keown (Everton), Pearce (Nottingham Forest), Rocastle (Arsenal), Walker (Nottingham Forest), Mabbutt (Tottenham Hotspur), Platt (Bari), Merson (Arsenal), Clough (Nottingham Forest), Hateley (Glasgow Rangers), Barnes (Liverpool)   *Subs*   Dixon (Arsenal) for Rocastle, Stewart (Tottenham Hotspur) for Clough, Dorigo (Leeds United) for Barnes, Lineker (Tottenham Hotspur) for Mabbutt

Moscow, 29 April 1992
CIS v England

Friendly, drew 2–2 (Lineker, Steven)

Woods (Sheffield Wednesday), Stevens (Glasgow Rangers), Sinton (Queen's Park Rangers), Palmer (Sheffield Wednesday), Walker (Nottingham Forest), Keown (Everton), Platt (Bari), Steven (Marseille), Shearer (Southampton), Lineker (Tottenham Hotspur), Daley (Aston Villa)   *Subs*   Curle (Manchester City) for Sinton, Clough (Nottingham Forest) for Shearer, Martyn (Crystal Palace) for Woods

Budapest, 12 May 1992
Hungary v England

Friendly, won 1–0 (Webb)

Martyn (Crystal Palace), Stevens (Glasgow Rangers), Dorigo (Leeds United), Curle (Manchester City), Walker (Nottingham Forest), Keown (Everton), Webb (Manchester United), Palmer (Sheffield Wednesday), Merson (Arsenal), Lineker (Tottenham Hotspur), Daley (Aston Villa)   *Subs*   Smith (Arsenal) for Merson, Sinton (Queen's Park Rangers) for Curle, Seaman (Arsenal) for Martyn, Wright (Arsenal) for Lineker, Batty (Leeds United) for Webb

Wembley, 17 May 1992
England v Brazil

Friendly, drew 1–1 (Platt)

Woods (Sheffield Wednesday), Stevens (Glasgow Rangers), Dorigo (Leeds United), Palmer (Sheffield Wednesday), Walker (Nottingham Forest), Keown (Everton), Daley (Aston Villa), Steven (Marseille), Platt (Bari), Lineker (Tottenham Hotspur), Sinton (Queen's Park Rangers) *Subs* Rocastle (Arsenal) for Sinton, Webb (Manchester United) for Steven, Merson (Arsenal) for Daley, Pearce (Nottingham Forest) for Dorigo

Helsinki, 3 June 1992
Finland v England

Friendly, won 2–1 (Platt 2)

Woods (Sheffield Wednesday), Stevens (Glasgow Rangers), Pearce (Nottingham Forest), Keown (Everton), Walker (Nottingham Forest), Wright (Liverpool), Platt (Bari), Steven (Marseille), Webb (Manchester United), Lineker (Tottenham Hotspur), Barnes (Liverpool) *Subs* Merson (Arsenal) for Barnes, Daley (Aston Villa) for Steven, Palmer (Sheffield Wednesday) for Stevens

Malmö, 11 June 1992
England v Denmark

European Championship, drew 0–0

Woods (Sheffield Wednesday), Curle (Manchester City), Pearce (Nottingham Forest), Keown (Everton), Walker (Nottingham Forest), Platt (Bari), Steven (Marseille), Lineker (Tottenham Hotspur), Palmer (Sheffield Wednesday), Merson (Arsenal), Smith (Arsenal) *Subs* Tony Daley (Aston Villa) for Curle, Neil Webb (Manchester United) for Merson

England were once again left to bemoan their missed chances as a first half of control gave way to a second of anxiety in their opening European Championship game.

Graham Taylor had reverted to the orthodox English formation, abandoning the temptation to play with a sweeper against the eventual surprise winners.

David Platt had two good chances in the opening half and Alan Smith, a surprise choice, forced Schmeichel into a good diving save.

But the tide turned in the second half and the Danes, late entrants into the competition after Yugoslavia's expulsion, took command. John Jensen should perhaps have finished England off in the 66th minute rolling his shot beyond Chris Woods and against the inside of the upright.

Malmö, 14 June 1992
England v France

European Championship, drew 0–0

Woods (Sheffield Wednesday), Steven (Marseille), Pearce (Nottingham Forest), Keown (Everton), Walker (Nottingham Forest), Palmer (Sheffield Wednesday), Sinton (QPR), Platt (Bari), Batty (Leeds United), Lineker (Tottenham Hotspur), Shearer (Southampton)

This was a disappointing match with the French, one of the favourites to win the competition, unable to find their sophisticated stride.

For England the problem again was a shortage of supply into the penalty area and though this was not the result Graham Taylor hoped for at least it could be claimed England were going for the victory whereas France seemed content with a draw.

Indeed, this game will be remembered for a Stuart Pearce free-kick from 25 yards that made the crossbar of French goalkeeper Bruno Martini quiver. On that coat of paint England's hopes stumbled.

Stockholm, 17 June 1992
England v Sweden

European Championship, lost 1–2

Woods (Sheffield Wednesday), Batty (Leeds United), Pearce (Nottingham Forest), Keown (Everton), Walker (Nottingham Forest), Palmer (Sheffield Wednesday), Platt (Bari), Webb (Manchester United), Sinton (QPR), Lineker (Tottenham Hotspur), Daley (Sheffield Wednesday)   *Subs*   Smith (Arsenal) for Lineker, Merson (Arsenal) for Sinton

England had the perfect start to a match that was to see their exit from the European Championships as David Platt scored England's first goal of the finals after four minutes.

His conversion from Gary Lineker's cross might have been the platform for victory but once again chances were not taken and England were made to pay a heavy price.

Six minutes into the second half Jan Eriksson equalised. Lineker was controversially withdrawn in the 62nd minute, a sad way for his England career to end. A winner from Tomas Brolin nine minutes from time sealed England's fate.

Under-21
Scunthorpe, 10 September 1991
England v Germany

Friendly, won 2–1 (Johnson, Ebbrell)

Jones (Watford), Dodd (Southampton), Vinnicombe (Glasgow Rangers), Ebbrell (Everton), Tiler (Nottingham Forest), Warhurst (Sheffield Wednesday), Johnson (Notts County), Draper (Notts County), Shearer (Southampton), Williams (Derby County), Campbell (Arsenal)   *Subs*   Matthew (Chelsea) for Draper

Under-21
Reading, 15 October 1991
England v Turkey

UEFA Under-21 Championship, won 2–0 (Shearer 2)

James (Watford), Charles (Nottingham Forest), Vinnicombe (Glasgow Rangers), Ebbrell (Everton), Tiler (Nottingham Forest), Atherton (Coventry City), Johnson (Notts County), Matthew (Chelsea), Shearer (Southampton), Williams (Derby County), Campbell (Arsenal)   *Subs*   Blake (Aston Villa) for Matthew

Under-21
Pila, 12 November 1991
Poland v England

UEFA Under-21 Championship, lost 1–2 (Kitson)

James (Watford), Dodd (Southampton), Vinnicombe (Glasgow Rangers), Blake (Aston Villa), Cundy (Chelsea), Lee (Chelsea), Kitson (Leicester City), Draper (Notts County), Shearer (Southampton), Williams (Derby County), Johnson (Notts County)   *Subs*   Atkinson (Sunderland) for Vinnicombe, Olney (Aston Villa) for Blake

Under-21
Vac, 12 May 1992
Hungary v England

Friendly, drew 2-2 (Allen, Cole)

Walker (Tottenham Hotspur), Jackson (Everton), Minto (Charlton), Sutch (Norwich), Ehiogu (Aston Villa), Hendon (Tottenham Hotspur), Sheron (Manchester City), Parlour (Arsenal), Cole (Arsenal), Allen (Queen's Park Rangers), Heaney (Arsenal)
Subs Hall (Southampton) for Cole, Ashcroft (Preston) for Jackson, Bazeley (Watford) for Hendon

Castellon de la Plana, 18 December 1991
England B v Spain B

Friendly, won 1–0 (Merson)

Seaman (Arsenal), Barrett (Oldham Athletic), Winterburn (Arsenal), Webb (Manchester United), Keown (Everton), Curle (Manchester City), Rocastle (Arsenal), Campbell (Arsenal), Hirst (Sheffield Wednesday), Palmer (Sheffield Wednesday), Merson (Arsenal) *Subs* Slater (West Ham United) for Campbell, Deane (Sheffield United) for Merson

Queen's Park Rangers, 18 February 1992
England B v France B

Friendly, won 3–0 (Merson, Stewart, Dumas og)

Seaman (Arsenal), Curle (Manchester City), Dorigo (Leeds United), Stewart (Tottenham Hotspur), Mabbutt (Tottenham Hotspur), Pallister (Manchester United), Ince (Manchester United), Merson (Arsenal), Wright (Arsenal), Palmer (Sheffield Wednesday), Sinton (Queen's Park Rangers) *Subs* Coton (Manchester City) for Seaman, White (Manchester City) for Wright, Le Tissier (Southampton) for Ince

Ceske Budejovice, 24 March 1992
Czechoslovakia B v England B

Friendly, won 1–0 (Smith)

Martyn (Crystal Palace), Barrett (Aston Villa), Dicks (West Ham United), Batty (Leeds United), Jobson (Oldham Athletic), Palmer (Sheffield Wednesday), Sinton (Queen's Park Rangers), Thomas (Liverpool), Smith (Arsenal), Shearer (Southampton), Le Tissier (Southampton) *Subs* Dorigo (Leeds United) for Smith, Hirst (Sheffield Wednesday) for Shearer

Graham Taylor at an
England training
session

Moscow, 28 April 1992
CIS B v England B

Friendly, drew 1–1 (Smith)

Seaman (Arsenal), Dixon (Arsenal), Dicks (West Ham United), Webb
(Manchester United), Mabbutt (Tottenham Hotspur), Jobson
(Oldham Athletic), Rocastle (Arsenal), Beardsley (Everton), Smith
(Arsenal), Thomas (Crystal Palace), Sharpe (Manchester United)
Subs Le Tissier (Southampton) for Sharpe, Le Saux (Chelsea) for
Beardsley

CHAPTER NINE

RECORD SECTION

OBITUARIES

BILL FOX *Died December 1991*

Born in Blackburn on 6 January 1928, Bill Fox became chairman of Blackburn Rovers in 1982, a member of the Football League management committee in 1985 and president of the Football League in 1989.

Fox was deeply concerned about the game in England. He proposed that the League and the FA amalgamate and give the national team greater priority; he advocated players' representation in the game's council chambers and was the main influence behind the publication of the Football League's *One Game, One Team, One Voice* in 1990, a document which spelled out his beliefs.

Bill Fox fierce resisted all attempts to split the Football League – especially the formation of the FA Premier League, a resistance ultimately doomed to failure.

DR JOHN O'HARA *Died February 1992*

A vice-president of the FA, Dr John O'Hara was a driving force behind the improvement of the Association's medical facilities and awareness. A former Scottish amateur international of the 1920s, he also played for Glasgow University and made a number of appearances for Glasgow Celtic. He became chairman of the Weardale FA in 1930 and president of the Sussex FA in 1958. He was also president of the Sussex County League, the Sussex Schools FA and the Brighton League.

LORD WESTWOOD *Died November 1991*

Lord Westwood, 'the Peer with the black eye patch', was a Scotsman (born in Dundee on 25 December, 1907) who settled in Newcastle. A tall, flamboyant figure, he was a successful industrialist, initially in the cinema and later in toy manufacturing.

He followed in his father's footsteps by joining the board of Newcastle United FC in 1960. He became chairman of the club in 1964.

Lord Westwood joined the Football League management committee in 1970 and was elected president of the League four years later, a position he retained until his retirement from Newcastle in 1981.

Amendments to the Laws of the Game

At its annual meeting in Newport, Wales, on 30 May 1992, the International Football Association Board made a number of amendments to the Laws of the Game which were subsequently enforced on 25 July 1992.

The *Punishment* section of *Law IV (Players' Equipment)* was lengthened in order to further assist referees with its application.

Law V (Referees): clause (e) [misconduct or ungentlemanly conduct] was altered to include specific reference to the yellow card, while *clause (h)* [violent conduct, serious foul play, the use of foul or abusive language] was altered to include specific reference to the red card, thereby making these cards mandatory at all levels of the game. (Previously these clauses made no mention of the cards.)

Furthermore, if a player is sent off for a *second cautionable offence*, the referee must show both the yellow and the red card simultaneously in one hand, in order to differentiate between a second cautionable offence and an offence requiring immediate expulsion.

A new paragraph was inserted into *Law XII (Fouls and misconduct)*, concerning the deliberate pass back to the goalkeeper. It is no longer permissible for the goalkeeper to touch the ball *with his hands*, from a pass which has been *kicked* to him (although it is permissible for a goalkeeper to handle a ball played with the head, chest or the knee, or by deflection). An infringement of this Law is punishable by an indirect free-kick taken from the place where the infringement occurred – subject to the over-riding conditions of *Law XIII* (Free-Kick).

A stricter implementation of *Law XII decision 17 (Control of the ball by the goalkeeper)* was also insisted upon; as was the rule regarding the wearing of cycling shorts. These must now be of the same colour as the team shorts, and must extend no farther than the top of the knee.

In order to help reduce time wasting, *Law XIII (Free-Kick)* now allows a free-kick awarded to the defending team inside its goal-area, to be taken from *any* point within the goal-area. (Previously the free-kick had to be taken within the *half* of the goal-area in which it had been awarded.) Likewise, *Law XVI (Goal-kick)* was simplified to allow a goal-kick to be taken from *any* point within the goal area.

The Board also insisted that referees be *much stricter when dealing with time-wasting tactics*. In particular, the referee *must caution* the following: a player guilty of kicking the ball away after a free-kick has been given; a player encroaching from a 'wall'; a player who stands in front of the ball when a free-kick has been given against his team.

Fixtures – Season 1992–93

SATURDAY, 15 AUGUST, 1992
FA Premier League
Arsenal v Norwich City
Chelsea v Oldham Athletic
Coventry City v Middlesbrough
Crystal Palace v Blackburn Rovers
Everton v Sheffield Wednesday
Ipswich Town v Aston Villa
Leeds United v Wimbledon
Sheffield United v Manchester United
Southampton v Tottenham Hotspur

Barclays League

DIVISION ONE
Barnsley v West Ham United
Birmingham City v Notts County
Brentford v Wolverhampton Wanderers
Bristol City v Portsmouth
Charlton Athletic v Grimsby Town
Leicester City v Luton Town
Newcastle United v Southend United
Oxford United v Bristol Rovers
Peterborough United v Derby County
Swindon Town v Sunderland
Tranmere Rovers v Cambridge United
Watford v Millwall

DIVISION TWO
Bolton Wanderers v Huddersfield Town
Bradford City v Chester City
Burnley v Swansea City
Exeter City v Rotherham United
Hartlepool United v Reading
Hull City v Stoke City
Leyton Orient v Brighton & Hove Albion
Mansfield Town v Plymouth Argyle
Port Vale v Fulham
Preston North End v A.F.C. Bournemouth
West Bromwich Albion v Blackpool
Wigan Athletic v Stockport County

DIVISION THREE
Cardiff City v Darlington
Carlisle United v Walsall
Chesterfield v Barnet
Colchester United v Lincoln City
Crewe Alexandra v Torquay United
Doncaster Rovers v Bury
Gillingham v Northampton Town
Hereford United v Scarborough
Rochdale v Halifax Town
Scunthorpe United v Maidstone United
York City v Shrewsbury Town

SUNDAY, 16 AUGUST, 1992
FA Premier League
Nottingham Forest v Liverpool

MONDAY, 17 AUGUST, 1992
FA Premier League
Manchester City v Queen's Park Rangers

TUESDAY, 18 AUGUST, 1992
FA Premier League
Blackburn Rovers v Arsenal
Wimbledon v Ipswich Town

Barclays League
DIVISION ONE
Cambridge United v Charlton Athletic
Wolverhampton Wanderers v Leicester
City

WEDNESDAY, 19 AUGUST, 1992
FA Premier League
Aston Villa v Leeds United
Liverpool v Sheffield United
Manchester United v Everton
Middlesbrough v Manchester City
Norwich City v Chelsea
Oldham Athletic v Crystal Palace
Queen's Park Rangers v Southampton
Sheffield Wednesday v Nottingham Forest
Tottenham Hotspur v Coventry City

Barclays League
DIVISION ONE
Bristol Rovers v Swindon Town

FRIDAY, 21 AUGUST, 1992
Barclays League
DIVISION THREE
Barnet v Colchester United
Darlington v Hereford United

SATURDAY, 22 AUGUST, 1992
FA Premier League
Aston Villa v Southampton
Blackburn Rovers v Manchester City
Manchester United v Ipswich Town
Middlesbrough v Leeds United
Norwich City v Everton
Oldham Athletic v Nottingham Forest
Queen's Park Rangers v Sheffield United
Sheffield Wednesday v Chelsea
Tottenham Hotspur v Crystal Palace
Wimbledon v Coventry City

Barclays League
DIVISION ONE
Bristol Rovers v Brentford
Cambridge United v Birmingham City
Derby County v Newcastle United
Grimsby Town v Watford
Luton Town v Bristol City
Millwall v Oxford United
Notts County v Leicester City
Portsmouth v Barnsley
Southend United v Peterborough United
Sunderland v Tranmere Rovers
West Ham United v Charlton Athletic
Wolverhampton Wanderers v Swindon
Town

DIVISION TWO
A.F.C. Bournemouth v Port Vale
Blackpool v Exeter City
Brighton & Hove Albion v Bolton
Wanderers
Fulham v Preston North End
Huddersfield Town v West Bromwich
Albion
Hull City v Chester City
Plymouth Argyle v Bradford City
Reading v Leyton Orient
Rotherham United v Hartlepool United
Stockport County v Burnley
Stoke City v Wigan Athletic
Swansea City v Mansfield Town

DIVISION THREE
Bury v Gillingham
Halifax Town v Scunthorpe United
Lincoln City v York City
Maidstone United v Carlisle United
Scarborough v Crewe Alexandra
Shrewsbury Town v Doncaster Rovers
Walsall v Cardiff City
Wrexham v Rochdale

SUNDAY, 23 AUGUST, 1992
FA Premier League
Liverpool v Arsenal

MONDAY, 24 AUGUST, 1992
FA Premier League
Southampton v Manchester United

TUESDAY, 25 AUGUST, 1992
FA Premier League
Crystal Palace v Sheffield Wednesday
Everton v Aston Villa
Ipswich Town v Liverpool
Leeds United v Tottenham Hotspur
Sheffield United v Wimbledon
Barclays League
DIVISION ONE
Charlton Athletic v Bristol Rovers
Notts County v Watford

WEDNESDAY, 26 AUGUST, 1992
FA Premier League
Arsenal v Oldham Athletic
Chelsea v Blackburn Rovers
Coventry City v Queen's Park Rangers
Manchester City v Norwich City
Barclays League
DIVISION ONE
Leicester City v Derby County

FRIDAY, 28 AUGUST, 1992
Barclays League
DIVISION ONE
Tranmere Rovers v Bristol Rovers

DIVISION TWO
Hull City v Plymouth Argyle

DIVISION THREE
Crewe Alexandra v Northampton Town

SATURDAY, 29 AUGUST, 1992
FA Premier League
Arsenal v Sheffield Wednesday
Chelsea v Queen's Park Rangers
Coventry City v Blackburn Rovers
Crystal Palace v Norwich City
Everton v Wimbledon
Leeds United v Liverpool
Manchester City v Oldham Athletic
Nottingham Forest v Manchester United
Sheffield United v Aston Villa
Southampton v Middlesbrough
Barclays League
DIVISION ONE
Barnsley v Millwall
Birmingham City v Grimsby Town
Brentford v Southend United
Bristol City v Sunderland
Charlton Athletic v Luton Town
Leicester City v Portsmouth
Newcastle United v West Ham United
Oxford United v Wolverhampton
Wanderers
Peterborough United v Notts County
Swindon Town v Cambridge United
Watford v Derby County

DIVISION TWO
Bolton Wanderers v Reading
Bradford City v Brighton & Hove Albion
Burnley v Rotherham United
Exeter City v Stoke City
Hartlepool United v Huddersfield Town
Leyton Orient v Blackpool
Mansfield Town v Fulham
Port Vale v Stockport County
Preston North End v Chester City
West Bromwich Albion v A.F.C.
Bournemouth
Wigan Athletic v Swansea City

DIVISION THREE
Cardiff City v Halifax Town
Carlisle United v Lincoln City
Chesterfield v Bury
Colchester United v Darlington
Doncaster Rovers v Torquay United
Gillingham v Barnet
Hereford United v Walsall
Rochdale v Scarborough
Scunthorpe United v Shrewsbury Town
York City v Wrexham

SUNDAY, 30 AUGUST, 1992
FA Premier League
Ipswich Town v Tottenham Hotspur

MONDAY, 31 AUGUST, 1992
FA Premier League
Norwich City v Nottingham Forest

TUESDAY, 1 SEPTEMBER, 1992
FA Premier League
Liverpool v Southampton
Middlesbrough v Ipswich Town
Oldham Athletic v Leeds United
Wimbledon v Manchester City
Barclays League
DIVISION ONE
Barnsley v Wolverhampton Wanderers
Birmingham City v Southend United
Brentford v Portsmouth

DIVISION TWO
Bolton Wanderers v Blackpool
Exeter City v Brighton & Hove Albion
Hartlepool United v Chester City
Hull City v Swansea City
Leyton Orient v Huddersfield Town
Mansfield Town v A.F.C. Bournemouth
Port Vale v Rotherham United
Wigan Athletic v Fulham

DIVISION THREE
Cardiff City v Northampton Town
Carlisle United v Bury
Chesterfield v Darlington
Colchester United v Shrewsbury Town
Doncaster Rovers v Barnet
Gillingham v Wrexham
Hereford United v Lincoln City
Rochdale v Maidstone United
Scunthorpe United v Walsall
York City v Torquay United

WEDNESDAY, 2 SEPTEMBER, 1992
FA Premier League
Aston Villa v Chelsea
Manchester United v Crystal Palace
Queen's Park Rangers v Arsenal
Sheffield Wednesday v Coventry City
Tottenham Hotspur v Sheffield United
Barclays League
DIVISION ONE
Newcastle United v Luton Town

DIVISION TWO
Bradford City v Stoke City
West Bromwich Albion v Stockport
County

FRIDAY, 4 SEPTEMBER, 1992
Barclays League
DIVISION ONE
Cambridge United v Brentford

SATURDAY, 5 SEPTEMBER, 1992
FA Premier League
Aston Villa v Crystal Palace
Blackburn Rovers v Nottingham Forest
Liverpool v Chelsea
Norwich City v Southampton
Oldham Athletic v Coventry City
Queen's Park Rangers v Ipswich Town
Sheffield Wednesday v Manchester City
Tottenham Hotspur v Everton
Wimbledon v Arsenal

Barclays League
DIVISION ONE
Bristol Rovers v Newcastle United
Derby County v Bristol City
Grimsby Town v Oxford United
Luton Town v Tranmere Rovers
Millwall v Swindon Town
Notts County v Barnsley
Portsmouth v Birmingham City
Southend United v Leicester City
Sunderland v Charlton Athletic
West Ham United v Watford
Wolverhampton Wanderers v
Peterborough United

DIVISION TWO
A.F.C. Bournemouth v Hartlepool United
Blackpool v Mansfield Town
Brighton & Hove Albion v Preston North
End
Chester City v Burnley
Fulham v West Bromwich Albion
Plymouth Argyle v Leyton Orient
Reading v Hull City
Rotherham United v Wigan Athletic
Stockport County v Exeter City
Stoke City v Bolton Wanderers
Swansea City v Port Vale

DIVISION THREE
Barnet v Carlisle United
Bury v Colchester United
Darlington v Crewe Alexandra
Lincoln City v Scunthorpe United
Maidstone United v Chesterfield
Scarborough v Gillingham
Shrewsbury Town v Rochdale
Torquay United v Cardiff City
Walsall v York City
Wrexham v Doncaster Rovers

SUNDAY, 6 SEPTEMBER, 1992
FA Premier League
Manchester United v Leeds United
Barclays League
DIVISION TWO
Huddersfield Town v Bradford City

DIVISION THREE
Northampton Town v Hereford United

MONDAY, 7 SEPTEMBER, 1992
FA Premier League
Middlesbrough v Sheffield United

TUESDAY, 8 SEPTEMBER, 1992
Barclays League
DIVISION THREE
Cardiff City v Carlisle United

WEDNESDAY, 9 SEPTEMBER, 1992
Barclays League
DIVISION TWO
West Bromwich Albion v Reading

FRIDAY, 11 SEPTEMBER, 1992
Barclays League
DIVISION TWO
Wigan Athletic v Hartlepool United

SATURDAY, 12 SEPTEMBER, 1992
FA Premier League
Arsenal v Blackburn Rovers
Chelsea v Norwich City
Crystal Palace v Oldham Athletic
Everton v Manchester United
Ipswich Town v Wimbledon
Manchester City v Middlesbrough
Nottingham Forest v Sheffield Wednesday
Sheffield United v Liverpool
Southampton v Queen's Park Rangers
Barclays League
DIVISION ONE
Barnsley v Derby County
Brentford v Luton Town
Bristol City v Southend United
Charlton Athletic v Cambridge United
Leicester City v Wolverhampton
Wanderers
Millwall v Birmingham City
Newcastle United v Portsmouth
Oxford United v Sunderland
Peterborough United v West Ham United
Swindon Town v Bristol Rovers
Tranmere Rovers v Grimsby Town
Watford v Notts County

DIVISION TWO
A.F.C. Bournemouth v Fulham
Brighton & Hove Albion v Huddersfield
Town
Leyton Orient v Chester City

Mansfield Town v Bradford City
Plymouth Argyle v Stoke City
Port Vale v Exeter City
Preston North End v Burnley
Rotherham United v Bolton Wanderers
Stockport County v Hull City
Swansea City v Blackpool

DIVISION THREE
Bury v Barnet
Carlisle United v York City
Colchester United v Walsall
Crewe Alexandra v Doncaster Rovers
Darlington v Maidstone United
Gillingham v Chesterfield
Lincoln City v Halifax Town
Northampton Town v Scunthorpe United
Scarborough v Torquay United
Wrexham v Shrewsbury Town

SUNDAY, 13 SEPTEMBER, 1992
FA Premier League
Leeds United v Aston Villa
Barclays League
DIVISION THREE
Hereford United v Cardiff City

MONDAY, 14 SEPTEMBER, 1992
FA Premier League
Coventry City v Tottenham Hotspur

TUESDAY, 15 SEPTEMBER, 1992
FA Premier League
Blackburn Rovers v Everton
Barclays League
DIVISION ONE
Bristol City v West Ham
Oxford United v Cambridge United
Peterborough United v Millwall

DIVISION TWO
Blackpool v A.F.C. Bournemouth
Bolton Wanderers v West Bromwich
Albion
Burnley v Port Vale
Chester City v Mansfield Town
Exeter City v Wigan Athletic
Fulham v Swansea City
Hartlepool United v Leyton Orient
Huddersfield Town v Plymouth Argyle
Hull City v Preston North End

DIVISION THREE
Barnet v Northampton Town
Chesterfield v Crewe Alexandra
Doncaster Rovers v Colchester United
Halifax Town v Darlington
Maidstone United v Lincoln City
Rochdale v Gillingham
Shrewsbury Town v Scarborough
Torquay United v Wrexham
Walsall v Bury
York City v Hereford United

WEDNESDAY, 16 SEPTEMBER, 1992
Barclays League
DIVISION TWO
Bradford City v Stockport County
Reading v Rotherham United
Stoke City v Brighton & Hove Albion

FRIDAY, 18 SEPTEMBER, 1992
Barclays League
DIVISION ONE
Southend United v Portsmouth
Tranmere Rovers v Charlton Athletic

DIVISION THREE
Doncaster Rovers v Lincoln City

SATURDAY, 19 SEPTEMBER, 1992
FA Premier League
Aston Villa v Liverpool
Everton v Crystal Palace
Norwich City v Sheffield Wednesday
Nottingham Forest v Coventry City
Oldham Athletic v Ipswich Town
Queen's Park Rangers v Middlesbrough
Sheffield United v Arsenal
Southampton v Leeds United
Tottenham Hotspur v Manchester United
Wimbledon v Blackburn Rovers

Barclays League
DIVISION ONE
Barnsley v Peterborough United
Bristol Rovers v Grimsby Town
Cambridge United v Sunderland
Leicester City v Brentford
Luton Town v Birmingham City
Millwall v Notts County
Newcastle United v Bristol City
Swindon Town v Oxford United
West Ham United v Derby County
Wolverhampton Wanderers v Watford

DIVISION TWO
Blackpool v Brighton & Hove Albion
Bolton Wanderers v A.F.C. Bournemouth
Bradford City v Preston North End
Burnley v Mansfield Town
Chester City v Stockport County
Exeter City v Leyton Orient
Fulham v Plymouth Argyle
Hartlepool United v Port Vale
Huddersfield Town v Swansea City
Hull City v Rotherham United
Reading v Wigan Athletic
Stoke City v West Bromwich Albion

DIVISION THREE
Barnet v Hereford United
Cardiff City v Gillingham
Chesterfield v Carlisle United
Halifax Town v Scarborough
Maidstone United v Wrexham
Rochdale v Darlington
Scunthorpe United v Crewe Alexandra

Shrewsbury Town v Bury
Torquay United v Northampton Town
York City v Colchester United

SUNDAY, 20 SEPTEMBER, 1992
FA Premier League
Manchester City v Chelsea

FRIDAY, 25 SEPTEMBER, 1992
Barclays League
DIVISION TWO
Stockport County v Fulham

DIVISION THREE
Darlington v York City

SATURDAY, 26 SEPTEMBER, 1992
FA Premier League
Blackburn Rovers v Oldham Athletic
Chelsea v Nottingham Forest
Coventry City v Norwich City
Crystal Palace v Southampton
Ipswich Town v Sheffield United
Leeds United v Everton
Liverpool v Wimbledon
Manchester United v Queen's Park
Rangers
Middlesbrough v Aston Villa

Barclays League
DIVISION ONE
Birmingham City v Wolverhampton
Wanderers
Brentford v Millwall
Bristol City v Barnsley
Charlton Athletic v Swindon Town
Derby County v Southend United
Grimsby Town v Cambridge United
Notts County v Luton Town
Oxford United v Tranmere Rovers
Peterborough United v Newcastle United
Portsmouth v West Ham United
Sunderland v Bristol Rovers
Watford v Leicester City

DIVISION TWO
A.F.C. Bournemouth v Huddersfield Town
Brighton & Hove Albion v Reading
Leyton Orient v Hull City
Mansfield Town v Stoke City
Plymouth Argyle v Bolton Wanderers
Port Vale v Chester City
Preston North End v Hartlepool United
Rotherham United v Blackpool
Swansea City v Bradford City
West Bromwich Albion v Exeter City
Wigan Athletic v Burnley

DIVISION THREE
Bury v Torquay United
Carlisle United v Scunthorpe United
Colchester United v Chesterfield
Crewe Alexandra v Maidstone United
Gillingham v Walsall

218

Hereford United v Rochdale
Lincoln City v Shrewsbury Town
Northampton Town v Halifax Town
Scarborough v Doncaster Rovers
Wrexham v Barnet

SUNDAY, 27 SEPTEMBER, 1992
FA Premier League
Sheffield Wednesday v Tottenham
Hotspur

MONDAY, 28 SEPTEMBER, 1992
FA Premier League
Arsenal v Manchester City

TUESDAY, 29 SEPTEMBER, 1992
Barclays League
DIVISION ONE
Swindon Town v Grimsby Town
Tranmere Rovers v Notts County
Watford v Sunderland

DIVISION TWO
Burnley v Plymouth Argyle

FRIDAY, 2 OCTOBER, 1992
Barclays League
DIVISION TWO
Reading v Fulham

DIVISION THREE
Darlington v Torquay United

SATURDAY, 3 OCTOBER, 1992
FA Premier League
Arsenal v Chelsea
Blackburn Rovers v Norwich City
Coventry City v Crystal Palace
Ipswich Town v Leeds United
Liverpool v 3heffield Wednesday
Manchester City v Nottingham Forest
Middlesbrough v Manchester United
Queen's Park Rangers v Tottenham
Hotspur
Sheffield United v Southampton
Wimbledon v Aston Villa

Barclays League
DIVISION ONE
Brentford v Newcastle United
Bristol Rovers v Notts County
Cambridge United v Derby County
Charlton Athletic v Southend United
Grimsby Town v Peterborough United
Leicester City v Barnsley
Luton Town v Portsmouth
Oxford United v Birmingham City
Sunderland v Millwall
Swindon Town v Watford
Tranmere Rovers v Bristol City
Wolverhampton Wanderers v West Ham
United

DIVISION TWO
Burnley v West Bromwich Albion
Chester City v Stoke City

Exeter City v A.F.C. Bournemouth
Hull City v Bradford City
Leyton Orient v Bolton Wanderers
Port Vale v Brighton & Hove Albion
Preston North End v Plymouth Argyle
Rotherham United v Huddersfield Town
Stockport County v Swansea City
Wigan Athletic v Mansfield Town

DIVISION THREE
Barnet v Shrewsbury Town
Bury v Scarborough
Cardiff City v Rochdale
Carlisle United v Halifax Town
Chesterfield v Scunthorpe United
Gillingham v Crewe Alexandra
Hereford United v Wrexham
Northampton Town v Lincoln City
Walsall v Maidstone United
York City v Doncaster Rovers

SUNDAY, 4 OCTOBER, 1992
FA Premier League
Oldham Athletic v Everton

Barclays League
DIVISION TWO
Hartlepool United v Blackpool

SATURDAY, 10 OCTOBER, 1992
Barclays League
DIVISION ONE
Barnsley v Luton Town
Birmingham City v Leicester City
Bristol City v Charlton Athletic
Derby County v Oxford United
Millwall v Cambridge United
Newcastle United v Tranmere Rovers
Notts County v Grimsby Town
Peterborough United v Brentford
Portsmouth v Swindon Town
Southend United v Wolverhampton
Wanderers
Watford v Bristol Rovers
West Ham United v Sunderland

DIVISION TWO
A.F.C. Bournemouth v Rotherham United
Blackpool v Preston North End
Bolton Wanderers v Hartlepool United
Brighton & Hove Albion v Wigan Athletic
Fulham v Hull City
Huddersfield Town v Reading
Mansfield Town v Stockport County
Plymouth Argyle v Chester City
Stoke City v Leyton Orient
Swansea City v Exeter City
West Bromwich Albion v Port Vale

DIVISION THREE
Crewe Alexandra v Cardiff City
Doncaster Rovers v Gillingham
Halifax Town v Colchester United
Lincoln City v Walsall
Maidstone United v Barnet

Rochdale v Carlisle United
Scarborough v Northampton Town
Scunthorpe United v York City
Shrewsbury Town v Darlington
Torquay United v Chesterfield
Wrexham v Bury

SUNDAY, 11 OCTOBER, 1992
Barclays League
DIVISION TWO
Bradford City v Burnley

TUESDAY, 13 OCTOBER, 1992
Barclays League
DIVISION THREE
Northampton Town v Chesterfield

FRIDAY, 16 OCTOBER, 1992
DIVISION TWO
Stockport County v Blackpool

DIVISION THREE
Colchester United v Crewe Alexandra

SATURDAY, 17 OCTOBER, 1992
FA Premier League
Chelsea v Ipswich Town
Crystal Palace v Manchester City
Everton v Coventry City
Leeds United v Sheffield United
Norwich City v Queen's Park Rangers
Nottingham Forest v Arsenal
Sheffield Wednesday v Oldham Athletic
Southampton v Wimbledon
Tottenham Hotspur v Middlesbrough

Barclays League
DIVISION ONE
Brentford v Watford
Bristol Rovers v West Ham United
Cambridge United v Bristol City
Charlton Athletic v Millwall
Grimsby Town v Southend United
Leicester City v Peterborough United
Luton Town v Derby County
Oxford United v Barnsley
Swindon Town v Notts County
Tranmere Rovers v Birmingham City
Wolverhampton Wanderers v Portsmouth

DIVISION TWO
Burnley v Fulham
Chester City v Bolton Wanderers
Exeter City v Mansfield Town
Hartlepool United v Swansea City
Hull City v Huddersfield Town
Leyton Orient v A.F.C. Bournemouth
Port Vale v Plymouth Argyle
Preston North End v Stoke City
Reading v Bradford City
Rotherham United v Brighton & Hove
Albion
Wigan Athletic v West Bromwich Albion

DIVISION THREE
Barnet v Scunthorpe United
Bury v Lincoln City
Cardiff City v Maidstone United
Carlisle United v Wrexham
Chesterfield v Shrewsbury Town
Darlington v Scarborough
Hereford United v Torquay United
Northampton Town v Doncaster Rovers
Walsall v Halifax Town
York City v Rochdale

SUNDAY, 18 OCTOBER, 1992
FA Premier League
Manchester United v Liverpool
Barclays League
DIVISION ONE
Sunderland v Newcastle United

MONDAY, 19 OCTOBER, 1992
FA Premier League
Aston Villa v Blackburn Rovers

TUESDAY, 20 OCTOBER, 1992
Barclays League
DIVISION TWO
Preston North End v Reading

WEDNESDAY, 21 OCTOBER, 1992
FA Premier League
Nottingham Forest v Middlesbrough

FRIDAY, 23 OCTOBER, 1992
Barclays League
DIVISION THREE
Doncaster Rovers v Hereford United

SATURDAY, 24 OCTOBER, 1992
FA Premier League
Arsenal v Everton
Blackburn Rovers v Manchester United
Coventry City v Chelsea
Ipswich Town v Crystal Palace
Liverpool v Norwich City
Manchester City v Southampton
Middlesbrough v Sheffield Wednesday
Oldham Athletic v Aston Villa
Queen's Park Rangers v Leeds United
Sheffield United v Nottingham Forest
Barclays League
DIVISION ONE
Barnsley v Brentford
Birmingham City v Bristol Rovers
Bristol City v Leicester City
Derby County v Charlton Athletic
Millwall v Wolverhampton Wanderers
Newcastle United v Grimsby Town
Notts County v Oxford United
Peterborough United v Luton Town
Portsmouth v Sunderland
Watford v Tranmere Rovers
West Ham United v Swindon Town

DIVISION TWO
A.F.C. Bournemouth v Stockport County
Blackpool v Burnley
Bolton Wanderers v Hull City
Bradford City v Leyton Orient
Brighton & Hove Albion v Hartlepool
United
Fulham v Chester City
Huddersfield Town v Exeter City
Mansfield Town v Preston North End
Plymouth Argyle v Wigan Athletic
Stoke City v Port Vale
Swansea City v Reading
West Bromwich Albion v Rotherham
United

DIVISION THREE
Crewe Alexandra v Bury
Halifax Town v Gillingham
Lincoln City v Barnet
Maidstone United v York City
Rochdale v Walsall
Scarborough v Chesterfield
Scunthorpe United v Colchester United
Shrewsbury Town v Cardiff City
Torquay United v Carlisle United
Wrexham v Northampton Town

SUNDAY, 25 OCTOBER, 1992
FA Premier League
Wimbledon v Tottenham Hotspur

Barclays League
DIVISION ONE
Southend United v Cambridge United

FRIDAY, 30 OCTOBER, 1992
Barclays League
DIVISION ONE
Tranmere Rovers v Peterborough United

DIVISION TWO
Stockport County v Huddersfield Town

DIVISION THREE
Colchester United v Wrexham

SATURDAY, 31 OCTOBER, 1992
FA Premier League
Chelsea v Sheffield United
Everton v Manchester City
Leeds United v Coventry City
Manchester United v Wimbledon
Norwich City v Middlesbrough
Nottingham Forest v Ipswich Town
Sheffield Wednesday v Blackburn Rovers
Southampton v Oldham Athletic
Tottenham Hotspur v Liverpool

Barclays League
DIVISION ONE
Brentford v Bristol City
Bristol Rovers v Millwall
Cambridge United v West Ham United

Charlton Athletic v Birmingham City
Grimsby Town v Portsmouth
Leicester City v Newcastle United
Luton Town v Southend United
Oxford United v Watford
Sunderland v Notts County
Swindon Town v Barnsley
Wolverhampton Wanderers v Derby
County

DIVISION TWO
Burnley v Stoke City
Chester City v Brighton & Hove Albion
Exeter City v Fulham
Hartlepool United v Bradford City
Hull City v West Bromwich Albion
Leyton Orient v Swansea City
Port Vale v Blackpool
Preston North End v Bolton Wanderers
Reading v Plymouth Argyle
Rotherham United v Mansfield Town
Wigan Athletic v A.F.C. Bournemouth

DIVISION THREE
Barnet v Crewe Alexandra
Bury v Maidstone United
Cardiff City v Scunthorpe United
Carlisle United v Scarborough
Chesterfield v Rochdale
Darlington v Lincoln City
Gillingham v Torquay United
Hereford United v Halifax Town
Northampton Town v Shrewsbury Town
Walsall v Doncaster Rovers

SUNDAY, 1 NOVEMBER, 1992
FA Premier League
Aston Villa v Queen's Park Rangers

MONDAY, 2 NOVEMBER, 1992
FA Premier League
Crystal Palace v Arsenal

TUESDAY, 3 NOVEMBER, 1992
Barclays League
DIVISION ONE
Birmingham City v Newcastle United
Bristol Rovers v Barnsley
Cambridge United v Luton Town
Charlton Athletic v Leicester City
Grimsby Town v West Ham United
Notts County v Derby County
Oxford United v Portsmouth
Sunderland v Wolverhampton Wanderers
Swindon Town v Brentford
Tranmere Rovers v Southend United
Watford v Peterborough United

DIVISION TWO
A.F.C. Bournemouth v Brighton & Hove
Albion
Blackpool v Huddersfield Town
Burnley v Reading

Exeter City v Bolton Wanderers
Fulham v Stoke City
Mansfield Town v Hull City
Port Vale v Leyton Orient
Rotherham United v Chester City
Stockport County v Preston North End
Swansea City v Plymouth Argyle
Wigan Athletic v Bradford City

DIVISION THREE
Barnet v Walsall
Bury v York City
Chesterfield v Cardiff City
Colchester United v Carlisle United
Doncaster Rovers v Maidstone United
Gillingham v Hereford United
Northampton Town v Darlington
Scarborough v Lincoln City
Shrewsbury Town v Halifax Town
Torquay United v Rochdale
Wrexham v Scunthorpe United

WEDNESDAY, 4 NOVEMBER, 1992
Barclays League
DIVISION ONE
Millwall v Bristol City

DIVISION TWO
West Bromwich Albion v Hartlepool
United

SATURDAY, 7 NOVEMBER, 1992
FA Premier League
Arsenal v Coventry City
Aston Villa v Manchester United
Blackburn Rovers v Tottenham Hotspur
Chelsea v Crystal Palace
Ipswich Town v Southampton
Liverpool v Middlesbrough
Manchester City v Leeds United
Nottingham Forest v Everton
Oldham Athletic v Norwich City
Wimbledon v Queen's Park Rangers

Barclays League
DIVISION ONE
Barnsley v Watford
Brentford v Charlton Athletic
Bristol City v Birmingham City
Derby County v Millwall
Leicester City v Tranmere Rovers
Luton Town v Grimsby Town
Newcastle United v Swindon Town
Peterborough United v Sunderland
Portsmouth v Cambridge United
Southend United v Oxford United
West Ham United v Notts County
Wolverhampton Wanderers v Bristol
Rovers

DIVISION TWO
Bolton Wanderers v Port Vale
Bradford City v Fulham
Brighton & Hove Albion v Stockport
County

Chester City v Swansea City
Hartlepool United v Exeter City
Huddersfield Town v Mansfield Town
Hull City v Burnley
Leyton Orient v West Bromwich Albion
Plymouth Argyle v Rotherham United
Preston North End v Wigan Athletic
Reading v Blackpool
Stoke City v A.F.C. Bournemouth

DIVISION THREE
Cardiff City v Colchester United
Carlisle United v Gillingham
Darlington v Bury
Halifax Town v Torquay United
Hereford United v Chesterfield
Lincoln City v Wrexham
Maidstone United v Shrewsbury Town
Rochdale v Crewe Alexandra
Scunthorpe United v Doncaster Rovers
Walsall v Scarborough
York City v Barnet

SUNDAY, 8 NOVEMBER, 1992
FA Premier League
Sheffield United v Sheffield Wednesday

SATURDAY, 14 NOVEMBER, 1992
Barclays League
DIVISION ONE
Bristol Rovers v Derby County
Cambridge United v Barnsley
Charlton Athletic v Newcastle United
Grimsby Town v Bristol City
Notts County v Wolverhampton
Wanderers
Oxford United v Luton Town
Sunderland v Leicester City
Swindon Town v Southend United
Tranmere Rovers v Brentford
Watford v Portsmouth

SUNDAY, 15 NOVEMBER, 1992
Barclays League
DIVISION ONE
Millwall v West Ham United

FRIDAY, 20 NOVEMBER, 1992
Barclays League
DIVISION TWO
Stockport County v Plymouth Argyle
Swansea City v Brighton & Hove Albion

SATURDAY, 21 NOVEMBER, 1992
FA Premier League
Coventry City v Manchester City
Crystal Palace v Nottingham Forest
Everton v Chelsea
Leeds United v Arsenal
Manchester United v Oldham Athletic
Middlesbrough v Wimbledon
Norwich City v Sheffield United
Sheffield Wednesday v Ipswich Town

Southampton v Blackburn Rovers
Tottenham Hotspur v Aston Villa
Barclays League
DIVISION ONE
Barnsley v Birmingham City
Brentford v Grimsby Town
Bristol City v Swindon Town
Derby County v Sunderland
Leicester City v Cambridge United
Luton Town v Millwall
Newcastle United v Watford
Peterborough United v Bristol Rovers
Portsmouth v Tranmere Rovers
Southend United v Notts County
West Ham United v Oxford United
Wolverhampton Wanderers v Charlton
Athletic

DIVISION TWO
A.F.C. Bournemouth v Reading
Blackpool v Stoke City
Burnley v Huddersfield Town
Exeter City v Chester City
Fulham v Bolton Wanderers
Mansfield Town v Hartlepool United
Port Vale v Hull City
Rotherham United v Preston North End
West Bromwich Albion v Bradford City
Wigan Athletic v Leyton Orient

DIVISION THREE
Bury v Hereford United
Colchester United v Rochdale
Crewe Alexandra v Lincoln City
Doncaster Rovers v Carlisle United
Gillingham v Darlington
Northampton Town v York City
Scarborough v Maidstone United
Shrewsbury Town v Walsall
Torquay United v Scunthorpe United
Wrexham v Halifax Town

SUNDAY, 22 NOVEMBER, 1992
Barclays League
DIVISION THREE
Barnet v Cardiff City

MONDAY, 23 NOVEMBER, 1992
FA Premier League
Queen's Park Rangers v Liverpool

FRIDAY, 27 NOVEMBER, 1992
Barclays League
DIVISION TWO
Chester City v Wigan Athletic

SATURDAY, 28 NOVEMBER, 1992
FA Premier League
Arsenal v Manchester United
Aston Villa v Norwich City
Blackburn Rovers v Queen's Park
Rangers
Chelsea v Leeds United

Ipswich Town v Everton
Liverpool v Crystal Palace
Manchester City v Tottenham Hotspur
Nottingham Forest v Southampton
Oldham Athletic v Middlesbrough
Sheffield United v Coventry City
Wimbledon v Sheffield Wednesday
Barclays League
DIVISION ONE
Barnsley v Charlton Athletic
Brentford v Oxford United
Bristol City v Notts County
Derby County v Tranmere Rovers
Leicester City v Bristol Rovers
Luton Town v Watford
Newcastle United v Cambridge United
Peterborough United v Swindon Town
Portsmouth v Millwall
Southend United v Sunderland
West Ham United v Birmingham City
Wolverhampton Wanderers v Grimsby
Town

DIVISION TWO
Bolton Wanderers v Burnley
Bradford City v Rotherham United
Brighton & Hove Albion v Fulham
Hartlepool United v Stockport County
Huddersfield Town v Port Vale
Hull City v Blackpool
Leyton Orient v Mansfield Town
Plymouth Argyle v A.F.C. Bournemouth
Preston North End v West Bromwich
Albion
Reading v Exeter City
Stoke City v Swansea City

DIVISION THREE
Cardiff City v Bury
Carlisle United v Northampton Town
Darlington v Barnet
Halifax Town v Chesterfield
Hereford United v Colchester United
Lincoln City v Gillingham
Maidstone United v Torquay United
Rochdale v Doncaster Rovers
Scunthorpe United v Scarborough
Walsall v Wrexham
York City v Crewe Alexandra

FRIDAY, 4 DECEMBER, 1992
Barclays League
DIVISION ONE
Tranmere Rovers v West Ham United

SATURDAY, 5 DECEMBER, 1992
FA Premier League
Coventry City v Ipswich Town
Crystal Palace v Sheffield United
Leeds United v Nottingham Forest
Manchester United v Manchester City
Middlesbrough v Blackburn Rovers
Norwich City v Wimbledon

Queen's Park Rangers v Oldham Athletic
Sheffield Wednesday v Aston Villa
Southampton v Arsenal
Tottenham Hotspur v Chelsea

Barclays League

DIVISION ONE

Birmingham City v Brentford
Bristol Rovers v Luton Town
Cambridge United v Wolverhampton
Wanderers
Charlton Athletic v Portsmouth
Grimsby Town v Leicester City
Millwall v Southend United
Notts County v Newcastle United
Oxford United v Peterborough United
Sunderland v Barnsley
Swindon Town v Derby County
Watford v Bristol City

MONDAY, 7 DECEMBER, 1992
FA Premier League
Everton v Liverpool

FRIDAY, 11 DECEMBER, 1992
DIVISION TWO
Stockport County v Bolton Wanderers

DIVISION THREE
Colchester United v Torquay United
Doncaster Rovers v Cardiff City

SATURDAY, 12 DECEMBER, 1992
FA Premier League
Aston Villa v Nottingham Forest
Ipswich Town v Manchester City
Leeds United v Sheffield Wednesday
Liverpool v Blackburn Rovers
Manchester United v Norwich City
Middlesbrough v Chelsea
Queen's Park Rangers v Crystal Palace
Sheffield United v Everton
Southampton v Coventry City
Tottenham Hotspur v Arsenal
Wimbledon v Oldham Athletic

Barclays League

DIVISION ONE

Barnsley v Newcastle United
Bristol Rovers v Bristol City
Derby County v Birmingham City
Millwall v Grimsby Town
Notts County v Cambridge United
Oxford United v Leicester City
Peterborough United v Portsmouth
Sunderland v Brentford
Swindon Town v Tranmere Rovers
Watford v Charlton Athletic
West Ham United v Southend United
Wolverhampton Wanderers v Luton Town

DIVISION TWO
Bradford City v A.F.C. Bournemouth
Burnley v Leyton Orient
Chester City v Reading

Fulham v Rotherham United
Hull City v Exeter City
Mansfield Town v Brighton & Hove
Albion
Plymouth Argyle v Hartlepool United
Preston North End v Port Vale
Stoke City v Huddersfield Town
Swansea City v West Bromwich Albion
Wigan Athletic v Blackpool

DIVISION THREE
Barnet v Rochdale
Bury v Northampton Town
Carlisle United v Crewe Alexandra
Maidstone United v Halifax Town
Scunthorpe United v Hereford United
Shrewsbury Town v Gillingham
Walsall v Darlington
Wrexham v Scarborough
York City v Chesterfield

SATURDAY, 19 DECEMBER, 1992
FA Premier League
Arsenal v Middlesbrough
Blackburn Rovers v Sheffield United
Chelsea v Manchester United
Coventry City v Liverpool
Crystal Palace v Leeds United
Everton v Southampton
Manchester City v Aston Villa
Oldham Athletic v Tottenham Hotspur
Sheffield Wednesday v Queen's Park
Rangers

Barclays League

DIVISION ONE

Birmingham City v Watford
Bristol City v Peterborough United
Charlton Athletic v Oxford United
Grimsby Town v Derby County
Luton Town v Sunderland
Newcastle United v Millwall
Portsmouth v Notts County
Southend United v Barnsley
Tranmere Rovers v Wolverhampton
Wanderers

DIVISION TWO
A.F.C. Bournemouth v Hull City
Blackpool v Fulham
Bolton Wanderers v Bradford City
Brighton & Hove Albion v Plymouth
Argyle
Exeter City v Burnley
Huddersfield Town v Chester City
Port Vale v Wigan Athletic
Reading v Stockport County

DIVISION THREE
Chesterfield v Doncaster Rovers
Darlington v Scunthorpe United
Halifax Town v Bury
Hereford United v Carlisle United
Rochdale v Lincoln City
Scarborough v York City

224

SUNDAY, 20 DECEMBER, 1992
FA Premier League
Nottingham Forest v Wimbledon
Barclays League
DIVISION ONE
Brentford v West Ham United
Leicester City v Swindon Town

DIVISION TWO
Hartlepool United v Stoke City
West Bromwich Albion v Mansfield Town

DIVISION THREE
Northampton Town v Maidstone United
Torquay United v Shrewsbury Town

MONDAY, 21 DECEMBER, 1992
FA Premier League
Norwich City v Ipswich Town

SATURDAY, 26 DECEMBER, 1992
FA Premier League
Arsenal v Ipswich Town
Blackburn Rovers v Leeds United
Chelsea v Southampton
Coventry City v Aston Villa
Crystal Palace v Wimbledon
Everton v Middlesbrough
Manchester City v Sheffield United
Norwich City v Tottenham Hotspur
Nottingham Forest v Queen's Park
Rangers
Oldham Athletic v Liverpool
Sheffield Wednesday v Manchester United
Barclays League
DIVISION ONE
Birmingham City v Sunderland
Brentford v Derby County
Bristol City v Oxford United
Cambridge United v Peterborough United
Charlton Athletic v West Ham United
Grimsby Town v Barnsley
Leicester City v Notts County
Luton Town v Swindon Town
Newcastle United v Wolverhampton
Wanderers
Portsmouth v Bristol Rovers
Southend United v Watford
Tranmere Rovers v Millwall

DIVISION TWO
A.F.C. Bournemouth v Swansea City
Blackpool v Bradford City
Bolton Wanderers v Wigan Athletic
Brighton & Hove Albion v Burnley
Exeter City v Plymouth Argyle
Hartlepool United v Hull City
Huddersfield Town v Preston North End
Leyton Orient v Fulham
Port Vale v Mansfield Town
Reading v Stoke City
Rotherham United v Stockport County
West Bromwich Albion v Chester City

DIVISION THREE
Cardiff City v York City
Chesterfield v Lincoln City
Crewe Alexandra v Wrexham
Darlington v Carlisle United
Gillingham v Maidstone United
Halifax Town v Doncaster Rovers
Hereford United v Shrewsbury Town
Northampton Town v Colchester United
Rochdale v Scunthorpe United
Scarborough v Barnet
Torquay United v Walsall

MONDAY, 28 DECEMBER, 1992
FA Premier League
Aston Villa v Arsenal
Ipswich Town v Blackburn Rovers
Leeds United v Norwich City
Liverpool v Manchester City
Manchester United v Coventry City
Middlesbrough v Crystal Palace
Queen's Park Rangers v Everton
Southampton v Sheffield Wednesday
Tottenham Hotspur v Nottingham Forest
Wimbledon v Chelsea
Barclays League
DIVISION ONE
Barnsley v Tranmere Rovers
Bristol Rovers v Southend United
Derby County v Portsmouth
Millwall v Leicester City
Notts County v Brentford
Oxford United v Newcastle United
Peterborough United v Charlton Athletic
Sunderland v Grimsby Town
Watford v Cambridge United
West Ham United v Luton Town
Wolverhampton Wanderers v Bristol City

DIVISION TWO
Bradford City v Port Vale
Burnley v A.F.C. Bournemouth
Chester City v Blackpool
Fulham v Hartlepool United
Hull City v Brighton & Hove Albion
Mansfield Town v Reading
Plymouth Argyle v West Bromwich
Albion
Preston North End v Exeter City
Stockport County v Leyton Orient
Stoke City v Rotherham United
Swansea City v Bolton Wanderers
Wigan Athletic v Huddersfield Town

DIVISION THREE
Barnet v Torquay United
Bury v Rochdale
Doncaster Rovers v Darlington
Lincoln City v Cardiff City
Maidstone United v Hereford United
Scunthorpe United v Gillingham
Shrewsbury Town v Crewe Alexandra
Walsall v Northampton Town

Wrexham v Chesterfield
York City v Halifax Town

TUESDAY, 29 DECEMBER, 1992
FA Premier League
Sheffield United v Oldham Athletic
Barclays League
DIVISION ONE
Swindon Town v Birmingham City

DIVISION THREE
Colchester United v Scarborough

SATURDAY, 2 JANUARY, 1993
Barclays League
DIVISION ONE
Birmingham City v Peterborough United

DIVISION TWO
Blackpool v Swansea City
Bolton Wanderers v Rotherham United
Bradford City v Mansfield Town
Burnley v Preston North End
Chester City v Leyton Orient
Exeter City v Port Vale
Fulham v A.F.C. Bournemouth
Hartlepool United v Wigan Athletic
Huddersfield Town v Brighton & Hove
Albion
Hull City v Stockport County
Reading v West Bromwich Albion
Stoke City v Plymouth Argyle

DIVISION THREE
Barnet v Bury
Cardiff City v Hereford United
Chesterfield v Gillingham
Doncaster Rovers v Crewe Alexandra
Halifax Town v Lincoln City
Maidstone United v Darlington
Scunthorpe United v Northampton Town
Shrewsbury Town v Wrexham
Torquay United v Scarborough
Walsall v Colchester United
York City v Carlisle United

FRIDAY, 8 JANUARY, 1993
Barclays League
DIVISION THREE
Colchester United v Doncaster Rovers
Gillingham v Rochdale
Northampton Town v Barnet

SATURDAY, 9 JANUARY, 1993
FA Premier League
Arsenal v Sheffield United
Blackburn Rovers v Wimbledon
Chelsea v Manchester City
Coventry City v Nottingham Forest
Crystal Palace v Everton
Ipswich Town v Oldham Athletic
Leeds United v Southampton
Liverpool v Aston Villa
Manchester United v Tottenham Hotspur

Middlesbrough v Queen's Park Rangers
Sheffield Wednesday v Norwich City

Barclays League
DIVISION ONE
Birmingham City v Luton Town
Brentford v Leicester City
Bristol City v Newcastle United
Charlton Athletic v Tranmere Rovers
Derby County v West Ham United
Grimsby Town v Bristol Rovers
Notts County v Millwall
Oxford United v Swindon Town
Peterborough United v Barnsley
Portsmouth v Southend United
Sunderland v Cambridge United
Watford v Wolverhampton Wanderers

DIVISION TWO
A.F.C. Bournemouth v Blackpool
Brighton & Hove Albion v Stoke City
Leyton Orient v Hartlepool United
Mansfield Town v Chester City
Plymouth Argyle v Huddersfield Town
Port Vale v Burnley
Preston North End v Hull City
Rotherham United v Reading
Stockport County v Bradford City
Swansea City v Fulham
West Bromwich Albion v Bolton
Wanderers
Wigan Athletic v Exeter City

DIVISION THREE
Bury v Walsall
Carlisle United v Cardiff City
Crewe Alexandra v Chesterfield
Darlington v Halifax Town
Hereford United v York City
Lincoln City v Maidstone United
Scarborough v Shrewsbury Town
Wrexham v Torquay United

FRIDAY, 15 JANUARY, 1993
Barclays League
Tranmere Rovers v Oxford United

SATURDAY, 16 JANUARY, 1993
FA Premier League
Aston Villa v Middlesbrough
Everton v Leeds United
Manchester City v Arsenal
Norwich City v Coventry City
Nottingham Forest v Chelsea
Oldham Athletic v Blackburn Rovers
Queen's Park Rangers v Manchester
United
Sheffield United v Ipswich Town
Southampton v Crystal Palace
Tottenham Hotspur v Sheffield
Wednesday
Wimbledon v Liverpool

Barclays League
DIVISION ONE
Barnsley v Bristol City
Bristol Rovers v Sunderland
Cambridge United v Grimsby Town
Leicester City v Watford
Luton Town v Notts County
Millwall v Brentford
Newcastle United v Peterborough United
Southend United v Derby County
Swindon Town v Charlton Athletic
West Ham United v Portsmouth
Wolverhampton Wanderers v
Birmingham City

DIVISION TWO
Blackpool v Rotherham United
Bolton Wanderers v Plymouth Argyle
Bradford City v Swansea City
Burnley v Wigan Athletic
Chester City v Port Vale
Exeter City v West Bromwich Albion
Fulham v Stockport County
Hartlepool United v Preston North End
Huddersfield Town v A.F.C. Bournemouth
Hull City v Leyton Orient
Reading v Brighton & Hove Albion
Stoke City v Mansfield Town

DIVISION THREE
Barnet v Wrexham
Chesterfield v Colchester United
Doncaster Rovers v Scarborough
Halifax Town v Northampton Town
Maidstone United v Crewe Alexandra
Rochdale v Hereford United
Scunthorpe United v Carlisle United
Shrewsbury Town v Lincoln City
Torquay United v Bury
Walsall v Gillingham
York City v Darlington

WEDNESDAY, 20 JANUARY, 1993
Barclays League
DIVISION ONE
Southend United v Newcastle United

FRIDAY, 22 JANUARY, 1993
Barclays League
DIVISION TWO
Stockport County v Chester City

DIVISION THREE
Colchester United v York City

SATURDAY, 23 JANUARY, 1993
Barclays League
DIVISION TWO
A.F.C. Bournemouth v Bolton Wanderers
Brighton & Hove Albion v Blackpool
Leyton Orient v Exeter City
Mansfield Town v Burnley
Plymouth Argyle v Fulham
Port Vale v Hartlepool United

Preston North End v Bradford City
Rotherham United v Hull City
Swansea City v Huddersfield Town
West Bromwich Albion v Stoke City
Wigan Athletic v Reading

DIVISION THREE
Bury v Shrewsbury Town
Carlisle United v Chesterfield
Crewe Alexandra v Scunthorpe United
Darlington v Rochdale
Gillingham v Cardiff City
Hereford United v Barnet
Lincoln City v Doncaster Rovers
Northampton Town v Torquay United
Scarborough v Halifax Town
Wrexham v Maidstone United

TUESDAY, 26 JANUARY, 1993
FA Premier League
Blackburn Rovers v Coventry City
Middlesbrough v Southampton
Oldham Athletic v Manchester City
Tottenham Hotspur v Ipswich Town
Wimbledon v Everton
Barclays League
DIVISION ONE
Cambridge United v Oxford United
Grimsby Town v Swindon Town
Notts County v Tranmere Rovers
Portsmouth v Brentford
Sunderland v Watford
Wolverhampton Wanderers v Barnsley

DIVISION TWO
A.F.C. Bournemouth v West Bromwich
Albion
Blackpool v Leyton Orient
Chester City v Preston North End
Fulham v Mansfield Town
Plymouth Argyle v Hull City
Rotherham United v Burnley
Stockport County v Port Vale
Swansea City v Wigan Athletic

DIVISION THREE
Barnet v Gillingham
Bury v Chesterfield
Darlington v Colchester United
Halifax Town v Cardiff City
Lincoln City v Carlisle United
Northampton Town v Crewe Alexandra
Scarborough v Rochdale
Shrewsbury Town v Scunthorpe United
Torquay United v Doncaster Rovers
Walsall v Hereford United
Wrexham v York City

WEDNESDAY, 27 JANUARY, 1993
FA Premier League
Aston Villa v Sheffield United
Liverpool v Leeds United
Manchester United v Nottingham Forest
Norwich City v Crystal Palace

Queen's Park Rangers v Chelsea
Sheffield Wednesday v Arsenal
Barclays League
DIVISION ONE
Bristol Rovers v Charlton Athletic
Derby County v Leicester City
Luton Town v Newcastle United
Millwall v Peterborough United
Southend United v Birmingham City
West Ham United v Bristol City

DIVISION TWO
Brighton & Hove Albion v Bradford City
Huddersfield Town v Hartlepool United
Reading v Bolton Wanderers
Stoke City v Exeter City

FRIDAY, 29 JANUARY, 1993
Barclays League
DIVISION THREE
Colchester United v Barnet
Doncaster Rovers v Shrewsbury Town

SATURDAY, 30 JANUARY, 1993
FA Premier League
Arsenal v Liverpool
Chelsea v Sheffield Wednesday
Coventry City v Wimbledon
Crystal Palace v Tottenham Hotspur
Everton v Norwich City
Ipswich Town v Manchester United
Leeds United v Middlesbrough
Manchester City v Blackburn Rovers
Nottingham Forest v Oldham Athletic
Sheffield United v Queen's Park Rangers
Southampton v Aston Villa
Barclays League
DIVISION ONE
Barnsley v Portsmouth
Birmingham City v Cambridge United
Brentford v Bristol Rovers
Bristol City v Luton Town
Charlton Athletic v Notts County
Leicester City v West Ham United
Newcastle United v Derby County
Oxford United v Millwall
Peterborough United v Southend United
Swindon Town v Wolverhampton
Wanderers
Tranmere Rovers v Sunderland
Watford v Grimsby Town

DIVISION TWO
Bolton Wanderers v Brighton & Hove
Albion
Bradford City v Plymouth Argyle
Burnley v Stockport County
Chester City v Hull City
Exeter City v Blackpool
Hartlepool United v Rotherham United
Leyton Orient v Reading
Mansfield Town v Swansea City
Port Vale v A.F.C. Bournemouth

Preston North End v Fulham
West Bromwich Albion v Huddersfield
Town
Wigan Athletic v Stoke City

DIVISION THREE
Cardiff City v Walsall
Carlisle United v Maidstone United
Chesterfield v Northampton Town
Crewe Alexandra v Scarborough
Gillingham v Bury
Hereford United v Darlington
Rochdale v Wrexham
Scunthorpe United v Halifax Town
York City v Lincoln City

FRIDAY, 5 FEBRUARY, 1993
Barclays League
DIVISION TWO
Stockport County v Wigan Athletic
Swansea City v Burnley

SATURDAY, 6 FEBRUARY, 1993
FA Premier League
Aston Villa v Ipswich Town
Blackburn Rovers v Crystal Palace
Liverpool v Nottingham Forest
Manchester United v Sheffield United
Middlesbrough v Coventry City
Norwich City v Arsenal
Oldham Athletic v Chelsea
Queen's Park Rangers v Manchester City
Sheffield Wednesday v Everton
Tottenham Hotspur v Southampton
Wimbledon v Leeds United
Barclays League
DIVISION ONE
Bristol Rovers v Oxford United
Cambridge United v Tranmere Rovers
Derby County v Peterborough United
Grimsby Town v Charlton Athletic
Luton Town v Leicester City
Millwall v Watford
Notts County v Birmingham City
Portsmouth v Bristol City
Sunderland v Swindon Town
West Ham United v Barnsley
Wolverhampton Wanderers v Brentford

DIVISION TWO
A.F.C. Bournemouth v Preston North End
Blackpool v West Bromwich Albion
Brighton & Hove Albion v Leyton Orient
Chester City v Bradford City
Fulham v Port Vale
Huddersfield Town v Bolton Wanderers
Plymouth Argyle v Mansfield Town
Reading v Hartlepool United
Rotherham United v Exeter City
Stoke City v Hull City

DIVISION THREE
Barnet v Chesterfield
Bury v Doncaster Rovers

Darlington v Cardiff City
Halifax Town v Rochdale
Lincoln City v Colchester United
Maidstone United v Scunthorpe United
Northampton Town v Gillingham
Scarborough v Hereford United
Shrewsbury Town v York City
Torquay United v Crewe Alexandra
Walsall v Carlisle United

TUESDAY, 9 FEBRUARY, 1993
FA Premier League
Arsenal v Wimbledon
Crystal Palace v Aston Villa
Ipswich Town v Queen's Park Rangers
Leeds United v Manchester United
Sheffield United v Middlesbrough
Barclays League
DIVISION ONE
Birmingham City v Millwall
Grimsby Town v Tranmere Rovers
Portsmouth v Newcastle United
Sunderland v Oxford United

WEDNESDAY, 10 FEBRUARY, 1993
FA Premier League
Chelsea v Liverpool
Coventry City v Oldham Athletic
Everton v Tottenham Hotspur
Manchester City v Sheffield Wednesday
Nottingham Forest v Blackburn Rovers
Southampton v Norwich City
Barclays League
DIVISION ONE
Derby County v Barnsley
Luton Town v Brentford
Southend United v Bristol City
West Ham United v Peterborough United

SATURDAY, 13 FEBRUARY, 1993
FA Premier League
Arsenal v Queen's Park Rangers
Chelsea v Aston Villa
Coventry City v Sheffield Wednesday
Crystal Palace v Manchester United
Everton v Blackburn Rovers
Ipswich Town v Middlesbrough
Leeds United v Oldham Athletic
Manchester City v Wimbledon
Nottingham Forest v Norwich City
Sheffield United v Tottenham Hotspur
Southampton v Liverpool
Barclays League
DIVISION ONE
Barnsley v Notts County
Birmingham City v Portsmouth
Bristol City v Derby County
Charlton Athletic v Sunderland
Leicester City v Southend United
Newcastle United v Bristol Rovers
Oxford United v Grimsby Town

Peterborough United v Wolverhampton
Wanderers
Swindon Town v Millwall
Tranmere Rovers v Luton Town
Watford v West Ham United

DIVISION TWO
Bolton Wanderers v Stoke City
Burnley v Chester City
Exeter City v Stockport County
Hartlepool United v A.F.C. Bournemouth
Hull City v Reading
Leyton Orient v Plymouth Argyle
Mansfield Town v Blackpool
Port Vale v Swansea City
Preston North End v Brighton & Hove
Albion
West Bromwich Albion v Fulham
Wigan Athletic v Rotherham United

DIVISION THREE
Cardiff City v Torquay United
Carlisle United v Barnet
Chesterfield v Maidstone United
Colchester United v Bury
Crewe Alexandra v Darlington
Doncaster Rovers v Wrexham
Gillingham v Scarborough
Hereford United v Northampton Town
Rochdale v Shrewsbury Town
Scunthorpe United v Lincoln City
York City v Walsall

SUNDAY, 14 FEBRUARY, 1993
Barclays League
DIVISION ONE
Brentford v Cambridge United

DIVISION TWO
Bradford City v Huddersfield Town

FRIDAY, 19 FEBRUARY, 1993
Barclays League
DIVISION THREE
Northampton Town v Cardiff City

SATURDAY, 20 FEBRUARY, 1993
FA Premier League
Aston Villa v Everton
Blackburn Rovers v Chelsea
Liverpool v Ipswich Town
Manchester United v Southampton
Middlesbrough v Nottingham Forest
Norwich City v Manchester City
Oldham Athletic v Arsenal
Queen's Park Rangers v Coventry City
Sheffield Wednesday v Crystal Palace
Tottenham Hotspur v Leeds United
Wimbledon v Sheffield United
Barclays League
DIVISION ONE
Bristol Rovers v Tranmere Rovers
Cambridge United v Swindon Town
Derby County v Watford

Grimsby Town v Birmingham City
Luton Town v Charlton Athletic
Millwall v Barnsley
Notts County v Peterborough United
Portsmouth v Leicester City
Sunderland v Bristol City
West Ham United v Newcastle United
Wolverhampton Wanderers v Oxford United

DIVISION TWO
A.F.C. Bournemouth v Mansfield Town
Blackpool v Bolton Wanderers
Brighton & Hove Albion v Exeter City
Chester City v Hartlepool United
Fulham v Wigan Athletic
Huddersfield Town v Leyton Orient
Plymouth Argyle v Burnley
Reading v Preston North End
Rotherham United v Port Vale
Stockport County v West Bromwich Albion
Stoke City v Bradford City
Swansea City v Hull City

DIVISION THREE
Barnet v Doncaster Rovers
Bury v Carlisle United
Darlington v Chesterfield
Halifax Town v Crewe Alexandra
Lincoln City v Hereford United
Maidstone United v Rochdale
Shrewsbury Town v Colchester United
Torquay United v York City
Walsall v Scunthorpe United
Wrexham v Gillingham

SUNDAY, 21 FEBRUARY, 1993
Barclays League
DIVISION ONE
Southend United v Brentford

FRIDAY, 26 FEBRUARY, 1993
Barclays League
DIVISION TWO
Rotherham United v A.F.C. Bournemouth
Stockport County v Mansfield Town

DIVISION THREE
Colchester United v Halifax Town

SATURDAY, 27 FEBRUARY, 1993
FA Premier League
Aston Villa v Wimbledon
Chelsea v Arsenal
Crystal Palace v Coventry City
Everton v Oldham Athletic
Leeds United v Ipswich Town
Manchester United v Middlesbrough
Norwich City v Blackburn Rovers
Nottingham Forest v Manchester City
Sheffield Wednesday v Liverpool
Southampton v Sheffield United
Tottenham Hotspur v Queen's Park Rangers

Barclays League
DIVISION ONE
Brentford v Peterborough United
Bristol Rovers v Watford
Cambridge United v Millwall
Charlton Athletic v Bristol City
Grimsby Town v Notts County
Leicester City v Birmingham City
Luton Town v Barnsley
Oxford United v Derby County
Sunderland v West Ham United
Swindon Town v Portsmouth
Tranmere Rovers v Newcastle United
Wolverhampton Wanderers v Southend United

DIVISION TWO
Burnley v Bradford City
Chester City v Plymouth Argyle
Exeter City v Swansea City
Hartlepool United v Bolton Wanderers
Hull City v Fulham
Leyton Orient v Stoke City
Port Vale v West Bromwich Albion
Preston North End v Blackpool
Reading v Huddersfield Town
Wigan Athletic v Brighton & Hove Albion

DIVISION THREE
Barnet v Maidstone United
Bury v Wrexham
Cardiff City v Crewe Alexandra
Carlisle United v Rochdale
Chesterfield v Torquay United
Darlington v Shrewsbury Town
Gillingham v Doncaster Rovers
Northampton Town v Scarborough
Walsall v Lincoln City
York City v Scunthorpe United

FRIDAY, 5 MARCH, 1993
Barclays League
DIVISION TWO
Swansea City v Stockport County

DIVISION THREE
Doncaster Rovers v York City

SATURDAY, 6 MARCH, 1993
FA Premier League
Arsenal v Nottingham Forest
Blackburn Rovers v Aston Villa
Coventry City v Everton
Ipswich Town v Chelsea
Liverpool v Manchester United
Manchester City v Crystal Palace
Middlesbrough v Tottenham Hotspur
Oldham Athletic v Sheffield Wednesday
Queen's Park Rangers v Norwich City
Wimbledon v Southampton

Barclays League
DIVISION ONE
Barnsley v Leicester City
Birmingham City v Oxford United

Bristol City v Tranmere Rovers
Derby County v Cambridge United
Millwall v Sunderland
Newcastle United v Brentford
Notts County v Bristol Rovers
Peterborough United v Grimsby Town
Portsmouth v Luton Town
Southend United v Charlton Athletic
Watford v Swindon Town
West Ham United v Wolverhampton
Wanderers

DIVISION TWO
A.F.C. Bournemouth v Exeter City
Blackpool v Hartlepool United
Bolton Wanderers v Leyton Orient
Bradford City v Hull City
Brighton & Hove Albion v Port Vale
Fulham v Reading
Huddersfield Town v Rotherham United
Mansfield Town v Wigan Athletic
Plymouth Argyle v Preston North End
Stoke City v Chester City
West Bromwich Albion v Burnley

DIVISION THREE
Crewe Alexandra v Gillingham
Halifax Town v Carlisle United
Lincoln City v Northampton Town
Maidstone United v Walsall
Rochdale v Cardiff City
Scarborough v Bury
Scunthorpe United v Chesterfield
Shrewsbury Town v Barnet
Torquay United v Darlington
Wrexham v Hereford United

SUNDAY, 7 MARCH, 1993
FA Premier League
Sheffield United v Leeds United

TUESDAY, 9 MARCH, 1993
FA Premier League
Arsenal v Leeds United
Blackburn Rovers v Southampton
Ipswich Town v Sheffield Wednesday
Oldham Athletic v Manchester United
Wimbledon v Middlesbrough
Barclays League
DIVISION ONE
Barnsley v Cambridge United
Brentford v Tranmere Rovers
Bristol City v Millwall
Peterborough United v Birmingham City
Portsmouth v Watford
Wolverhampton Wanderers v Notts
County

DIVISION TWO
Bolton Wanderers v Mansfield Town
Chester City v A.F.C. Bournemouth
Hartlepool United v Burnley
Hull City v Wigan Athletic
Leyton Orient v Rotherham United

Plymouth Argyle v Blackpool
Preston North End v Swansea City

DIVISION THREE
Cardiff City v Scarborough
Carlisle United v Shrewsbury Town
Darlington v Wrexham
Halifax Town v Barnet
Hereford United v Crewe Alexandra
Lincoln City v Torquay United
Maidstone United v Colchester United
Rochdale v Northampton Town
Scunthorpe United v Bury
Walsall v Chesterfield
York City v Gillingham

WEDNESDAY, 10 MARCH, 1993
FA Premier League
Aston Villa v Tottenham Hotspur
Chelsea v Everton
Liverpool v Queen's Park Rangers
Manchester City v Coventry City
Nottingham Forest v Crystal Palace
Sheffield United v Norwich City

Barclays League
DIVISION ONE
Derby County v Bristol Rovers
Leicester City v Sunderland
Luton Town v Oxford United
Newcastle United v Charlton Athletic
Southend United v Swindon Town
West Ham United v Grimsby Town

DIVISION TWO
Bradford City v Exeter City
Brighton & Hove Albion v West
Bromwich Albion
Huddersfield Town v Fulham
Reading v Port Vale
Stoke City v Stockport County

FRIDAY, 12 MARCH, 1993
Barclays League
DIVISION TWO
Wigan Athletic v Preston North End

DIVISION THREE
Colchester United v Cardiff City
Crewe Alexandra v Rochdale

SATURDAY, 13 MARCH, 1993
FA Premier League
Coventry City v Arsenal
Crystal Palace v Chelsea
Everton v Nottingham Forest
Leeds United v Manchester City
Manchester United v Aston Villa
Middlesbrough v Liverpool
Norwich City v Oldham Athletic
Queen's Park Rangers v Wimbledon
Southampton v Ipswich Town
Tottenham Hotspur v Blackburn Rovers

Barclays League
DIVISION ONE
Birmingham City v Bristol City
Bristol Rovers v Wolverhampton
Wanderers
Cambridge United v Portsmouth
Charlton Athletic v Brentford
Grimsby Town v Luton Town
Millwall v Derby County
Notts County v West Ham United
Oxford United v Southend United
Sunderland v Peterborough United
Swindon Town v Newcastle United
Tranmere Rovers v Leicester City
Watford v Barnsley

DIVISION TWO
A.F.C. Bournemouth v Stoke City
Blackpool v Reading
Burnley v Hull City
Exeter City v Hartlepool United
Fulham v Bradford City
Mansfield Town v Huddersfield Town
Port Vale v Bolton Wanderers
Rotherham United v Plymouth Argyle
Stockport County v Brighton & Hove
Albion
Swansea City v Chester City
West Bromwich Albion v Leyton Orient

DIVISION THREE
Barnet v York City
Bury v Darlington
Chesterfield v Hereford United
Doncaster Rovers v Scunthorpe United
Gillingham v Carlisle United
Scarborough v Walsall
Shrewsbury Town v Maidstone United
Torquay United v Halifax Town
Wrexham v Lincoln City

SUNDAY, 14 MARCH, 1993
FA Premier League
Sheffield Wednesday v Sheffield United

TUESDAY, 16 MARCH, 1993
Barclays League
DIVISION TWO
Port Vale v Stoke City

FRIDAY, 19 MARCH, 1993
Barclays League
DIVISION TWO
Chester City v Rotherham United

SATURDAY, 20 MARCH, 1993
FA Premier League
Arsenal v Southampton
Aston Villa v Sheffield Wednesday
Blackburn Rovers v Middlesbrough
Chelsea v Tottenham Hotspur
Ipswich Town v Coventry City
Liverpool v Everton
Manchester City v Manchester United

Nottingham Forest v Leeds United
Oldham Athletic v Queen's Park Rangers
Sheffield United v Crystal Palace
Wimbledon v Norwich City
Barclays League
DIVISION ONE
Barnsley v Sunderland
Brentford v Birmingham City
Bristol City v Watford
Derby County v Swindon Town
Leicester City v Grimsby Town
Luton Town v Bristol Rovers
Newcastle United v Notts County
Peterborough United v Oxford United
Portsmouth v Charlton Athletic
Southend United v Millwall
West Ham United v Tranmere Rovers
Wolverhampton Wanderers v Cambridge
United

DIVISION TWO
Bolton Wanderers v Exeter City
Bradford City v Wigan Athletic
Brighton & Hove Albion v A.F.C.
Bournemouth
Hartlepool United v West Bromwich
Albion
Huddersfield Town v Blackpool
Hull City v Mansfield Town
Leyton Orient v Port Vale
Plymouth Argyle v Swansea City
Preston North End v Stockport County
Reading v Burnley
Stoke City v Fulham

DIVISION THREE
Cardiff City v Chesterfield
Carlisle United v Colchester United
Darlington v Northampton Town
Halifax Town v Shrewsbury Town
Hereford United v Gillingham
Lincoln City v Scarborough
Maidstone United v Doncaster Rovers
Rochdale v Torquay United
Scunthorpe United·v Wrexham
Walsall v Barnet
York City v Bury

TUESDAY, 23 MARCH, 1993
FA Premier League
Crystal Palace v Liverpool
Leeds United v Chelsea
Middlesbrough v Oldham Athletic
Tottenham Hotspur v Manchester City
Barclays League
DIVISION ONE
Birmingham City v Barnsley
Cambridge United v Leicester City
Charlton Athletic v Wolverhampton
Wanderers
Grimsby Town v Brentford
Notts County v Southend United
Oxford United v West Ham United

232

Sunderland v Derby County
Swindon Town v Bristol City
Watford v Newcastle United

DIVISION TWO
A.F.C. Bournemouth v Plymouth Argyle
Blackpool v Hull City
Burnley v Bolton Wanderers
Exeter City v Reading
Fulham v Brighton & Hove Albion
Mansfield Town v Leyton Orient
Port Vale v Huddersfield Town
Rotherham United v Bradford City
Stockport County v Hartlepool United
Swansea City v Stoke City
Wigan Athletic v Chester City

DIVISION THREE
Barnet v Darlington
Bury v Cardiff City
Chesterfield v Halifax Town
Colchester United v Hereford United
Crewe Alexandra v York City
Doncaster Rovers v Rochdale
Gillingham v Lincoln City
Northampton Town v Carlisle United
Scarborough v Scunthorpe United
Torquay United v Maidstone United
Wrexham v Walsall

WEDNESDAY, 24 MARCH, 1993
FA Premier League
Coventry City v Sheffield United
Everton v Ipswich Town
Manchester United v Arsenal
Norwich City v Aston Villa
Queen's Park Rangers v Blackburn
Rovers
Sheffield Wednesday v Wimbledon
Southampton v Nottingham Forest

Barclays League
DIVISION ONE
Bristol Rovers v Peterborough United
Millwall v Luton Town

DIVISION TWO
West Bromwich Albion v Preston North
End

FRIDAY, 26 MARCH, 1993
Barclays League
DIVISION ONE
Southend United v Tranmere Rovers

DIVISION THREE
Halifax Town v Wrexham
York City v Northampton Town

SATURDAY, 27 MARCH, 1993
Barclays League
DIVISION ONE
Barnsley v Bristol Rovers
Brentford v Swindon Town

Bristol City v Grimsby Town
Derby County v Notts County
Leicester City v Charlton Athletic
Luton Town v Cambridge United
Newcastle United v Birmingham City
Peterborough United v Watford
Portsmouth v Oxford United
West Ham United v Millwall
Wolverhampton Wanderers v Sunderland

DIVISION TWO
Bolton Wanderers v Fulham
Bradford City v West Bromwich Albion
Brighton & Hove Albion v Swansea City
Chester City v Exeter City
Hartlepool United v Mansfield Town
Huddersfield Town v Burnley
Hull City v Port Vale
Leyton Orient v Wigan Athletic
Plymouth Argyle v Stockport County
Preston North End v Rotherham United
Reading v A.F.C. Bournemouth
Stoke City v Blackpool

DIVISION THREE
Cardiff City v Barnet
Carlisle United v Doncaster Rovers
Darlington v Gillingham
Hereford United v Bury
Lincoln City v Crewe Alexandra
Maidstone United v Scarborough
Rochdale v Colchester United
Scunthorpe United v Torquay United
Walsall v Shrewsbury Town

FRIDAY, 2 APRIL, 1993
Barclays League
DIVISION ONE
Tranmere Rovers v Derby County

DIVISION TWO
Fulham v Huddersfield Town

DIVISION THREE
Crewe Alexandra v Hereford United
Gillingham v York City
Northampton Town v Rochdale
Wrexham v Darlington

SATURDAY, 3 APRIL, 1993
FA Premier League
Arsenal v Tottenham Hotspur
Blackburn Rovers v Liverpool
Chelsea v Middlesbrough
Coventry City v Southampton
Crystal Palace v Queen's Park Rangers
Everton v Sheffield United
Manchester City v Ipswich Town
Norwich City v Manchester United
Nottingham Forest v Aston Villa
Oldham Athletic v Wimbledon
Sheffield Wednesday v Leeds United

Barclays League
DIVISION ONE
Birmingham City v West Ham United
Bristol Rovers v Leicester City

Cambridge United v Newcastle United
Charlton Athletic v Barnsley
Grimsby Town v Wolverhampton Wanderers
Millwall v Portsmouth
Notts County v Bristol City
Oxford United v Brentford
Sunderland v Southend United
Swindon Town v Peterborough United
Tranmere Rovers v Derby County
Watford v Luton Town

DIVISION TWO
A.F.C. Bournemouth v Chester City
Blackpool v Plymouth Argyle
Burnley v Hartlepool United
Exeter City v Bradford City
Mansfield Town v Bolton Wanderers
Port Vale v Reading
Rotherham United v Leyton Orient
Stockport County v Stoke City
Swansea City v Preston North End
West Bromwich Albion v Brighton & Hove Albion
Wigan Athletic v Hull City

DIVISION THREE
Barnet v Halifax Town
Bury v Scunthorpe United
Chesterfield v Walsall
Colchester United v Maidstone United
Scarborough v Cardiff City
Shrewsbury Town v Carlisle United
Torquay United v Lincoln City

TUESDAY, 6 APRIL, 1993
Barclays League
DIVISION ONE
Birmingham City v Derby County
Brentford v Sunderland
Bristol City v Bristol Rovers
Cambridge United v Notts County
Charlton Athletic v Watford
Grimsby Town v Millwall
Portsmouth v Peterborough United
Tranmere Rovers v Swindon Town

DIVISION TWO
A.F.C. Bournemouth v Bradford City
Blackpool v Wigan Athletic
Bolton Wanderers v Stockport County
Exeter City v Hull City
Hartlepool United v Plymouth Argyle
Leyton Orient v Burnley
Port Vale v Preston North End
Rotherham United v Fulham

DIVISION THREE
Cardiff City v Doncaster Rovers
Chesterfield v York City
Crewe Alexandra v Carlisle United
Darlington v Walsall
Gillingham v Shrewsbury Town
Halifax Town v Maidstone United
Hereford United v Scunthorpe United

Northampton Town v Bury
Rochdale v Barnet
Scarborough v Wrexham
Torquay United v Colchester United

WEDNESDAY, 7 APRIL, 1993
Barclays League
DIVISION ONE
Leicester City v Oxford United
Luton Town v Wolverhampton Wanderers
Newcastle United v Barnsley
Southend United v West Ham United

DIVISION TWO
Brighton & Hove Albion v Mansfield Town
Huddersfield Town v Stoke City
Reading v Chester City
West Bromwich Albion v Swansea City

FRIDAY, 9 APRIL, 1993
FA Premier League
Tottenham Hotspur v Norwich City
Barclays League
DIVISION TWO
Stockport County v Rotherham United

DIVISION THREE
Colchester United v Northampton Town

SATURDAY, 10 APRIL, 1993
FA Premier League
Aston Villa v Coventry City
Ipswich Town v Arsenal
Leeds United v Blackburn Rovers
Liverpool v Oldham Athletic
Manchester United v Sheffield Wednesday
Middlesbrough v Everton
Queen's Park Rangers v Nottingham Forest
Sheffield United v Manchester City
Southampton v Chelsea
Wimbledon v Crystal Palace

Barclays League
DIVISION ONE
Barnsley v Grimsby Town
Bristol Rovers v Portsmouth
Derby County v Brentford
Millwall v Tranmere Rovers
Notts County v Charlton Athletic
Oxford United v Bristol City
Peterborough United v Cambridge United
Sunderland v Birmingham City
Swindon Town v Luton Town
Watford v Southend United
West Ham United v Leicester City
Wolverhampton Wanderers v Newcastle United

DIVISION TWO
Bradford City v Blackpool
Burnley v Brighton & Hove Albion
Chester City v West Bromwich Albion

Fulham v Leyton Orient
Hull City v Hartlepool United
Mansfield Town v Port Vale
Plymouth Argyle v Exeter City
Preston North End v Huddersfield Town
Stoke City v Reading
Swansea City v A.F.C. Bournemouth
Wigan Athletic v Bolton Wanderers

DIVISION THREE
Barnet v Scarborough
Carlisle United v Darlington
Doncaster Rovers v Halifax Town
Lincoln City v Chesterfield
Maidstone United v Gillingham
Scunthorpe United v Rochdale
Shrewsbury Town v Hereford United
Walsall v Torquay United
Wrexham v Crewe Alexandra
York City v Cardiff City

MONDAY, 12 APRIL, 1993
FA Premier League
Arsenal v Aston Villa
Blackburn Rovers v Ipswich Town
Chelsea v Wimbledon
Coventry City v Manchester United
Crystal Palace v Middlesbrough
Everton v Queen's Park Rangers
Manchester City v Liverpool
Nottingham Forest v Tottenham Hotspur
Oldham Athletic v Sheffield United
Sheffield Wednesday v Southampton
Barclays League
DIVISION ONE
Birmingham City v Swindon Town
Brentford v Notts County
Bristol City v Wolverhampton Wanderers
Charlton Athletic v Peterborough United
Grimsby Town v Sunderland
Newcastle United v Oxford United
Portsmouth v Derby County
Tranmere Rovers v Barnsley

DIVISION TWO
Bolton Wanderers v Swansea City
Exeter City v Preston North End
Hartlepool United v Fulham
Huddersfield Town v Wigan Athletic
Leyton Orient v Stockport County
Reading v Mansfield Town
Rotherham United v Stoke City
West Bromwich Albion v Plymouth
Argyle

DIVISION THREE
Cardiff City v Lincoln City
Chesterfield v Wrexham
Crewe Alexandra v Shrewsbury Town
Darlington v Doncaster Rovers
Gillingham v Scunthorpe United
Halifax Town v York City
Hereford United v Maidstone United

Northampton Town v Walsall
Rochdale v Bury

TUESDAY, 13 APRIL, 1993
Barclays League
DIVISION ONE
Cambridge United v Watford
Leicester City v Millwall
Luton v West Ham United

DIVISION TWO
A.F.C. Bournemouth v Burnley
Blackpool v Chester City
Port Vale v Bradford City

DIVISION THREE
Scarborough v Colchester United
Torquay United v Barnet

WEDNESDAY, 14 APRIL, 1993
FA Premier League
Norwich City v Leeds United
Barclays League
DIVISION ONE
Southend United v Bristol Rovers

DIVISION TWO
Brighton & Hove Albion v Hull City

FRIDAY, 16 APRIL, 1993
Barclays League
DIVISION TWO
Stockport County v Reading

DIVISION THREE
Colchester United v Gillingham

SATURDAY, 17 APRIL, 1993
FA Premier League
Aston Villa v Manchester City
Ipswich Town v Norwich City
Leeds United v Crystal Palace
Liverpool v Coventry City
Manchester United v Chelsea
Middlesbrough v Arsenal
Queen's Park Rangers v Sheffield
Wednesday
Sheffield United v Blackburn Rovers
Southampton v Everton
Tottenham Hotspur v Oldham Athletic
Wimbledon v Nottingham Forest
Barclays League
DIVISION ONE
Barnsley v Southend United
Bristol Rovers v Cambridge United
Derby County v Grimsby Town
Millwall v Newcastle United
Notts County v Portsmouth
Oxford United v Charlton Athletic
Peterborough United v Bristol City
Sunderland v Luton Town
Swindon Town v Leicester City
Watford v Birmingham City

West Ham United v Brentford
Wolverhampton Wanderers v Tranmere Rovers

DIVISION TWO
Bradford City v Bolton Wanderers
Burnley v Exeter City
Chester City v Huddersfield Town
Fulham v Blackpool
Hull City v A.F.C. Bournemouth
Mansfield Town v West Bromwich Albion
Plymouth Argyle v Brighton & Hove Albion
Preston North End v Leyton Orient
Stoke City v Hartlepool United
Swansea City v Rotherham United
Wigan Athletic v Port Vale

DIVISION THREE
Bury v Halifax Town
Carlisle United v Hereford United
Doncaster Rovers v Chesterfield
Lincoln City v Rochdale
Maidstone United v Northampton Town
Scunthorpe United v Darlington
Shrewsbury Town v Torquay United
Walsall v Crewe Alexandra
Wrexham v Cardiff City
York City v Scarborough

FRIDAY, 23 APRIL, 1993
Barclays League
DIVISION ONE
Southend United v Grimsby Town

SATURDAY, 24 APRIL, 1993
Barclays League
DIVISION ONE
Barnsley v Oxford United
Birmingham City v Tranmere Rovers
Bristol City v Cambridge United
Derby County v Luton Town
Millwall v Charlton Athletic
Notts County v Swindon Town
Peterborough United v Leicester City
Portsmouth v Wolverhampton Wanderers
Watford v Brentford
West Ham United v Bristol Rovers

DIVISION TWO
A.F.C. Bournemouth v Leyton Orient
Blackpool v Stockport County
Bolton Wanderers v Chester City
Bradford City v Reading
Brighton & Hove Albion v Rotherham United
Fulham v Burnley
Huddersfield Town v Hull City
Mansfield Town v Exeter City
Plymouth Argyle v Port Vale
Stoke City v Preston North End
Swansea City v Hartlepool United
West Bromwich Albion v Wigan Athletic

DIVISION THREE
Crewe Alexandra v Colchester United
Doncaster Rovers v Northampton Town
Halifax Town v Walsall
Lincoln City v Bury
Maidstone United v Cardiff City
Rochdale v York City
Scarborough v Darlington
Scunthorpe United v Barnet
Shrewsbury Town v Chesterfield
Torquay United v Hereford United
Wrexham v Carlisle United

SUNDAY, 25 APRIL, 1993
Barclays League
DIVISION ONE
Newcastle United v Sunderland

TUESDAY, 27 APRIL, 1993
Barclays League
DIVISION THREE
Northampton Town v Wrexham

FRIDAY, 30 APRIL, 1993
Barclays League
DIVISION TWO
Hull City v Bolton Wanderers

SATURDAY, 1 MAY, 1993
FA Premier League
Aston Villa v Oldham Athletic
Chelsea v Coventry City
Crystal Palace v Ipswich Town
Everton v Arsenal
Leeds United v Queen's Park Rangers
Manchester United v Blackburn Rovers
Norwich City v Liverpool
Nottingham Forest v Sheffield United
Sheffield Wednesday v Middlesbrough
Southampton v Manchester City
Tottenham Hotspur v Wimbledon

Barclays League
DIVISION ONE
Brentford v Barnsley
Bristol Rovers v Birmingham City
Cambridge United v Southend United
Charlton Athletic v Derby County
Grimsby Town v Newcastle United
Leicester City v Bristol City
Luton Town v Peterborough United
Oxford United v Notts County
Sunderland v Portsmouth
Swindon Town v West Ham United
Tranmere Rovers v Watford
Wolverhampton Wanderers v Millwall

DIVISION TWO
Burnley v Blackpool
Chester City v Fulham
Exeter City v Huddersfield Town
Hartlepool United v Brighton & Hove Albion

Leyton Orient v Bradford City
Preston North End v Mansfield Town
Reading v Swansea City
Rotherham United v West Bromwich Albion
Stockport County v A.F.C. Bournemouth
Wigan Athletic v Plymouth Argyle

DIVISION THREE
Barnet v Lincoln City
Bury v Crewe Alexandra
Cardiff City v Shrewsbury Town
Carlisle United v Torquay United
Chesterfield v Scarborough
Colchester United v Scunthorpe United
Gillingham v Halifax Town
Hereford United v Doncaster Rovers
Walsall v Rochdale
York City v Maidstone United

SATURDAY, 8 MAY, 1993
FA Premier League
Arsenal v Crystal Palace
Blackburn Rovers v Sheffield Wednesday
Coventry City v Leeds United
Ipswich Town v Nottingham Forest
Liverpool v Tottenham Hotspur
Manchester City v Everton
Middlesbrough v Norwich City
Oldham Athletic v Southampton
Queen's Park Rangers v Aston Villa
Sheffield United v Chelsea
Wimbledon v Manchester United

Barclays League
DIVISION ONE
Barnsley v Swindon Town
Birmingham City v Charlton Athletic

Bristol City v Brentford
Derby County v Wolverhampton Wanderers
Millwall v Bristol Rovers
Newcastle United v Leicester City
Notts County v Sunderland
Peterborough United v Tranmere Rovers
Portsmouth v Grimsby Town
Southend United v Luton Town
Watford v Oxford United
West Ham United v Cambridge United

DIVISION TWO
A.F.C. Bournemouth v Wigan Athletic
Blackpool v Port Vale
Bolton Wanderers v Preston North End
Bradford City v Hartlepool United
Brighton & Hove Albion v Chester City
Fulham v Exeter City
Huddersfield Town v Stockport County
Mansfield Town v Rotherham United
Plymouth Argyle v Reading
Stoke City v Burnley
Swansea City v Leyton Orient
West Bromwich Albion v Hull City

DIVISION THREE
Crewe Alexandra v Barnet
Doncaster Rovers v Walsall
Halifax Town v Hereford United
Lincoln City v Darlington
Maidstone United v Bury
Rochdale v Chesterfield
Scarborough v Carlisle United
Scunthorpe United v Cardiff City
Shrewsbury Town v Northampton Town
Torquay United v Gillingham
Wrexham v Colchester United

League Tables 1991-92

BARCLAYS LEAGUE DIVISION 1

| | P | HOME | | | | | AWAY | | | | | | Goal |
		W	D	L	F	A	W	D	L	F	A	Pts	Diff
Leeds United	42	13	8	0	38	13	9	8	4	36	24	82	37+
Manchester United	42	12	7	2	34	13	9	8	4	29	30	78	30+
Sheffield Wednesday	42	13	5	3	39	24	8	7	6	23	25	75	13+
Arsenal	42	12	7	2	51	22	7	8	6	30	24	72	35+
Manchester City	42	13	4	4	32	14	7	8	6	29	34	70	13+
Liverpool	42	13	5	3	34	17	3	11	7	13	23	64	7+
Aston Villa	42	13	3	5	31	16	4	6	11	17	28	60	4+
Nottingham Forest	42	10	7	4	36	27	6	4	11	24	31	59	2+
Sheffield United	42	9	6	6	29	23	7	3	11	36	40	57	2+
Crystal Palace	42	7	8	6	24	25	7	7	7	29	36	57	8-
Queen's Park Rangers	42	6	10	5	25	21	6	8	7	23	26	54	1+
Everton	42	8	8	5	28	19	5	6	10	24	32	53	1+
Wimbledon	42	10	5	6	32	20	3	9	9	21	33	53	0
Chelsea	42	7	8	6	31	30	6	6	9	19	30	53	10-
Tottenham Hotspur	42	7	3	11	33	35	8	4	9	25	28	52	5-
Southampton	42	7	5	9	17	28	7	5	9	22	27	52	16-
Oldham Athletic	42	11	5	5	46	36	3	4	14	17	31	51	4-
Norwich City	42	8	6	7	29	28	3	6	12	18	35	45	16-
Coventry City	42	6	7	8	18	15	5	4	12	17	29	44	9-
Luton Town	42	10	7	4	25	17	0	5	16	13	54	42	33-
Notts County	42	7	5	9	24	29	3	5	13	16	33	40	22-
West Ham United	42	6	6	9	22	24	3	5	13	15	35	38	22-

BARCLAYS LEAGUE DIVISION 2

| | P | HOME | | | | | AWAY | | | | | | Goal |
		W	D	L	F	A	W	D	L	F	A	Pts	Diff
Ipswich Town	46	16	3	4	42	22	8	9	6	28	28	84	20+
Middlesbrough	46	15	6	2	37	13	8	5	10	21	28	80	17+
Derby County	46	11	4	8	35	24	12	5	6	34	27	78	18+
Leicester City	46	14	4	5	41	24	9	4	10	21	31	77	7+
Cambridge United	46	10	9	4	34	19	9	8	6	31	28	74	18+
*Blackburn Rovers	46	14	5	4	41	21	7	6	10	29	32	74	17+
Charlton Athletic	46	9	7	7	25	23	11	4	8	29	25	71	6+
Swindon Town	46	15	3	5	38	22	3	12	8	31	33	69	14+
Portsmouth	46	15	6	2	41	12	4	6	13	24	39	69	14+
Watford	46	9	5	9	25	23	9	6	8	26	25	65	3+
Wolverhampton Wanderers	46	11	·6	6	36	24	7	4	12	25	30	64	7+
Southend United	46	11	5	7	37	26	6	6	11	26	37	62	0
Bristol Rovers	46	11	9	3	43	29	5	5	13	17	34	62	3-
Tranmere Rovers	46	9	9	5	37	32	5	10	8	19	24	61	0
Millwall	46	10	4	9	32	32	7	6	10	32	39	61	7-

Blackburn Rovers promoted via play-offs

238

	P	W	D	L	F	A	W	D	L	F	A	Pts	Goal Diff
		HOME					AWAY						Goal
Barnsley	46	11	4	8	27	25	5	7	11	19	32	59	11−
Bristol City	46	10	8	5	30	24	3	7	13	25	47	54	16−
Sunderland	46	10	8	5	36	23	4	3	16	25	42	53	4−
Grimsby Town	46	7	5	11	25	28	7	6	10	22	34	53	15−
Newcastle United	46	9	8	6	38	30	4	5	14	28	54	52	18−
Oxford United	46	10	6	7	39	30	3	5	15	27	43	50	7−
Plymouth Argyle	46	11	5	7	26	26	2	4	17	16	38	48	22−
Brighton & Hove Albion	46	7	7	9	36	37	5	4	14	20	40	47	21−
Port Vale	46	7	8	8	23	25	3	7	13	19	34	45	17−

BARCLAYS LEAGUE DIVISION 3

		HOME					AWAY						Goal
	P	W	D	L	F	A	W	D	L	F	A	Pts	Diff
Brentford	46	17	2	4	55	29	8	5	10	26	26	82	26+
Birmingham City	46	15	6	2	42	22	8	6	9	27	30	81	17+
Huddersfield Town	46	15	4	4	36	15	7	8	8	23	23	78	21+
Stoke City	46	14	5	4	45	24	7	9	7	24	25	77	20+
Stockport County	46	15	5	3	47	19	7	5	11	28	32	76	24+
*Peterborough United	46	13	7	3	38	20	7	7	9	27	38	74	7+
West Bromwich Albion	46	12	6	5	45	25	7	8	8	19	24	71	15+
AFC Bournemouth	46	13	4	6	33	18	7	7	9	19	30	71	4+
Fulham	46	11	7	5	29	16	8	6	9	23	37	70	1−
Leyton Orient	46	12	7	4	36	18	6	4	13	26	34	65	10+
Hartlepool United	46	12	5	6	30	21	6	6	11	27	36	65	0
Reading	46	9	8	6	33	27	7	5	11	26	35	61	3−
Bolton Wanderers	46	10	9	4	26	19	4	8	11	31	37	59	1+
Hull City	46	9	4	10	28	23	7	7	9	26	31	59	0
Wigan Athletic	46	11	6	6	33	21	4	8	11	25	43	59	6−
Bradford City	46	8	10	5	36	30	5	9	9	26	31	58	1+
Preston North End	46	12	7	4	42	32	3	5	15	19	40	57	11−
Chester City	46	10	6	7	34	29	4	8	11	22	30	56	3−
Swansea City	46	10	9	4	35	24	4	5	14	20	41	56	10−
Exeter City	46	11	7	5	34	25	3	4	16	23	55	53	23−
Bury	46	8	7	8	31	31	5	5	13	24	43	51	19−
Shrewsbury Town	46	7	7	9	30	31	5	4	14	23	37	47	15−
Torquay United	46	13	3	7	29	19	0	5	18	13	49	47	26−
Darlington	46	5	5	13	31	39	5	2	16	25	51	37	34−

Peterborough United promoted via play-offs

BARCLAYS LEAGUE DIVISION 4

| | P | | HOME | | | | | AWAY | | | | | Goal |
		W	D	L	F	A	W	D	L	F	A	Pts	Diff
Burnley	42	14	4	3	42	16	11	4	6	37	27	83	36+
Rotherham United	42	12	6	3	38	16	10	5	6	32	21	77	33+
Mansfield Town	42	13	4	4	43	26	10	4	7	32	27	77	22+
*Blackpool	42	17	3	1	48	13	5	7	9	23	32	76	26+
Scunthorpe United	42	14	5	2	39	18	7	4	10	25	41	72	5+
Crewe Alexandra	42	12	6	3	33	20	8	4	9	33	31	70	15+
Barnet	42	16	1	4	48	23	5	5	11	33	38	69	20+
Rochdale	42	12	6	3	34	22	6	7	8	23	31	67	4+
Cardiff City	42	13	3	5	42	26	4	12	5	24	27	66	13+
Lincoln City	42	9	5	7	21	24	8	6	7	29	20	62	6+
Gillingham	42	12	5	4	41	19	3	7	11	22	34	57	10+
Scarborough	42	12	5	4	39	28	3	7	11	25	40	57	4−
Chesterfield	42	6	7	8	26	28	8	4	9	23	33	53	12−
Wrexham	42	11	4	6	31	26	3	5	13	21	47	51	21−
Walsall	42	5	10	6	28	26	7	3	11	20	32	49	10−
Northampton Town	42	5	9	7	25	23	6	4	11	21	34	46	11−
Hereford United	42	9	4	8	31	24	3	4	14	13	33	44	13−
Maidstone United	42	6	9	6	24	22	2	9	10	21	34	42	11−
York City	42	6	9	6	26	23	2	7	12	16	35	40	16−
Halifax Town	42	7	5	9	23	35	3	3	15	11	40	38	41−
Doncaster Rovers	42	6	2	13	21	35	3	6	12	19	30	35	25−
Carlisle United	42	5	9	7	24	27	2	4	15	17	40	34	26−

Blackpool promoted via play-offs
Aldershot disbanded, all results removed
Colchester United promoted from GM Vauxhall Conference

European Past Winners

EUROPEAN CHAMPION CLUBS' CUP

Year/venue	Winner		Runner-up	Result
1956 Paris	Real Madrid	v	Stade de Rheims	4–3
1957 Madrid	Real Madrid	v	Fiorentina	2–0
1958 Brussels	Real Madrid	v	AC Milan	3–2*
1959 Stuttgart	Real Madrid	v	Stade de Rheims	2–0
1960 Glasgow	Real Madrid	v	Eintracht Frankfurt	7–3
1961 Berne	Benfica	v	Barcelona	3–2
1962 Amsterdam	Benfica	v	Real Madrid	5–3
1963 Wembley	AC Milan	v	Benfica	2–1
1964 Vienna	Inter Milan	v	Real Madrid	3–1
1965 Madrid	Inter Milan	v	Benfica	1–0
1966 Brussels	Real Madrid	v	Partizan Belgrade	2–1
1967 Lisbon	Celtic	v	Inter Milan	2–1
1968 Wembley	Manchester United	v	Benfica	4–1*
1969 Madrid.	AC Milan	v	Ajax Amsterdam	4–1
1970 Milan	Feyenoord	v	Celtic	2–1*

Year/venue	Winner		Runner-up	Result
1971 Wembley	Ajax Amsterdam	v	Panathinaikos	2–0
1972 Rotterdam	Ajax Amsterdam	v	Inter Milan	2–0
1973 Belgrade	Ajax Amsterdam	v	Juventus	1–0
1974 Brussels	Bayern Munich	v	Atletico Madrid	1–1
Brussels	*Bayern*	v	*Madrid*	*4–0*
1975 Paris	Bayern Munich	v	Leeds United	2–0
1976 Glasgow	Bayern Munich	v	St Etienne	1–0
1977 Rome	Liverpool	v	Borussia Möenchengladbach	3–1
1978 Wembley	Liverpool	v	FC Bruges	1–0
1979 Munich	Nottingham Forest	v	Malmø	1–0
1980 Madrid	Nottingham Forest	v	Hamburg	1–0
1981 Paris	Liverpool	v	Real Madrid	1–0
1982 Rotterdam	Aston Villa	v	Bayern Munich	1–0
1983 Athens	Hamburg	v	Juventus	1–0
1984 Rome	Liverpool	v	Roma	1–1**
1985 Brussels	Juventus	v	Liverpool	1–0
1986 Seville	Steaua Bucharest	v	Barcelona	0–0**
1987 Vienna	Porto	v	Bayern Munich	2–1
1988 Stuttgart	PSV Eindhoven	v	Benfica	0–0**
1989 Barcelona	AC Milan	v	Steaua Bucharest	4–0
1990 Vienna	AC Milan	v	Benfica	1–0
1991 Bari	Red Star Belgrade	v	Marseille	0–0**
1992 Wembley	Barcelona	v	Sampdoria	1–0*

* after extra time
** match won on penalties

EUROPEAN CUP WINNERS' CUP

Year/venue	Winner		Runner-up	Result
1961	Fiorentina	v	Rangers	4–1†
1962 Glasgow	Atletico Madrid	v	Fiorentina	1–1
Stuttgart	Atletico Madrid	v	Fiorentina	3–0
1963 Rotterdam	Tottenham Hotspur	v	Atletico Madrid	5–1
1964 Brussels	Sporting Lisbon	v	MTK Budapest	3–3*
Antwerp	Sporting Lisbon	v	MTK Budapest	1–0
1965 Wembley	West Ham United	v	Munich 1860	2–0
1966 Glasgow	Borussia Dortmund	v	Liverpool	2–1*
1967 Nuremberg	Bayern Munich	v	Rangers	1–0*
1968 Rotterdam	AC Milan	v	Hamburg	2–0
1969 Basle	Slovan Bratislava	v	Barcelona	3–2
1970 Vienna	Manchester City	v	Gornik Zabrze	2–1
1971 Athens	Chelsea	v	Real Madrid	1–1*
Athens	Chelsea	v	Real Madrid	2–1
1972 Barcelona	Glasgow Rangers	v	Moscow Dynamo	3–2
1973 Salonika	AC Milan	v	Leeds United	1–0
1974 Rotterdam	FC Magdeburg	v	AC Milan	2–0
1975 Basle	Dynamo Kiev	v	Ferencvaros	3–0
1976 Brussels	Anderlecht	v	West Ham	4–2

† two legs
* after extra time

Year/venue	Winner		Runner-up	Result
1977 Amsterdam	Hamburg	v	Anderlecht	2–0
1978 Paris	Anderlecht	v	Austria Vienna	4–0
1979 Basle	Barcelona	v	Fortuna Düsseldorf	4–3*
1980 Brussels	Valencia	v	Arsenal	0–0**
1981 Düsseldorf	Dynamo Tbilisi	v	Carl Zeiss Jena	2–1
1982 Barcelona	Barcelona	v	Standard Liège	2–1
1983 Gothenburg	Aberdeen	v	Real Madrid	2–1*
1984 Basle	Juventus	v	Porto	2–1
1985 Rotterdam	Everton	v	Rapid Vienna	3–1
1986 Lyon	Dynamo Kiev	v	Atletico Madrid	3–0
1987 Athens	Ajax Amsterdam	v	Lokomotiv Leipzig	1–0
1988 Strasbourg	Mechelen	v	Ajax Amsterdam	1–0
1989 Berne	Barcelona	v	Sampdoria	2–0
1990 Gothenburg	Sampdoria	v	Anderlecht	2–0*
1991 Rotterdam	Manchester United	v	Barcelona	2–1
1992 Lisbon	Werder Bremen	v	Monaco	2–0

after extra time
** *match won on penalties*

UEFA CUP

(Known also as the Inter Cities Fairs' Cup until 1971. Two-leg finals except in 1964 and 1965. Aggregate scores.)

Year	Winner		Runner-up	Result
1958	Barcelona	v	London	8–2
1960	Barcelona	v	Birmingham	4–1
1961	Roma	v	Birmingham	4–2
1962	Valencia	v	Barcelona	7–3
1963	Valencia	v	Dynamo Zagreb	4–1
1964	Zaragoza	v	Valencia	2–1
1965	Ferencvaros	v	Juventus	1–0
1966	Barcelona	v	Zaragoza	4–3
1967	Dynamo Zagreb	v	Leeds United	2–0
1968	Leeds	v	Ferencvaros	1–0
1969	Newcastle United	v	Ujpest Dozsa	6–2
1970	Arsenal	v	Anderlecht	4–3
1971	Leeds	v	Juventus	3–3†
1972	Tottenham Hotspur	v	Wolverhampton Wanderers	3–2
1973	Liverpool	v	Borussia Möenchengladbach	3–2
1974	Feyenoord	v	Tottenham Hotspur	4–2
1975	Borussia Möenchengladbach	v	Twente Enschede	5–1
1976	Liverpool	v	FC Bruges	4–3
1977	Juventus	v	Bilbao	2–2†
1978	PSV Eindhoven	v	Bastia	3–0
1979	Borussia Möenchengladbach	v	Red Star Belgrade	2–1
1980	Eintracht Frankfurt	v	Borussia Möenchengladbach	3–3†
1981	Ipswich Town	v	AZ 67 Alkmaar	5–4
1982	IFK Gothenburg	v	Hamburg	4–0
1983	Anderlecht	v	Benfica	2–1

† *tie won on away goals*

Year/venue	Winner		Runner-up	Result
1984	Tottenham Hotspur	v	Anderlecht	2–2**
1985	Real Madrid	v	Videoton	3–1
1986	Real Madrid	v	Cologne	5–3
1987	IFK Gothenburg	v	Dundee United	2–1
1988	Bayer Leverkusen	v	Espanol	3–3**
1989	Napoli	v	Stuttgart	5–4
1990	Juventus	v	Fiorentina	3–1
1991	Inter Milan	v	Roma	2–1
1992	Ajax Amsterdam	v	Torino	2–2†

** *tie won on penalties*
† *tie won on away goals*

WORLD CLUB CHAMPIONSHIP

(Played annually until 1974 and then the tournament became disjointed. It was revived when it became a single game for the Toyota Cup and has been played in Tokyo since 1980.)

Year/venue	Winner		Runner-up	Result
1960	Real Madrid	v	Penarol	5–1
1961	Penarol	v	Benfica	7–2†
1962	Santos	v	Benfica	8–4
1963	Santos	v	AC Milan	7–6†
1964	Inter Milan	v	Independiente	3–1†
1965	Inter Milan	v	Independiente	3–0
1966	Penarol	v	Real Madrid	4–0
1967	Racing Club	v	Celtic	3–2†
1968	Estudiantes	v	Manchester United	2–1
1969	AC Milan	v	Estudiantes	4–2
1970	Feyenoord	v	Estudiantes	3–2
1971	Nacional	v	Panathinaikos	3–2
1972	Ajax Amsterdam	v	Independiente	4–1
1973	Independiente	v	Juventus	1–0
1974	Atletico Madrid	v	Independiente	2–1
1975		Not played		
1976	Bayern Munich	v	Cruzeiro	2–0
1977	Boca Juniors	v	Borussia Möenchengladbach	5–2
1978		Not played		
1979	Olimpia	v	Malmö	3–1
1980 Tokyo	Nacional	v	Nottingham Forest	1–0
1981 Tokyo	Flamengo	v	Liverpool	3–0
1982 Tokyo	Penarol	v	Aston Villa	2–0
1983 Tokyo	Gremio Porte Alegre	v	Hamburg	2–1
1984 Tokyo	Independiente	v	Liverpool	1–0
1985 Tokyo	Juventus	v	Argentinos Juniors	2–2**
1986 Tokyo	River Plate	v	Steaua Bucharest	1–0
1987 Tokyo	Porto	v	Penarol	2–1*
1988 Tokyo	Nacional (Uruguay)	v	PSV Eindhoven	1–1**
1989 Tokyo	AC Milan	v	Nacional (Colombia)	1–0*
1990 Tokyo	AC Milan	v	Olimpia	3–0
1991 Tokyo	Red Star Belgrade	v	Colo Colo (Chile)	3–0

* *after extra time*   ** *match won on penalties*   † *three matches*

243

EUROPEAN SUPER CUP

(Played [normally over two legs] between the winners of the European Cup and the Cup Winners' Cup. Introduced in 1972 because of European disillusionment with the World Club Championship.)

Year				Result
1972	Ajax Amsterdam	v	Rangers	6–3
1973	Ajax Amsterdam	v	AC Milan	6–1
1974	Not played			
1975	Dynamo Kiev	v	Bayern Munich	3–0
1976	Anderlecht	v	Bayern Munich	5–3
1977	Liverpool	v	Hamburg	7–1
1978	Anderlecht	v	Liverpool	4–3
1979	Nottingham Forest	v	Barcelona	2–1
1980	Valencia	v	Nottingham Forest	2–2†
1981	Not played			
1982	Aston Villa	v	Barcelona	3–1
1983	Aberdeen	v	Hamburg	2–0
1984	Juventus	v	Liverpool	2–0††
1985	Not played because of UEFA ban on English teams (Everton qualified)			
1986	Steaua Bucharest	v	Dynamo Kiev	1–0††
1987	Porto	v	Ajax Amsterdam	2–0
1988	Mechelen	v	PSV Eindhoven	3–1
1989	AC Milan	v	Barcelona	2–1
1990	AC Milan	v	Sampdoria	3–1
1991	Manchester United (McClair, 67)	v	Red Star Belgrade	1–0††

Old Trafford, Manchester 19 November

Manchester United Schmeichel, Martin (Giggs), Irwin, Bruce, Webb, Pallister, Kanchelskis, Ince, McClair, Hughes, Blackmore.
Red Star Belgrade Milojevic, Radinovic, Vasilijevic, Tanjga, Belodedic, Najdoski, Stosic, Jugovic, Pancev, Savicevic (Ivic), Mihajlovic.
Referee M Van der Ende (Holland).

† *Valencia won on away goals*
†† *one match only*

Barclays Young Eagle of the Year 1992

ROY KEANE, of Nottingham Forest, was elected the 1992 Barclays Young Eagle of the Year by a committee chaired by England manager Graham Taylor and including Jack Charlton, Jimmy Armfield, Stan Cullis, Trevor Cherry, Bill Nicholson, Bill Dodgin and Terry Yorath.

In naming the lad snapped up from Cobh Ramblers for £25,000 by Brian Clough, the England manager Taylor said: 'I saw Roy make his debut for Nottingham Forest at Anfield against Liverpool in August 1990. He ended up running last season's winner, Lee Sharpe, very close and he has now convinced me that he has earned this year's award for his consistency over a two-year period.

'Some youngsters, and sometimes even the more experienced players, excel for one season, but a lot of them then find it hard to build on that the following year. But that is what Roy Keane has done.

'Not only is he good from box to box – and a good passer of the ball – he knows how to intercept and tackle, he scores goals and I don't think that you can ask for much more from a young player.'

Barclays Manager of the Year 1991-92

Howard Wilkinson of Leeds United.

Monthly winners:
August: Alex Ferguson (Manchester United)
September: Alex Ferguson (Manchester United)
October: Howard Wilkinson (Leeds United)
November: Howard Wilkinson (Leeds United)
December: Alex Ferguson (Manchester United)
January: Graeme Souness (Liverpool)
February: Brian Clough (Nottingham Forest)
March: Gerry Francis (Queen's Park Rangers)
April: Trevor Francis (Sheffield Wednesday)

Football Writers' Association Footballer of the Year 1948-92

1948: Stanley Matthews (Blackpool); 1949 Johnny Carey (Manchester United); 1950 Joe Mercer (Arsenal); 1951 Harry Johnston (Blackpool); 1952 Billy Wright (Wolverhampton Wanderers); 1953 Nat Lofthouse (Bolton); 1954 Tom Finney (Preston); 1955 Don Revie (Manchester City); 1956 Bert Trautmann (Manchester City); 1957 Tom Finney (Preston); 1958 Danny Blanchflower (Tottenham); 1959 Syd Owen (Luton); 1960 Bill Slater (Wolverhampton Wanderers); 1961 Danny Blanchflower (Tottenham); 1962 Jimmy Adamson (Burnley); 1963 Stanley Matthews (Stoke); 1964 Bobby Moore (West Ham); 1965 Bobby Collins (Leeds); 1966 Bobby Charlton (Manchester United); 1967 Jackie Charlton (Leeds); 1968 George Best (Manchester United); 1969 Dave Mackay (Derby) shared with Tony Book (Manchester City); 1970 Billy Bremner (Leeds); 1971 Frank McLintock (Arsenal); 1972 Gordon Banks (Stoke); 1973 Pat Jennings (Tottenham); 1974 Ian Callaghan (Liverpool); 1975 Alan Mullery (Fulham); 1976 Kevin Keegan (Liverpool); 1977 Emlyn Hughes (Liverpool); 1978 Kenny Burns (Nottingham Forest); 1979 Kenny Dalglish (Liverpool); 1980 Terry McDermott

Gary Lineker, the Football Writers' Association Footballer of the Year 1992

(Liverpool); 1981 Frans Thijssen (Ipswich); 1982 Steve Perryman (Tottenham); 1983 Kenny Dalglish (Liverpool); 1984 Ian Rush (Liverpool); 1985 Neville Southall (Everton); 1986 Gary Lineker (Everton); 1987 Clive Allen (Tottenham); 1988 John Barnes (Liverpool); 1989 Steve Nicol (Liverpool); 1990 John Barnes (Liverpool); 1991 Gordon Strachan (Leeds); **1992 Gary Lineker (Tottenham Hotspur).**

PFA Footballer of the Year 1974-92

1974 Norman Hunter (Leeds); 1975 Colin Todd (Derby); 1976 Pat Jennings (Tottenham); 1977 Andy Gray (Aston Villa); 1978 Peter Shilton (Nottingham Forest); 1979 Liam Brady (Arsenal); 1980 Terry McDermott (Liverpool); 1981 John Wark (Ipswich); 1982 Kevin Keegan (Southampton); 1983 Kenny Dalglish (Liverpool); 1984 Ian Rush (Liverpool); 1985 Peter Reid (Everton); 1986 Gary Lineker (Everton); 1987 Clive Allen (Tottenham); 1988 John Barnes (Liverpool); 1989 Mark Hughes (Manchester United); 1990 David Platt (Aston Villa); 1991 Mark Hughes (Manchester United); **1992 Gary Pallister (Manchester United).**

THE COCA-COLA FOOTBALL ASSOCIATION COACHING AND EDUCATION SCHEME

FOOTBALL IN THE COMMUNITY

■ SOCCER STAR SCHEME ■

* This unique soccer education programme has been developed by The Football Association to assist boys and girls to enjoy and improve their football whilst reinforcing good attitudes and behaviour.
Since 1988 The Football Association has processed test results for over 123,000 boys and 5,000 girls. Over 7,000 teachers, coaches and youth leaders have already conducted the Scheme and have appreciated the following benefits for their schools, clubs and sports centres :

1 All teachers and youth leaders receive a complimentary start pack with free posters and the 64 page Instructional Football Association Soccer Star Book
2 The Scheme focuses on 6 challenges which test the young players' ability in the most important soccer techniques.
3 The tests are relevant, valid and easy to administer. They require a minimum of equipment and facilities, are quickly organised and simple to record.
4 The Scheme is open to all teachers and youth leaders regardless of their own previous football experience or coaching qualifications.
5 The free Soccer Star Book outlines the tests and simple practices for boys and girls to master the technique and score highly on the tests.
6 On completion of the tests the results are sent to The Football Association who return to the teacher/youth leader a computerised graph of the group's performance.
7 The youngsters receive individual graphs, reports, badges, certificates and pennants.

■ PRELIMINARY SOCCER STAR ■

* The Preliminary Soccer Star Scheme is a soccer education programme based on the Soccer Star Scheme, for those with sensory or physical disabilities or for those individuals with learning difficulties. Because the techniques are the same, individuals involved in the Preliminary Soccer Star Scheme can and should be integrated with those working in the Soccer Star Scheme.

■ FUNWEEKS ■

* The Football Association's successful Funweeks is the largest activity holiday organisation.
Funweeks are the officially recognised non-residential and residential coaching courses of The Football Association. Since 1989 over 6500 courses have been organised attracting over 127,000 children - boys and girls aged 6-16 years. Funweeks take place during the school holidays at over 350 venues throughout England at sites approved by The Football Association.

The popularity of these courses is due largely to the quality and reliability of the experienced staff appointed. Qualified F.A. Coaches provide firm but fair discipline to allow children to enjoy themselves, learn new skills and make new friends.

All children enrolling on the 1992 courses will receive:

● **A Certificate signed by Graham Taylor**

● **A Cloth Badge**

● **An Autographed 1992 England Squad poster**

● **A Bannerette**

● **An Attendance Certificate**

● **An England lapel badge**

■ ADULT COURSES ■

* The Coaching and Education Department of The Football Association organises a wide programme of instructional courses for men and women. These courses include:

● FA Preliminary Award - a practical course of instruction to teach the most effective methods of coaching football techniques and principles of play.

● FA Teaching Certificate - a course for in-service teachers and teachers in training.

● FA Football Leaders - a course for youth leaders and Sunday managers.

FOR DETAILS OF FUNWEEKS (RESIDENTIAL AND NON-RESIDENTIAL), SOCCER STAR, FA PRELIMINARY AWARD, FA TEACHING CERTIFICATE AND FOOTBALL LEADERS COURSES
PLEASE TELEPHONE THE 24-HOUR ANSAPHONE SERVICE ON 0707 50057
OR WRITE TO: THE FOOTBALL ASSOCIATION, 9 WYLLYOTTS PLACE, POTTERS BAR, HERTS EN6 2JD

'Coca Cola' is a registered trade mark of The Coca-Cola Company.

Young Player of the Year 1974-92

1974 Kevin Beattie (Ipswich); 1975 Mervyn Day (West Ham); 1976 Peter Barnes (Manchester City); 1977 Andy Gray (Aston Villa); 1978 Tony Woodcock (Nottingham Forest); 1979 Cyrille Regis (West Brom); 1980 Glenn Hoddle (Tottenham); 1981 Gary Shaw (Aston Villa); 1982 Steve Moran (Southampton); 1983 Ian Rush (Liverpool); 1984 Paul Walsh (Luton Town); 1985 Mark Hughes (Manchester United); 1986 Tony Cottee (West Ham); 1987 Tony Adams (Arsenal); 1988 Paul Gascoigne (Newcastle United); 1989 Paul Merson (Arsenal); 1990 Matthew Le Tissier (Southampton); 1991 Lee Sharpe (Manchester United); **1992 Ryan Giggs (Manchester United).**

European Footballer of the Year 1956-91

1956 Stanley Matthews (Blackpool); 1957 Alfredo Di Stefano (Real Madrid); 1958 Raymond Kopa (Real Madrid); 1959 Alfredo Di Stefano (Real Madrid); 1960 Luis Saurez (Barcelona); 1961 Omar Sivori (Juventus); 1962 Josef Masopust (Dukla Prague); 1963 Lev Yashin (Moscow Dynamo); 1964 Denis Law (Manchester United); 1965 Eusebio (Benfica); 1966 Bobby Charlton (Manchester United); 1967 Florian Albert (Ferencvaros); 1968 George Best (Manchester United); 1969 Gianni Rivera (AC Milan); 1970 Gerd Muller (Bayern Munich); 1971 Johan Cruyff (Ajax); 1972 Franz Beckenbauer (Bayern Munich); 1973 Johan Cruyff (Ajax); 1974 Johan Cruyff (Ajax); 1975 Oleg Blokhin (Dynamo Kiev); 1976 Franz Beckenbauer (Bayern Munich); 1977 Allan Simonsen (Borussia Möenchengladbach); 1978 Kevin Keegan (SV Hamburg); 1979 Kevin Keegan (SV Hamburg); 1980 Karl-Heinz Rummenigge (Bayern Munich); 1981 Karl-Heinz Rummenigge (Bayern Munich); 1982 Paolo Rossi (Juventus); 1983, 84, 85 Michel Platini (Juventus); 1986 Igor Belanov (Dynamo Kiev); 1987 Ruud Gullit (AC Milan); 1988, 89 Marco Van Basten (AC Milan); 1990 Lothar Matthäus (Inter Milan); **1991 Jean Pierre Papin (Marseille).**

Presidents and other Officials of The Football Association

PRESIDENTS

1863-67: Arthur Pember

A London solicitor who was a member of the No Names club of Kilburn. He was elected president at the inaugural meeting of The Football Association on 26 October, 1863, at the Freemason's Tavern, Great Queen Street, Lincoln's Inn Field, London.

1867-74: E. C. Morley

Ebenezer Cobb Morley proposed the formation of The Football Association, drafted the playing laws of the game and is described as the father of organised football. He had previously been the FA's first secretary. Born in Hull in 1831 he moved to Barnes and formed the local club which was to produce three FA secretaries. He was a solicitor, a keen oarsman with London Rowing Club, a member of the Surrey Union Foxhounds, and the Devon and Somerset Staghounds.

1874-90: Major Sir Francis Marindin

A distinguished soldier, Sir Francis was founder, captain and full-back of the Royal Engineers and played in two Cup finals with the club. He also played as goalkeeper for the Old Etonians. He refereed nine Cup finals.

1890-1923: Lord Kinnaird

President for 33 years. Joined the FA committee at the age of 22 in 1869 and died just weeks before the first FA Cup final at Wembley Stadium. Like his predecessor he played in Cup finals – nine in all – and shares the record for the most winners' medals with fellow Wanderer Charles Wollaston and James Forrest of Blackburn Rovers. He was a Scottish international playing against England in 1873. He was also treasurer for 13 years.

1923-37: Sir Charles Clegg

Played for England in the first international against Scotland in 1872 and was the first man to be knighted for his services to football. Born in Sheffield he was a solicitor. He joined the FA in 1886, became chairman in 1889 and was president for fourteen years. He refereed the 1882 and 1892 Cup finals.

1937-39: William Pickford

1939-55: Earl of Athlone

1955-57: HRH The Duke of Edinburgh

1957-63: HRH The Duke of Gloucester

1963-71: The Earl of Harewood

1971-: HRH The Duke of Kent

CHAIRMEN

1938: A. G. Hines

1939-41: M. Frowde

1941-55: Sir Amos Brook Hirst

1955-61: Arthur Drewry

Born in Grimsby. He had been the president of the Football League between 1949 and 1955 before becoming chairman of the FA. He also moved on to be FIFA president, the second Englishman to hold that office. He was tour leader and selector in the 1950 World Cup.

1961-63: A. Graham Doggart

A fine footballer with Cambridge University, A. Graham Doggart won a cap for England and played cricket for Middlesex. He was a Corinthian who had helped to forge strong links between the FA and the Football League. He died suddenly at the FA's annual meeting in June 1963.

1963-66: Joe Mears

Chairman of Chelsea, he succeeded Graham Doggart and immediately became chairman of the World Cup committee planning the hosting of the tournament in England in 1966. Was responsible for the discovery of the man who stole the World Cup trophy from the Central Hall Westminster. Sadly he did not see the World Cup though. He died on the England tour before the tournament at the age of 61. Mr Mears had also been a member of the League Management Committee and an FA Councillor since 1948.

1966-76: Sir Andrew Stephen

Represented Sheffield Wednesday on the FA Council. A Scot.

Joe Mears

1976-81: Professor Sir Harold Thompson

The son of a Yorkshire colliery manager Thompson was an outstanding international scientist, knighted for his scientific work in 1968. He was a fellow of the Royal Society and President of the Great Britain-China Society. He played centre half for Oxford University and founded the Pegasus Club. He was a supporter of the scrapping of amateurism in 1974.

1981- : Sir Bert Millichip

FA chairman during one of the most turbulent eras of English football and knighted in 1991 for his services to the game. A former chairman of West Bromwich Albion for whom he played as an amateur. Sir Bert is a solicitor and the senior partner in the family firm. The longest serving FA chairman. Had the sad task of withdrawing English teams from Europe after the Heysel disaster of 1985. He worked hard to clean up the game and its image and to have English clubs readmitted to European competition in 1990.

SECRETARIES

1863-66: E. C. Morley

Not only was he the first secretary of the FA but also the president (see above).

1866-68: R. W. Willis

1868-70: R. G. Graham

1870-95: C. W. Alcock

Born in Sunderland and educated at Harrow, C. W. Alcock was the founding spirit of the FA Cup. He captained Middlesex and England, and captained Wanderers to the first-ever FA Cup success. He was a respected referee handling FA Cup finals and founder of the Referees Association. He played for Essex at cricket, was an outstanding sports journalist, chairman of Richmond Athletic Club and a vice president of the Mid Surrey Golf Club.

1895-1934: Sir Frederick Wall

Succeeded Alcock in 1985 and held the job for the longest-ever period – 39 years. He had worked at club and county level. As a player he had been a useful goalkeeper. He was a lawyer who became respected as a most able administrator. He was knighted in 1931.

1934-62: Sir Stanley Rous

Became the most influential administrator in world football. Sir Stanley was the third Englishman to become FIFA president and served the world game between 1962 and 1974. He was a schoolmaster at Watford Grammar School before going to the FA. He was one of the most celebrated referees, being in control of 34 internationals and the 1934 FA Cup final. He rewrote the Laws of the game and created the role of director of coaching (now known as England manager).

1962-73: Denis Follows

Won the vote for the job ahead of Walter Winterbottom. He had been the FA's honorary treasurer, a council member for 14 years and the secretary of the British Airline Pilots' Association. He retired to become chairman of the British Olympic Association and was knighted in 1978 – five years after his retirement from the FA.

1973-89: Ted Croker

Ted Croker brought a new, more commercial approach to the secretary's job. He enlightened the FA's thinking. A former Charlton defender, he was a successful businessman.

1989- : Graham Kelly

Former secretary of the Football League. He had become the youngest League secretary at the age of 33 when he succeeded Alan Hardaker. Appointed in the summer of 1988 but began work in early 1989. Immediately faced with the crisis over Hillsborough. Produced his *Blueprint for the Future of Football* in the spring of 1991 which changed the face of English football. It promoted the concept of the Premier League which begins in August 1992.

Denis Follows

FOOTBALL ASSOCIATION OFFICES

1881: First regular home of The Football Association was at 28 Paternoster Row, London, near St Paul's Cathedral.

1885: 51 Holborn Viaduct, London EC.

1892: 61 Chancery Lane, London WC.

1902: 104 High Holborn, London WC.

1910: 42 Russell Square, London WC1 in offices leased from the British Museum.

1929: 22 Lancaster Gate, London W2. Previous Eden Court Hotel premises.

1972: 16 Lancaster Gate, London W2. Exchanged premises with the Association of British Launderers and Cleaners.

ADDRESSES

Football Association: R. H. G. Kelly F.C.I.S., 16 Lancaster Gate, London W2 3LW. Tel: 071-262-4542

FA Premier League: R. Parry, 16 Lancaster Gate, London W2 3LW

Scottish FA: J. Farry, 6 Park Gardens, Glasgow G3 7YF. Tel: 041-332-6372

Northern Ireland: D. Bowen, 20 Windsor Avenue, Belfast BT9 6EG. Tel: 0232-669458

Wales: A. Evans, 3 Westgate Street, Cardiff, S. Glamorgan CF1 1JF. Tel: 0222-372325

Republic of Ireland: S. Connolly, 80 Merrion Square, Dublin 2. Tel: 010-3531-766864

UEFA: G. Aigner, Jupiterstrasse 33, PO Box 16, 3000 Berne 15, Switzerland. Tel: 010-41-31-9414121

FIFA: J. Blatter, PO Box 85, CH-8030 Zurich 30, Switzerland. Tel: 010-41-1-384-9595

World Cup 1994: Organising Committee: 1270 Avenue of Americas, New York City, New York. Tel: 0101-212-332-1994

Football League: J. Dent, The Football League, Lytham St Annes, Lancs FY8 1JG. Tel: 0253-729421

Scottish League: P. Donald, 188 West Regent Street, Glasgow G2 4RY. Tel: 041-248-3844

England Club Call: 0898-121196

FA Fixture Programme for 1992–93

August

Sat   1   Opening of Season
Sat   8   Tennents FA Charity Shield
Sat   15   FA Premier League and Football League programmes
          begin
Sat   29   FA Cup Preliminary Round

September

Sat   5   FA Vase Extra Preliminary Round
Wed   9   England v Continental Opposition
Sat   12   FA Cup First Qualifying Round
          FA Youth Cup Preliminary Round
Wed   16   European club competitions: First round, first leg
Sat   19   FA Trophy First Qualifying Round
Sat   26   FA Cup Second Qualifying Round
Wed   30   European club competitions: First Round, second leg

October

Sat   3   FA Vase Preliminary Round
          FA Youth Cup First Qualifying Round

Sat	10	FA Cup Third Qualifying Round
Sun	11	FA Sunday Cup First Round
Wed	14	England v Norway (World Cup)
Sat	17	FA Trophy Second Qualifying Round
		FA Youth Cup Second Qualifying Round
		FA County Youth Cup First Round
Wed	21	European club competitions: Second Round, first leg
Sat	24	FA Cup Fourth Qualifying Round
Sat	31	FA Vase First Round

November

© THE FOOTBALL ASSOCIATION

Wed	4	European club competitions: Second Round, second leg
Sun	8	FA Sunday Cup Second Round
Sat	14	FA Cup First Round
		FA Youth Cup First Round
Wed	18	England v Turkey (World Cup)
Sat	21	FA Vase Second Round
Wed	25	European Cup group matches; UEFA Cup Third Round, first leg
Sat	28	FA Trophy Third Qualifying Round
		FA County Youth Cup Second Round

December

Sat	5	FA Cup Second Round
Sun	6	FA Sunday Cup Third Round
Wed	9	European Cup group matches; UEFA Cup Third Round, second leg
Sat	12	FA Vase Third Round
		FA Youth Cup Second Round

January 1993

Sat	2	FA Cup Third Round
Sat	9	FA Trophy First Round
Sat	16	FA Vase Third Round
		FA Youth Cup Third Round
Sun	17	FA Sunday Cup Fourth Round
Sat	23	FA Cup Fourth Round
Sat	30	FA Trophy Second Round

February

Sat	6	FA Vase Fifth Round
		FA Youth Cup Fourth Round
Sat	13	FA Cup Fifth Round
Sun	14	FA Sunday Cup Fifth Round

Wed	17	England v San Marino (World Cup)
Sat	20	FA Trophy Third Round
		FA County Youth Cup Fourth Round
Sat	27	FA Vase Sixth Round

March

Wed	3	European Cup group matches; ECWC & UEFA Cup Quarter-final, first leg
Sat	6	FA Cup Sixth Round
		FA Youth Cup Fifth Round
Sat	13	FA Trophy Fourth Round
Wed	17	European Cup group matches; ECWC & UEFA Cup Quarter-final, second leg
Sat	20	FA Vase Semi-final, first leg
		FA County Youth Cup Semi-final
Sun	21	FA Sunday Cup Semi-final
Sat	27	FA Vase Semi-final, second leg
Wed	31	Turkey v England (World Cup)

April

Sat	3	FA Trophy Semi-final, first leg
		FA Youth Challenge Cup Semi-final
Sun	4	FA Cup Semi-finals
Wed	7	European Cup group matches; ECWC & UEFA Cup Semi-final, first leg
Sat	10	FA Trophy Semi-final, second leg
Wed	21	European Cup group matches; ECWC & UEFA Cup Semi-final, second leg
Wed	28	England v Holland (World Cup)

May

Sat	1	**FA County Youth Cup Final**
Sun	2	**FA Sunday Cup Final**
Wed	5	**UEFA Cup Final** first leg
Sat	8	**FA Vase Final**
		FA Youth Cup Final
Sun	9	**FA Trophy Final**
Wed	**12**	**European Cup Winners' Cup Final**
Sat	15	**FA Cup Final**
Wed	**19**	**UEFA Cup Final** second leg
Wed	26	**European Cup Final**
Sat	29	Poland v England (World Cup)

June

| Wed | 2 | Norway v England (World Cup) |